The Italian Model of Management

A Selection of Case Studies

T0383146

The Italian Model of
Management

A Selection of Case Studies

Luigi Serio

Greenleaf
PUBLISHING

© 2016 Greenleaf Publishing Limited

Published by Greenleaf Publishing Limited
Aizlewood's Mill
Nursery Street
Sheffield S3 8GG
UK
www.greenleaf-publishing.com

The right of Elio Borgonovi, Vladimir Nanut and Luigi Serio to be identified as Editors of this Work
has been asserted by them in accordance with sections 77 and 78 of the Copyright, Designs and
Patents Act 1988.

Cover by LaliAbril.com.
Printed and bound by Printondemand-worldwide.com, UK.

British Library Cataloguing in Publication Data:
   A catalogue record for this book is available from the British Library.

ISBN-13: 978-1-78353-428-9 [hardback]
ISBN-13: 978-1-78353-426-5 [paperback]
ISBN-13: 978-1-78353-424-1 [PDF ebook]
ISBN-13: 978-1-78353-425-8 [ePub ebook]

Contents

Foreword

Vladimir Nanut
President, ASFOR

The Annual Case Writing Competition edited by ASFOR for the last two years has met several objectives that I would like to elaborate on in this brief foreword.

First of all, this initiative is intended to stimulate and improve skills and practice in writing and adopting case studies in management education in Italy. It does this by incentivizing academics and practitioners at various levels to analyse and capitalize on their experiences of Italian management issues, either in Italian companies or in the domestic branches of multinationals. The idea is to add to the traditional repertory of "Harvard Style" case studies based on both Anglo-Saxon and universal managerial practices but explicitly from an Italian context and related to major issues that emerge from *day-to-day* activities. This can lead to the development of specific tools that help reflection on the blend of global and local and a deeper understanding of an Italian way of management that creates a "unique" and distinctive competitive advantage in the global market.

This development is not so obvious within the Italian management context for two different reasons. First, the production of Italian case studies is heavily blocked by the weak "scientific quality" of case studies in the evaluation and ranking of academics. Second, from the practical standpoint, entrepreneurs' traditional dislike of the sharing and spread of best practice for business and family reasons has reduced availability and caused tensions in documenting Italian examples. The result is meagre production of original materials and the adoption of international tools based on a universal view of management from a global perspective.

It was in this rather hostile context that ASFOR decided to launch the Annual Case Writing Competition. It aims at creating awareness about the Italian context and specific issues in our domestic environment to stimulate discussion about the Italian perspective within the global context.

The group of academic, independent and corporate members inside ASFOR has become a natural habitat for appreciating case studies that were largely adopted in the past in Italian management education but that have become recently less central to practice here in Italy.

The competition is run directly by ASFOR, with the contribution of a publishing company. In the first and second editions the publishers were Emerald Group Publishing, while for the third edition it is Greenleaf Publishing. The promoters provide two types of support:

- Financial support for the award

- Efforts in facilitating case study publication in leading international scientific and business magazines; for this reason we decided to open the competition only to materials written in English

Results from the first two editions have been impressive; in the first edition ASFOR collected 12 case studies including teaching notes while that number jumped to 22 case studies in the second edition. These were produced by 21 different institutions, both academic and business related. This volume presents a selection of ten case studies that come from seven institutions. These are mainly business schools – the institution that gave birth to the case study and embedded it from the beginning in education practices.

It is now time for the third edition. ASFOR's aim is to create awareness about taking managerial initiative, especially directed at the younger part of our communities. To this end Asfor has also linked the organization of a free seminar for members in order to share and improve knowledge about the practice of writing and adopting case studies in management education and stimulating interest in producing their own examples.

The next stage to reinforce the initiative will be to sustain the increased interest of Italian companies to become the subject of case studies as well as help researchers in understanding specific Italian factors and their link to global competition. As companies have learned over time, global competition is a combination of local and global factors that generate a unique formula for success. If local factors are ignored, any advantage a company may have is easily replicated. Failure to understand specific local factors would severely impact Italian companies' ability to be globally competitive. Meanwhile, Italian business schools should mirror these needs by creating the first step in an interesting sea change in the international educational environment, where interest in Italian companies, competences and business models has been growing in the last few years.

Introduction

Luigi Serio
Referent for the ASFOR Annual Case Writing Competition

This publication presents a selection of Italian management case studies that were prepared for the *Case Writing Competition* promoted by ASFOR Italian Association for Management Education.[1] The theme of the Italian model of management will be explored through two key perspectives:

- The first is the tool itself. The combination of "case study" and "management education" is seen as indissoluble and distinctive. This collection seeks to verify this perception.

- The second reflection deals with understanding whether or not there are unique approaches that exist in management in Italy and if these are of interest to the international community.

The case studies method: several contextual considerations

Although many consider it more a technique than a method, there is no doubt that the use of case studies in management education also implies a methodological choice. This choice is based on a clearly defined idea of education and learning that is widely shared: the use of active methods to stimulate diagnosis activities,

---

1 The top five case studies in the two case competitions were chosen, except those for which it was not possible to obtain the consent to publish. The Commission appointed by ASFOR was composed of: the Chairman of ASFOR, Vladimir Nanut, MIB School of Managment, Trieste; Elio Borgonovi, SDA Bocconi School of Management, Milan; Andrea Sianesi, MIP Politecnico di Milano; Luigi Serio, ISTUD Business School; and Mauro Meda, ASFOR. The first two editions of the *Case Writing Competition* were promoted by ASFOR in association with Emerald Group Publishing.

the choice between alternatives, simulated roles and the formation of work groups among the participants.

The case study method, and the discussion of its benefits, dominated the management education scene until the 1990s. It also acted as a selection criterion and lever of quality accreditation for schools which made significant use of the method and declared it as one of the distinctive factors of their offering.

The development of educational processes "outside and beyond the classroom" (Boldizzoni and Nacamulli, 2011) have led to the development of different forms, methods and techniques over recent years, leaving the case study method and the reflection on its goals in a state of *"almost"* total abandonment.

Consequently, a reflection on the *"use"* of the case study method today brings the focus back to the classroom and proposes a *"renewed"* approach. The case study method still facilitates a convergence of interests between the three main players comprising the key stakeholders in education, a convergence which is the foundation of a "good" educational initiative, regardless of the methods, places and timings developed. In this context, the case study method expresses the different priorities, but reconnects them in a common view. The players involved are: the researcher/teacher, the participant and the company.

For the researcher/teacher, the case study method facilitates the connection between theory and practice and improves the understanding of the key business issues. For the participant, the use of the case study method initiates learning in action, teamwork and the enhancement of ideas across team members. For the company which agrees to be the subject of a case study, the opportunity can stimulate internal change and can be used as an "employer branding" tool that consolidates its identity.

Cases studies and management education: a combination that is still inseparable

The starting point in understanding the value of the case study method in management education is to reflect on the perceptions, some might even say *prejudices*, that have come to characterize the relationship. More specifically, several basic considerations appear to characterize the subject of analysis:

- The connection between the *use of case studies* and *management education* is genetic and in some ways distinctive. It is genetic because the case study was born at and is developed by the Harvard Business School, the icon of management education, on which all business schools worldwide depend in terms of inspiration and didactic practices. It is distinctive because it is assumed that the use of the case study method distinguishes management education from broader education. For business schools, being different from the university system, while still remaining within it, is a prime concern.

- A widespread fatigue can be felt within the school system, driven by the competition between universities and by a market that is essentially, as far as Italy is concerned, compressed. This is reflected in the repeated use of educational materials produced in the past or borrowed from systems, mostly the Anglo-Saxon system, which is aimed at potentially different markets. Struggle, fatigue and the reduction of margins would seem to have affected the development of original thought. For schools integrated into the university system, what counts is the research done in the academy, even if much of it is unusable within companies. The knowledge gained by professionals remains implicit and is rarely shared. Therefore, less value is placed on it. The result of this situation is a dramatic reduction in the development of materials, while the market becomes less amenable towards the business school.

- The need to be *compliant* with the associations that internationally promote a case study *competition*. Strategically, ASFOR intends to occupy the space for reflection on the theme of adult education, strengthening the institutional dimension of management education schools, in addition to and differently from the university system.

- The intention to revitalize the ASFOR case studies centre, a place which had made case studies and teaching notes from Italian companies available to the school system and which for various reasons, formally connected with copyright, informally with the "tiredness" mentioned in the previous points, has experienced a slowing down.

- The desire to bring the managerial issue, but above all the managerial role, downsized by the crisis and by a general lack of trust in the role, back to the centre of the reflection. Focusing on the managerial issues and the dilemmas dealt with by managers on a day-to-day basis means bringing didactic exchange, rationale and methods back within a professional family which is experiencing a strong identity crisis, flattened between execution from the top and operation from the base.

In fact, with respect to the points mentioned, the proposed initiative presents a rather accurate picture, strengthening several possible scenarios and dispelling several prejudices.

As regards the development of case studies, the number of applications made in the two editions which compose our sample is certainly reassuring. In all, 26 didactic case studies were gathered, including teaching notes. The requirement to present the case studies in the Harvard Style reduced the eligible sample by approximately 25%. There were submissions from an interesting variety of schools and "corporate universities". The scientific and professional community in Italy – it can be said – is acquainted with the case studies and the underlying method, writes them with some frequency and uses the shared international standards.

As regards the potential "scientific space" occupied by the case study, it appears to be the corollary of a series of different activities for academics, while for those who come from the world of practice, the intention is to have their own didactic materials or to complete a term of office in the company with the completion of the work through the delivery of a specific company case study. The quality and the variety of the materials produced lead us to be able to say that the method is widely known, that the rationale of tackling managerial issues is still successful and that the case study completes the preparation of a teacher of management education, driving them to reflect on issues, rather than give solutions to questions given. Here too, it appears to be an original and distinctive way for schools to strengthen the professional scientific dimension of their activity, in addition to and differently from the extremes of the organizational field of management education, universities and the professional worlds. The impression is that the "tiredness" which we referred to exists, the scientific production of the professional world has fallen and yet an important space for reflection is present on managerial practices that the university world skims distractedly and the professional world rationalizes little and tacitly capitalizes on within its own restricted community.

If this data is cross-checked with participation in the seminar on how to write a case study, promoted by ASFOR in parallel with the award, which saw the participation of 26 educators, belonging to 17 different institutions, the situation becomes even more interesting; the community exists, moved by different motivations, but in any case of some note. The relationship between participation in the course and writing the case study for the competition is still not direct, but the connection between the two initiatives is clear and more direct results are expected over time.

Hence, considering the initiative from an institutional point of view, there is no doubt that the Italian system, while having its own peculiarity, interacts with its own institutional system and the case study method represents a code of uniformity and homologation which enables the development of common projects and the exchange of *know-how* at international level.

The second issue goes back to the existence of a possible peculiarity of the management model in Italy, to justify an interest in its national and foreign diffusion, but above all more generally on the meaning and role of managerial staff in Italy. This is probably the most interesting issue to which this publication draws attention.

In fact, if we take a closer look at the space generally dedicated to management in Italy, in international literature, the scene is occupied primarily by industrial districts, by the "industrial atmosphere" which regulates the functioning of these system areas. This reflection is essentially the only one present in literature. It refers to a very precise period of managerial dynamics in Italy, which is now suffering as a result of international economic dynamics and the affirmation of global strategies in competition. The subject of analysis is the business population. Only some companies have been studied in recent years at international level, large family-owned companies, considered more single episodes than carriers of their own managerial model. The reduced distribution of case studies from Italian companies and the relevant shortage of effort dedicated to the production of original didactic material

The managerial issues expressed by these companies can be reduced to three (Coltorti *et al.*, 2013; Serio, 2012):

- **Governance**. This deals primarily with the issues between firm and family: the relationship between family management and professional management. The use of the theme of networks, as integrative and, in perspective, complementary forms of governance, also falls within this category.

- **International strategies**. The search for new niches, strategic positioning and the role of human resources to support the internationalization processes in which Italian companies excel.

- **Focus strategies**. With regards to the new global supply chains, knowledge, technology and the role of intangibles in the construction of competitive advantage, based on flexible specialization and relationships in the supply chain.

Table 1 **Summary of case studies**

Case study	Typology of firm	Managerial issue	Hosting school
Hotel Stella	Family firm	Succession and strategy	CUOA Business School
Telespazio	Large Italian company	Strategy and people development	Joint effort between European University Rome, Luiss and Aquila University
UniManagement	Large Italian company	Strategy and executive development	Unimanagement
Fahrenheit Resort	Public and private companies	New company and strategy	SDA Bocconi
Dynamo Camp	Private company	New business model	SDA Bocconi
Mediolanum Bank	Private company	Strategy	SDA Bococni
Ametista	Family business	Strategy	Politecnico of Milan
Magneti Marelli and Mopar	Large private company	New business unit	SDA Bocconi
iGuzzini	Family business	Strategy and internationalization	ISTAO
MTV Italia	Branch of multinational	Strategy and competitive advantage	SDA Bocconi

The selected case studies, summarized in Table 1, move within this framework rebuilt in the three identified clusters, posing issues and dilemmas and, of course, behaviour, which help to trace the framework of the managerial priorities faced by companies in Italy. However, they are still dispersed in single stories, difficult to see internationally and still unable to outline the characteristics of an original model. Bearing this in mind, their study and this publication intend, on the one hand, to contribute shape and identity to the management model, which is still defined by its difference with respect to the international standards commonly adopted; and on the other, to give back several reflections on the role of relationships and intangibility, as a factor to create a competitive advantage, which in different forms appears to be the common thread that can be reconstructed in the three clusters. A perspective is proposed and a contribution to knowledge, which also and above all passes from the study and analysis in Italian and international classrooms of national companies which compete globally. To conclude, the ambition remains that of consolidating a *community* of academic staff, internal and external to the system of companies, carriers of critical views and generators of a specific reflection on the context of Italian firms, for too long considered "poor and smaller relations" of the British model of business, from which it has set itself apart by deep and significant differences in the basic characteristics which still succeed in making it interesting and worthy of international study. If knowledge passes through narration and capitalization, as it is often stated, then this book intends to move in this direction and start a reflection on the issue that our ASFOR observatory considers the most important, namely that of defining the management model in Italy.

References

Assens, C. & Baroncelli, A. (2005). Firms dynamics: The ineluctable "entanglement" of the organizational forms. *4th Global Conference on Business & Economics, Oxford: Oxford University, 26–28 June 2005.*

Boldizzoni, D. & Nacamulli, R. (2011). *Oltre l'aula.* Milan: Apogeo.

Boldizzoni, D. & Serio, L. (2008). L'impresa in tensione. *Il Sole 24 ORE.*

Coltorti, F., Resciniti, R., Tunisini, A., & Varaldo, R. (2013). *Mid-Sized Manufacturing Companies: The New Driver of Italian Competitiveness.* New York: Springer.

Masino, G. (2008). Culture and management in Italy: Tradition, modernization, new challenges. In: Eduardo Davel, Jean-Pierre Dupuis & Jean-François Chanlat (Eds.), *Gestion en contexte interculturel: Approches, problématiques, pratiques et plongées* (pp. 1-37). Québec: Presse de l'Université Laval et Télé-université (UQAM).

Serio, L. (2012). *La media Impresa e la crescita: Chiavi di lettura e opzioni di management,* Quaderni di Ricerca Fondazione Istud. Retrieved from http://www.istud.it/up_media/ricerche/report_quarto_capitalismo.pdf

All of the cases included in this book have excellent teaching notes, which are available for faculty, free of charge, by request from Greenleaf Publishing at the following link: **http://www.greeenleaf-publishing.com/asfor_notes**

1

The heart of business in an Italian family firm
The Hotel Stella case*

Alessandra Tognazzo
University of Padova, Italy

Paolo Gubitta
University of Padova and CUOA Business School, Italy

The case is about an *Italian entrepreneurial family* and its *second generation family hotel*. The protagonist is Rosa, who is torn between letting her daughter work in the family business and selling it. The historical background, values and rules of the family and the modes by which the family team was able to exploit environmental entrepreneurial opportunities are explained in detail. Hotel Stella is an organization which functioned according to informal family logics and dynamics. The firm's management and organization have been based on the family members' roles and connections. This was particularly important during the economic downturn in recent years. Hotel bookings are decreasing and it is time for innovation. The composition of the family has also changed over time. The Hotel Stella case triggers family business issues such as **succession, innovation, strategy**, and **human resources** and it is a comprehensive and stimulating real life example about a *family* and a *business*: these two strictly intertwined spheres can be the secret behind proactive and innovative entrepreneurial acts, but they can also hide risk-avoiding fears.

* The authors assume full responsibility for any mistakes in this document. Names of people and firms have been changed for privacy reasons. Places and facts correspond to reality.

It's 14 June 2010. Rosa, an elegant and charming 50-year-old woman, and her 25-year-old daughter, Giulia, are having dinner together at home. Rosa looks very tired. She is recovering after the surgery she's just had, even so she never comes home from work before 9 pm. Rosa has been working at Hotel Stella – her family's hotel – since 1983.

All of a sudden, Giulia asks, "Mom, do you think I could work at the hotel with you some time?" Rosa looks at her like she has been expecting this question for a long time, but she's never really been sure how to answer it. Her daughter's choice could be either the worst mistake of her life or their business salvation. Of course, she could give her the straight answer, "no", but she wonders what would be better: "The hotel is very stressful: can't you just keep doing what you are doing now and help me in your free time?" she manages finally. Giulia nods. The conversation apparently ends here.

1.1 Hotel Stella

1.1.1 Organization

Hotel Stella – a four-star hotel – is an enterprise with about 36 staff members (seven cooks and cooks' assistants, six waiters, two bartenders, two washerwomen, four chambermaids, two receptionists, two secretaries, one hairdresser and aesthetician, three masseurs, two mud therapists, two maintenance men, Rosa, her brother and her husband).

1.1.2 Building and facilities

The hotel has 30 single rooms and 58 double rooms, one indoor swimming pool and one outdoor one, a large hall with a bar, two meeting rooms (for 35 and 15 people), an attractive garden with a big terrace, a tennis court and bowls court, one restaurant, a kitchen and a wine cellar. On the first floor is the beauty, massage and inhalation therapy department; on the fourth and fifth floors are the thermal therapy departments. The whole hotel is accessible to clients, except for a laundry, three offices and the mud pond which have restricted access. Finally, an old swimming pool and an old tavern are used as warehouses.

1.1.3 History and location

The hotel is located in the centre of Abano Terme, in the north-eastern part of Italy. The town is quite well known for hotels with spas. Stella is one of the historic hotels in the town, founded in 1975 by a wealthy local family. Rosa's family bought it in 1983. In 1984 her daughter was born. After repaying the initial debt, the family has always financed the hotel with its own capital, without incurring other debts. Some additional financial data are reported in Table 1.1.

Rosa's father's family has a long entrepreneurial history, which still has a bearing on business conduct today.

Table 1.1 **Hotel Stella financial data**

Source: Data available at: https://aida.bvdep.com/ [accessed 16 October 2010]

	2010	2009	2008	2007	2006	2005	2004	2003	2002	2001	2000
Income	2,116,199	2,049,947	2,072,132	2,046,148	1,836,146	1,852,636	1,965,027	2,156,471	2,327,875	2,457,221	2,350,661
EBITDA	114,477	12,813	158,375	-81,510	15,316	-72	133,077	225,986	453,661	449,553	317,085
EBITDA/Income (%)	5.4	0.62	7.63	-3.98	0.83	0.00	6.76	10.45	19.41	18.26	13.47
ROS (%)	-0.41	-5.28	4.73	-7.70	-3.35	-4.13	3.03	6.54	15.32	15.08	10.55
Net income	-58,412	-152,848	44,021	-145,064	-76,670	-90,425	-4,358	59,715	145,746	243,497	92,609
Total assets	6,283,989	6,422,285	6,546,230	1,561,963	1,588,167	1,749,916	1,762,256	1,812,783	1,757,977	1,666,474	1,437,731
Net capital	5,579,628	5,638,041	5,790,884	866,088	1,011,153	1,087,822	1,178,246	1,181,568	1,121,853	976,107	732,610
Net financial position	-773,889	-863,297	-419,591	-280,575	-220,797	-1,023,454		-996,500	-857,585	-699,446	-439,090
ROA (%)	-0.14	-1.69	1.50	-10.10	-3.89	-4.40	3.39	7.80	20.38	22.28	17.28
ROE (%)	-1.05	-2.71	0.76	-16.75	-7.58	-8.31	-0.37	5.05	12.99	24.95	12.64
Invested capital turnover (no. of times)	0.34	0.32	0.32	1.31	1.16	1.06	1.12	1.19	1.32	1.47	1.63
Debt/Equity ratio	0	0.00	0.00	0.00	0.00	0.00		0.00	0.00	0.00	0.00
Debs vs. banks over income (%)	0	0.00	0.00	0.00	0.00	0.00		0.00	0.00	0.00	0.00
Debt/EBITDA ratio	0	0.00	0.00	0.00	0.00	0.00		0.00	0.00	0.00	0.00

Note: EBITDA, earnings before interest, taxes, depreciation and amortization; ROS, return on sales; ROA, return on assets; ROE, return on equity

1.2 The family background

Rosa's grandmother was Maria. "Mamma Maria", her husband, two daughters, and three little sons, Giuseppe, Salvo and Matteo: that's how it all started (Fig. 1.1).

Figure 1.1 **Simplified genogram of Rosa's family and businesses**

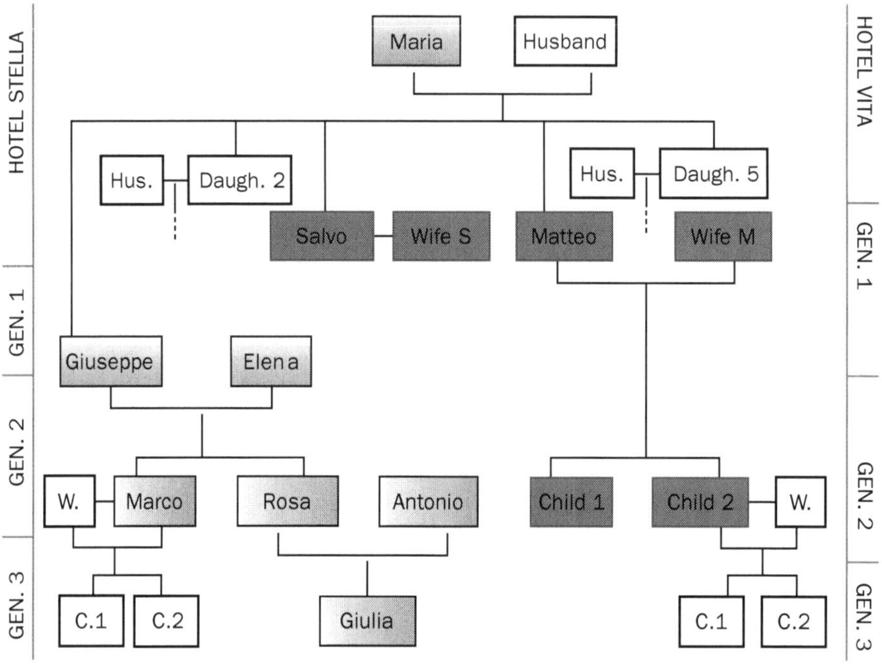

Notes: C.1 and 2 are less than 14 years old. W. do not feature in the case, but are present in real life. Light grey boxes indicate Hotel Stella; dark grey, Hotel Vita.

1.2.1 Traditional values and local roots

The Fontana family was a typical Catholic Italian middle-class family of the period after World War II. Everyone was used to working hard in the rural area where they lived. During the day, women stayed at home and cared for the children and the house, while their husbands worked in the fields and came back home at night for dinner. Men and older people were always served first, as a sign of respect.

The family was fairly well known in town, especially for their kindness and help-fulness. They were also considered wealthy, because they owned some fields. All the money they had was invested either in fields or in food. For them, work was a means of survival, and also something that could enhance their social status. They also loved nature; horses, fields and rivers were free amusement parks, where they could have fun and be carefree.

Mamma Maria was very important for everyone; she wanted her children to come together at night to feel part of one big united family.

1.2.2 The beginning of the entrepreneurial family

The Fontana family began its entrepreneurial adventure in the 1950s, when family members bought a grocery store in the town centre. It was soon after the war, a time of renaissance, growth and wellbeing. The business was going rather well. In the meantime, Maria's daughters got married and decided to start some new businesses with their husbands.

The three sons grew and got married and with their wives they decided to "get bigger". Therefore, they sold the grocery store and promptly bought a restaurant in town.

Giuseppe and Matteo both had two children. When the children grew up, they also had to help their parents with the business after school. It was a normal routine for them. Rosa says: "this was my everyday programme...come back from school, do my homework and then help mom and dad with the dishes."

The restaurant became quite famous and even had a picture of a well-known actor, who had lunch there, hanging on the wall!

The women made and served the food, did the dishes and the cleaning, while the men were in charge of the bar and of the food procurement. After work, the three men sat at the table and the women had to serve them. This was just the normal routine; no one ever complained.

When Rosa was little she was quite afraid of her dad, a big man who was always very strict. He never said "good job!" and never gave her attention, while her mother was always very busy working, but would have loved to. Since everyone was very busy, Rosa spent a lot of time with her grandmother, Maria. Work was hard for everyone, but they made good money, as Rosa says, "Nine adult hands and eight little hands were enough for being successful! Maybe, even too many for such a small business..."

1.3 Environmental changes and entrepreneurial opportunities

In the 1960s, the family's home town, Abano Terme, was becoming quite well developed thanks to the numerous hot water springs found there. Hotels were being established all over the town. The Italian public healthcare department was providing financial support to citizens for thermal treatments, as was German health care insurance. Thanks to this support, many hotels were built in the area. Here, the main form of treatment is still mud and inhalation therapy, which are recommended respectively for rheumatic illnesses and respiratory problems.

In a few years, there was a hotel in every corner of the town. Clients came mainly from Germany, along with visitors from Austria, Switzerland and France. The tourist season for foreigners ran from February until June and from September until November, while Italians came mainly in the summer. The average stay of each client was around 12–15 days, and clients used to come back year after year. The German mark was strong over the lira, which also helped to increase tourist traffic.

What still makes this area unique is that almost every hotel was founded by different owners, mainly local families, who built hotels as if they were their own houses. As a matter of fact, every hotel included not only rooms, a bar, a restaurant and a kitchen, but also its own thermal department and facilities (e.g. laundry). To offer a good service, everything had to be made "in house". This was a fairly common local belief that came from the rural culture, when the best things were "made by mom's hands". The associated costs could be afforded because there was no lack of income.

1.3.1 Hotel Romano

The Fontanas could not miss such an opportunity! In 1973 Salvo, the middle son, decided to buy a hotel – Hotel Romano – with his brothers. They took out a loan from the bank which they repaid in less than three years. In the 1970s the hotel was so full that some clients even had to sleep in the chambermaids' rooms. Meanwhile, barons, ministers and many other famous people started to come to Abano. It became a very attractive, elegant and luxurious town.

Rosa finished her studies when she was 16, in 1976. In that year, she started working full-time at the hotel, first in the front office and later in the back office. At school she was always a good student; she travelled in Switzerland and Germany to learn French and German, but she hated maths. Rosa remembers:

> I didn't like maths! I didn't like the back office work either. I always made a lot of mistakes with numbers, receipts, accounts. . . I had to do it, but I would have rather stayed talking or writing to clients for the bookings or information.

1.3.2 Hotel Vita and Rosa's love life

As there were enough family members to do the work, in less than three years another important decision was made. Salvo and his brothers decided to build another hotel on their own. In the meantime, their father passed away and Mamma Maria gave them her blessing.

In 1977, the new hotel was finished. They named it "Hotel Vita": a short name, which would have been cheap to light at night. Clients started to come and it was always full, just like Hotel Romano.

A young, proud and brilliant receptionist was hired; his name was Antonio. Rosa also went to work there. Antonio had been a hotel restaurant director before, but since he could speak other languages and was born in Abano, he thought he could also be a good receptionist. Antonio was so overconfident that he made a bet with another employee, "I bet that I will be able to date Rosa, the owner's daughter. If I win you owe me 20,000 lira".

Eventually, he did date Rosa! Of course, her father did not know anything about the relationship and Rosa didn't know about the bet. Giuseppe would have never let his daughter go out with that young man, who was so arrogant, and Rosa would have never agreed to go out with someone who just wanted to win a bet. In 1981 they got married and in 1984 their daughter, Giulia, was born.

1.3.3 Hotel Stella

In 1983, the hotel right in front of Hotel Romano was one of the most luxurious in town. The owners decided to put Hotel Romano up for sale, because they wanted to buy a bigger one. The three brothers didn't miss the opportunity. They sold Romano and bought the exclusive Hotel Stella. They were not afraid of having to pay off the loan they got from the bank again. They knew they were going to be successful if they worked hard, as they had always done. They felt like a winning team. They had a lot of energy, but also enough experience to accomplish their goals. They felt confident that the economy was growing and they felt they had the chance to be the winners again and again.

1.4 Hotel network and family relationships

1.4.1 The organization: family and business division

Giuseppe, the oldest son, stayed at Hotel Stella with his wife and their two children, Rosa and Marco. Since the family Fontana had to manage two hotels, Matteo's family remained at Hotel Vita where Matteo was mainly in charge of procurement. Relationships with suppliers were very friendly. They trusted each other; therefore he made the orders without looking too much at the prices.

Salvo also lived at Hotel Vita and was in charge of the finances for both the hotels. He paid the employees and he had the relationship with the banks and consultants. In short, he was considered the "head" of the entrepreneurial family. His relationship with the other hotel directors in Abano was relatively good. There was a local hotel consortium dominated by a small group, which then became a formal hotel group. No one was very confident about such an association, but for Salvo going to dinners was fun and rewarding. Also, consultants were treated almost like friends; the main business consultant of the family was – and still is – one of the three brothers' cousins.

The three brothers were all very proud of their accomplishments, even if they all had to work 24/7 and never enjoyed time with their families, because of their business.

1.4.2 Family and business roles

Hotel Stella, just like Hotel Vita, has never had a formal structure. It was the way the family was composed that made up the roles.

As we have already mentioned, Giuseppe, Elena, Rosa and her brother Marco were the family members working and managing Hotel Stella after 1983, although Salvo still had a relevant role.

At the time they bought the hotel, Giuseppe was in charge of gardening and maintenance. He had a rather severe and unsmiling character. He was always complaining about things. He was used to controlling people and didn't like to mix with clients. This was clear when, after the first secret dates, his daughter eventually fell in love with and married the reception manager, Antonio, who became his worst enemy.

Antonio was actually very highly skilled; he studied in Switzerland and travelled all around Europe. He also became the maître (director) of the restaurant at Stella. His capabilities were certainly superior to his role in the hotel, and he knew it, but he has never moved because of the love he felt for his wife.

Rosa was especially affectionate to her mother, Elena. When Rosa speaks about her, her voice trembles. . .

> She was the creative woman in the hotel. When she was young, she was one of the first women to wear trousers, in a time when only skirts were permitted for women. She had very progressive and forward-looking ideas. In the hotel, she controlled and managed the maids and the laundry work. She was always elegant and she loved to sew. In the winter time, when the hotel was closed, she sat for hours at her sewing machines to make decorations for her hotel, as if it was her home. She could not speak German or French but she stayed with the clients smiling at them and entertaining them with kind gestures. . . She was very special. . .

Giuseppe, Elena and Rosa's brother, Marco, lived on the 7th floor of the hotel, where they had a welcoming, comfortable flat. Rosa and Antonio lived in their own house, five minutes from the hotel; a house that Antonio built without any help from his wife's family.

After she married, Rosa continued to work in the front and back office. She used to get sick quite often because of the stress brought on by the fights between her husband and her father. For Rosa, work is something very important. She really cares about it and wants to do her best. She also used to feel a little inferior to her husband, Antonio, but she has found out that she has talents that he does not have. For instance, the hotel receptionist says:

> she is always caring with clients and when needed, she doesn't hesitate to leave her office to go to the hospital for the older guests, even twice or three times a day. She never forgets to call them at home after a surgery or to congratulate them for something important. She receives many letters from clients saying "thank you for how special you are". She dedicates them her time and her heart.

Everybody in the family considers her very kind, caring and sensitive. Perhaps too sensitive, unfortunately, which is why she gets sick so often. She cannot stop thinking about her responsibilities. Even the day before having her surgery she was thinking about how to organize the hotel work and had no concerns about her health at all.

Even if she always says she likes her work, just like her brother, she feels that she has never had the chance to really choose her job freely. Working at the hotel is what she had to do for her whole life. That's it.

Her daughter, Giulia, is sensitive too. Rosa is always there to help her whenever needed. A mother always knows the way her child feels, because they have the same blood and the same feelings too. Giulia has always been a well-educated girl and quite brilliant at school. She grew up thinking that working at weekends or on vacation is normal. Not because she worked at the hotel – her mother would have never let her – but because she saw her parents doing so. In the hotel she helps when she has some free time from school. When she was a child she didn't want to work at the hotel at all. The hotel was something that took away her parents' time and attention. She grew up with her grandmother, Elena, who loved to stay with her; she made her lunch and kept her for the whole day. Giulia was used to arriving at the hotel and asking, "Where is grandma?" and then she felt safe and useful. She never asked for her mother because she was busy and Giulia would have felt in her way all day long.

1.4.3 Italian values and family capital management

Following the Italian tradition, the ownership and money gained from the two businesses was divided into three equal parts, one for each brother. Women were given just a small part of the shares, but whenever they asked for money their husbands would always satisfy their needs and caprices. Their consultant and cousin, the family's most trusted advisor, made the calculations and helped them with the investments. The only thing that Giuseppe explicitly required was to invest some money in land. This is something that comes from his love for nature and his childhood memories.

Formally, Salvo was Stella's chairman. The board consisted of: Elena, Giuseppe, Matteo's wife and Salvo's wife. This decision (most board decisions were made informally, often at lunch or dinner meetings) was made with the condition that each brother had to be the chairman of one of the family's societies. Giuseppe wanted to be the chairman of the society that owns the land. Matteo, instead, took the responsibility for Vita. The board members were nominated in such a way that each of them was involved in at least two of the societies.

1.4.4 Employees and labour unions

The staff at the hotel were not always treated just as employees, they were considered people who had to work at least as much as the family did. Even if the family did not really fully trust them and therefore usually needed to work with them to control what they were doing, family members were always generous when paying them.

In Abano, there have been many strikes since the 1970s, for better contract terms. A strike for a hotel is a terrible event. Rosa says, "If all the workers are on strike, the hotel has to close and the clients have to go home and will probably never come back. The effects of one single strike can have consequences for years. . ." Therefore, in this town employment contracts are extremely favourable for workers, compared with other similar places in Italy.

Although Giuseppe complained a lot, personnel turnover was very low. Everyone received a salary, bonuses for good performance and generous tips from the clients. Moreover, even if the family expected a lot from the employees, when they needed a day off for personal reasons, they always found a way to meet their wishes.

1.4.5 How the family shaped the business

The structure of Hotel Stella had a classical style. The Fontanas made some renovations in the swimming pool, the bar and other parts of the hotel, because they felt they were needed and especially because of Elena who had many elegant and modern ideas. Many of these works were influenced by their own beliefs. For instance, Rosa reveals:

> there was a tavern which my grandpa decided to close and used it as a warehouse, because Giuseppe believed it could have been a place of perdition. He was Catholic and that was important for him to avoid alcohol and equivocal situations, even if this could have been a source of income.

The same happened with another large swimming pool that was too deep and therefore too dangerous to be left without a lifeguard. But paying one person to attend that swimming pool for the whole day would not have been viable. Therefore, they decided to use it as another warehouse. Other renovations however were very positive for attracting customers: for example they completely switched the entrance to the hotel so that it could be accessed from a central square in town and not only from a street nearby.

1.4.6 Market demand and internal organization

When the family bought the business in the 1980s, clients that came to the hotel stayed for 15 or even 20 days. Thermal cures started at 3 am until around 11 am; the night concierge woke the clients up by phone, they went to the thermal department which was located on the same floor as their bedrooms, and they would have the mud pack treatment. An employee would bring the mud on a trolley with some buckets.

After the mud treatment, in the same room the assistant would help them to shower and bathe in thermal water. Then, they had a massage for 25 minutes. Rosa laughs when thinking about this. . . "it was more some sort of a salami treatment as compared to the spa massage we think about today". Finally, the clients went back to bed for the sweating part of the treatment.

During the day clients usually stayed in the swimming pool, in the grotto or the fitness room and went out for some trips organized by a local travel agency. They were used to having breakfast, lunch and dinner at the hotel. They liked tasty Italian food and didn't care that much about their figures.

Some clients also had inhalations and aerosol treatments with thermal water. These treatments would cost clients almost nothing thanks to healthcare department funds. They would just pay for the hotel stay.

Until the 2000s the prices of the hotel were divided into three seasons, according to guest numbers (see Table 1.2). Low prices corresponded to the periods when there were fewer clients. The price list had to be made just once a year and no special offers or price cuts were offered. The family thought that this was the most honest way to work. The prices were set according to the competitors. More or less all the hotels of the same category in Abano had the same season and the same prices.

Table 1.2 **Full board prices per person per night, 2002**

	2–17 Mar	18–23 Mar	24 Mar– 18 May	19 May– 15 June	16 June– 10 Aug	11–31 Aug	1 Sep– 12 Oct	13 Oct– 2 Nov	3–30 Nov
Season	Low	Mid.	High	Mid.	Low	Mid.	High	Mid.	Low
Single room	€65	€75	€76	€75	€65	€75	€76	€75	€65
Double room	€60	€70	€76	€70	€60	€70	€76	€70	€60

Therefore, the hotel did not work with travel agencies because they would have been charged a 15% fee which was too much for them. Rosa was very proud of saying that Stella worked mainly with private clients. They only negotiated with two German travel agencies with which they contracted a charge of 13% per person per stay, and a couple of groups that came for the opening of the hotel which were granted 10% off the price.

1.5 Market revolution in the '90s

In the 1990s computers appeared on the Italian market and the first hotel software was available. In the late 1990s, clients started to book the hotel using the internet a few hours before arriving. The organization of the hotel became more difficult and work could not be programmed more than one or two weeks ahead. More flexibility was needed, but resources were scarce.

Professional further education institutions have lost their prestige over time. Workers were not easy to find, the local hotel school was regarded as the choice for people with low grades who didn't know what to do with their lives. There were no young, well-prepared professionals available in the market. Rosa used to believe that she would never hire graduates; she thought she would have felt inferior since she just had a professional education.

Also during this period, the German Government completely cut financial support for thermal cures and the Italian Government put many constraints on the benefits so that there was a sharp decrease in hotel bookings.

In 2002 the Euro was officially introduced as a currency. Italy and Abano became more expensive for German people, who used to find it convenient for vacations. Slovenia and other, cheaper places were starting to get more attractive to German visitors. More Italians started to come just for a weekend or for a few days. The average length of stay decreased to 4–5 days in the last few years (see Figures 1.2, 1.3 and Table 1.3).

Figure 1.2 **(a) Arrivals and (b) number of nights stayed in the Euganean district, 1997–2009**

Source: Data available at: http://statistica.regione.veneto.it/ [accessed 16 June 2011]

(a)

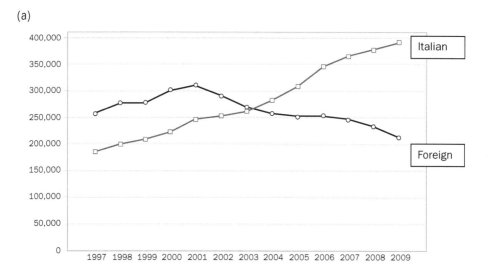

(b)

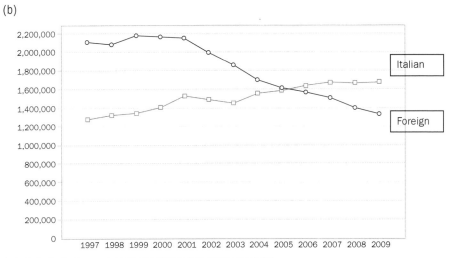

Arrivals indicate the number of new clients that arrive at a hotel

All the hotels in Abano started to offer "wellness packages" or "beauty treatments", like the Slovenian spas did. Everyone was looking after their own business, without thinking of Abano as a system that needed to be sustained. For instance, the mayor of the town was elected in 2007 and resigned the same year. Many people thought that the new mayor elected in 2011 seemed more interested in building houses than fostering tourism.

Figure 1.3 **Total monthly hotel bookings in the Euganean district (a) 1997–2000 and (b) 2006–2009**

Source: Data available at: http://statistica.regione.veneto.it/ [accessed 16 June 2011]

(a)

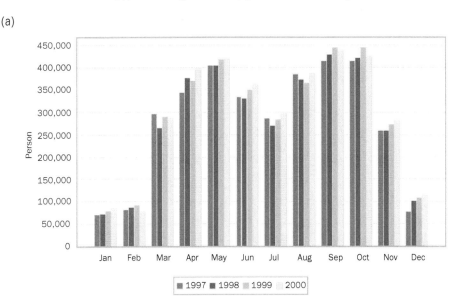

(b)

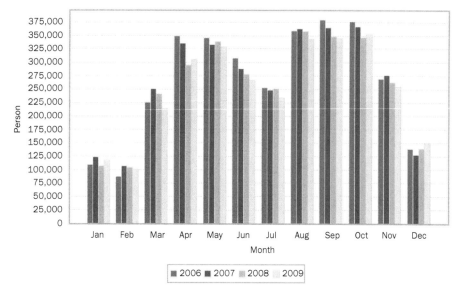

Some initiatives were taken by the Consortium and the Region, but all the initiatives were either quite limited in time or beneficial only for some hotels. Unfortunately, these marketing initiatives didn't cover any strategic and medium- or long-term coordinated action. Rosa's family was not into marketing, they didn't even know what it meant to have a sales department.

Table 1.3 **Foreign visitor numbers by country and hotel category in 1997 and 2009**

Source: Data available at: http://statistica.regione.veneto.it/ [accessed 16 June 2011]

1997	5 and 4 stars		3 stars and residence		2 and 1 stars		Hotels (total)	
	Arrivals	No. of nights stayed	Arrivals	No. of nights stayed	Arrivals	No. of nights stayed	Arrivals	No. of nights stayed
Austria	14,610	104,386	32,046	215,641	2,411	11,763	49,067	331,790
Belgium/Luxembourg	1,362	14,812	996	9,346	130	756	2,488	24,914
Denmark	117	645	79	304	58	284	254	1,233
France	5,676	56,767	4,575	40,765	389	1,927	10,640	99,459
Germany	63,713	597,866	67,772	639,058	3,570	22,103	135,055	1,259,027
Greece	571	3,169	219	1,193	33	91	823	4,453
Ireland	79	359	47	274	12	30	138	663
The Netherlands	513	3,113	322	1,948	108	251	943	5,312
Scandinavia	393	2,842	290	3,107	42	161	725	6,110
Portugal	112	868	104	364	31	52	247	1,284
UK	1,656	8,944	530	2,132	149	490	2,335	11,566
Spain	4,390	10,472	1,164	4,444	144	287	5,698	15,203
Russia	0	0	0	0	0	0	0	0
Switzerland/Liechtenstein,	7,935	78,607	13,971	138,639	758	5,168	22,664	222,414
Other European countries	2,213	10,654	1,821	9,866	2,261	6,540	6,295	27,060
Canada	321	2,105	163	1,008	109	290	593	3,403

1997	5 and 4 stars		3 stars and residence		2 and 1 stars		Hotels (total)	
	Arrivals	No. of nights stayed	Arrivals	No. of nights stayed	Arrivals	No. of nights stayed	Arrivals	No. of nights stayed
USA	1,992	14,335	1,215	6,056	122	268	3,329	20,659
Other American countries	690	4,073	267	869	195	659	1,152	5,601
Japan	367	1,117	136	377	28	67	531	1,561
South Africa	16	129	30	119	24	53	70	301
Australia	256	2,635	76	318	34	106	366	3,059
Other non-European countries	4,121	15,361	881	3,346	188	675	5,190	19,382
Total foreign states	111,103	933,259	126,704	1,079,174	10,796	52,021	248,603	2,064,454
Total Italy	56,833	328,452	89,619	659,988	36,883	262,574	183,335	1,251,014
Italy + foreign states	167,936	1,261,711	216,323	1,739,162	47,679	314,595	431,938	3,315,468

2009	5 and 4 stars		3 stars and residence		2 and 1 stars		Hotels (total)	
	Arrivals	No. of nights stayed	Arrivals	No. of nights stayed	Arrivals	No. of nights stayed	Arrivals	No. of nights stayed
Austria	25,234	130,725	22,704	124,033	167	862	48,105	255,620
Belgium/ Luxembourg	2,079	12,979	710	4,096	29	122	2,818	17,197
Denmark	277	1,396	304	1,674	16	108	597	3,178
France	9,599	63,825	2,517	16,403	248	698	12,364	80,926
Germany	51,332	418,689	27,327	229,270	493	1,958	79,152	649,917
Greece	457	2,738	59	172	4	9	520	2,919
Ireland	159	835	71	235	8	14	238	1,084
The Netherlands	1,609	6,454	609	1,792	102	347	2,320	8,593
Scandinavia	732	3,020	345	1,463	20	49	1,097	4,532
Portugal	343	981	102	394	10	80	455	1,455
Great Britain	1,604	8,284	957	3,661	39	95	2,600	12,040
Spain	1,391	3,505	349	1,171	36	79	1,776	4,755
Russia	3,707	25,550	560	2,850	26	65	4,293	28,465
Switzerland/ Liechtenstein	11,053	70,552	9,464	66,969	184	1,092	20,701	138,613
Other European countries	4,523	18,964	3,346	9,063	5,359	7,607	13,228	35,634
Canada	475	2,474	222	1,246	11	26	708	3,746
USA	2,205	10,447	823	3,885	98	182	3,126	14,514

2009	5 and 4 stars		3 stars and residence		2 and 1 stars		Hotels (total)	
	Arrivals	No. of nights stayed	Arrivals	No. of nights stayed	Arrivals	No. of nights stayed	Arrivals	No. of nights stayed
Other American countries	545	2,644	467	1,943	35	118	1,047	4,705
Japan	280	900	77	209	4	5	361	1,114
South Africa	66	254	17	88	0	0	83	342
Australia	211	1,415	114	518	15	30	340	1,963
Other non-European countries	4,184	15,344	2,598	5,903	43	118	6,825	21,365
Total foreign states	122,065	801,975	73,742	477,038	6,947	13,664	202,754	1,292,677
Total Italy	195,743	724,885	174,328	872,913	10,255	47,726	380,326	1,645,524
Italy + foreign states	317,808	1,526,860	248,070	1,349,951	17,202	61,390	583,080	2,938,201

1.5.1 Time for innovation?

Hotel Stella has always been renovated every year, but now the plumbing system is getting old. The decoration is classic, and it needs to be modernized somewhat. The swimming pools need more hydromassages; and more up-to-date spa facilities are probably needed.

Even today there are many loyal, older clients coming to the hotel year after year. They feel at home there. Any change to their favourite hotel is regarded as something quite personal. They appreciate some of the changes, but others can be regarded as detrimental.

The latest renovations were made in 2009. Antonio decided that it was time to renovate the breakfast buffet and he installed some self-service high-quality coffee machines. Many guests complained because they thought that the coffee was not good; this was not because of a change in the quality itself but because now they saw that the coffee came from such a machine. Formerly, the guests did not see anything because there was an old machine hidden in the kitchen and they thought the coffee was good.

In addition, some renovations to the building and repainting of the hall and entrance were needed. Giulia suggested to her mother that it was time to do some renovation work in the massage and beauty department and Rosa gave her the opportunity to manage the project. Also, Marco made some small changes to the garden, but unfortunately a storm damaged everything that was outside. He is also installing a new fire system, costing about €50,000, to comply with the new laws.

For older Italian people, the thermal treatments cost almost nothing thanks to the governments and healthcare department funds. As before, they just have to pay for the hotel stay. But the Italian clients are now more modest than those that used to come before in the "beautiful time". Nonetheless, Rosa is proud that they were able to keep some of the older, loyal and wealthy customers.

Besides these clients, there are also many guests that come just for 2 or 3 days, or even for a day spa. The thermal cures are still functioning, but now they usually start at 6 am and finish at midday. Rosa and Marco have also thought about changing the timetable of the therapies, but it is not permitted by local law. They also agreed not to sell packages of 1–2 or 3 days with mud packs, because the treatment is a medical one and therefore it should be done at least for 6 days.

Massages, instead, are frequently requested. Masseurs attend training courses and Rosa encourages them to go and even pays for some of them. It is quite difficult to organize everything and the receptionists are the ones in charge of making the appointments and setting the schedule for the day. The hairdresser and aesthetician, however, organizes the appointments by herself. The other types of treatment offered, inhalations and aerosols with thermal water, are still fairly popular, although less so than before. In terms of dining, guests are also just coming to breakfast and dinner. They would rather have a sandwich at the bar in the afternoon.

Antonio started to get information about computers in the 1990s and with the help of a programmer he started to write his own program for the hotel, because he was not satisfied with any others. He wanted a program that could be personalized for each guest and that could handle the whole schedule of thermal treatments and restaurant menu and table setting. He worked day and night for years and the program now makes it possible to see for each guest personal data, arrival date, accompanying guests, seating position, room number, thermal cures taken and the name of the therapist, and any particular requests for food or the room and so on.

At the beginning of the new century, Antonio started developing a very rudimentary website; he started to understand how the search engines worked and he understood immediately that the future depended on it. He could never express his ideas and nothing of what he had been suggesting for years had ever been taken into consideration. This was because he was an in-law of the family and also because he tended to be a little too arrogant sometimes. With the internet and the computer he had the real chance to realize everything that he wanted, to be autonomous.

One important decision was made by Rosa and Marco in 2009, with the agreement of the other relatives at Hotel Vita, to outsource the laundry. They looked for a laundry that offered them a good service (for example, whose detergents don't leave any smell) and now they are trialling the service with bed sheets. They are fairly satisfied, but many sheets are ruined during the washing, so they have a lot of waste. Moreover, the two employees that worked in the laundry are quite upset and are looking for other jobs.

1.5.2 Succession issues

The division of ownership of the hotels follows Italian hereditary rules. So when one of the three brothers dies half the inheritance goes to the wife and half to the sons/daughters (if any). Matteo passed away in 1996 and Elena died following a seizure in 2000. Rosa took on her mother's role at the hotel, but her father, Giuseppe, always prevented her from taking initiatives. Also, her brother started to help with the maintenance and administrative work. The family miss these two people greatly and find it a real challenge to face all the problems every day.

Giuseppe is in his 70s and sees that things are different now, but he probably doesn't know exactly why. He thinks that making an increase in prices would lead to a decrease in the number of guests coming to the hotel. The way they have always worked until now has been the right one, because it led them to success. Any changes could be too dangerous.

In the 2000s the family was hit by a series of deaths. In 2005 Matteo's first child died of a heart attack, just like his father. In 2008 Salvo died after going into a coma for one year and after a few months Giuseppe also died after a short illness.

The board and chairman of Stella had to be chosen again. Marco became the chairman and the board members were Rosa, Salvo's wife, Matteo's wife and Matteo's youngest child. Rosa was quite worried about her brother's decision. If something happened to the business he would have full responsibility.

2008, the year when both Salvo and Giuseppe passed away, saw the worst financial crises that the world has ever experienced. Now it's the three founders' sons and daughters who have to manage the businesses. In the same year Giulia started to help her mother a little in Hotel Stella. She asked her mother, "Mom, what is the breakeven point price?" Rosa stared at her like she was raving. When Giulia explained what the breakeven point is, Rosa said that she had always wished to know, but that she had no idea. Therefore, Giulia calculated the hotel bookings during 2007, looked at the other hotels' prices, took a look at some data (e.g. Figures 1.2 and 1.3 and Table 1.3), took a calendar of 2008 to check the holy days, and produced a proposal for prices for the next year. Rosa thought that her daughter was right. The prices of the hotel were divided into two seasons and, in 2010, Rosa set the prices with her daughter (see Table 1.4). They also decided to keep the hotel open in the first week of December.

Table 1.4 **Full board prices per person per night, 2010**

	27 Feb–31 Mar	1 Apr–2 June	3 June–4 Sep*	5 Sep–1 Nov	2 Nov–8 Dec
Season	Low	High	Low	High	Low
Single room	€73	€82	€73	€82	€73
Double room	€68	€77	€68	€77	€68

*Special promotion from 20 June to 7 August: reduction of €4 per person per night

Also, Giulia proposed to her mother a year-long programme for the packages, with special offers according to the periods and the treatments they offer. The new price list was issued in 2009. They also launched the "day spa" package which is actually attracting quite a lot of people, probably because it costs just €35 per person for the double room and use of the swimming pool. The hotel also maintained the same policy with travel agencies and groups.

The competitive arena has also changed over time. Every hotel now has its own strategy, some still stay attached to outdated prices and services, while others have completely rebuilt their hotel and reorganized the services.

Rosa and Marco are the ones who manage the relationships of the hotel. They pay the employees, they go to hotel directors meetings, they participate in meetings with the same consultant and relative that their parents had.

In their relationships with the employees they are always a little sceptical about what they do, but there are some members of staff that they really trust and appreciate their work. They thank them for what they do and reward them accordingly. Going to dinners with the other hotel directors is often very tiresome, occasionally fun, but they'd rather stay at home.

Today Rosa is starting to think that perhaps she should hire a graduate employee to help her with the front and back office work. Also her daughter tells her all the time that having a degree doesn't mean someone is capable of such a multi-tasking job. Despite this, Rosa is never completely satisfied with any candidate for the job.

She sees in her daughter someone who would be perfect in substituting her, but she doesn't dare to let her do so.

Rosa, Antonio and Marco are now getting tired because they work so hard, but the business is no longer profitable. Rosa doesn't want her daughter to go into the business because she sees no future there. They all know that some investment is needed. On one side, they would like to express themselves and build the hotel of their dreams, because they had never been able to do so before. On the other side, they are afraid that they would just incur a huge loss.

Initially, they talked about changing the hotel into a rest home for older people or into a medical spa. Unfortunately, legal constraints won't let them do so. Lately, they are considering the idea of selling the business although their consultant is very sceptical because after the 2008 crisis prices are still quite low. Rosa would never consider going into debt. In current economic times, it would be seen as an impending disaster. Investments are very risky and probably would not be repaid by this activity.

Giulia is very young and has a lot of energy. She still dreams a lot. Sometimes she reminds Rosa of her mother, especially in the way she is so creative. Though Rosa is not so sure that going into the family business would be the right decision for her.

Giulia packs her books for tomorrow: she has a final presentation for her management class at business school and she wants to present an extremely high standard of work.

Dinner is finished. It's better if Rosa goes to bed now.

Tomorrow will be another tough day.

2

Performance appraisal at Telespazio

Aligning strategic goals to people development*,**

Silvia Profili
European University of Rome, Italy

Alessia Sammarra
University of L'Aquila, Italy

Laura Innocenti
LUISS Guido Carli University, Italy

Gabriele Gabrielli
LUISS Guido Carli University, Italy

In 2011, Telespazio, a leading company in the aerospace industry, was dealing with the implementation of its new organizational model, a global matrix structure that the firm had adopted in 2010 to foster the process of international growth and integration. The challenge for the HR team was to align the HRM system to the company's new

* © HEC Montréal 2013. This case was originally published in the *International Journal of Case Studies in Management* (2013, Vol. 12 No. 1). © HEC Montreal, 2013. Reproduced with permission of HEC Montreal Case Centre.

** The authors wish to thank the Telespazio HR team, guided by Giorgio Dettori, for its continuous support. Particular thanks go to Marta Di Santo, who is in charge of the Organizational Development, Management and Training Function, for her input and enthusiastic involvement. Without her support, this case study would not have been possible. Special thanks also go to Stefania Tomassi, who heads the Development Function, for her valuable contributions to the writing of this case.

demands in order to improve strategic and organizational change. In this scenario, the case study focuses on the enhancement of the PAT programme, the performance appraisal system that Telespazio first introduced in 2005. The first part of the case illustrates the existing performance appraisal programme: what is assessed, who is in charge of the assessment, the steps involved. It ends in April 2011, when the HR team meets to evaluate the strengths and weaknesses of the system. The second part of the case describes the major revisions that were made to the appraisal programme, and brings a new challenge for the HR team: extending the implementation of the revised appraisal system worldwide to all of Telespazio's foreign subsidiaries by the end of 2014.

Dear colleague,

The Telespazio Performance Appraisal is one of the primary tools for human resource development and management, and its correct use is one of your main responsibilities.

Our organization sets important challenges at the transnational level, leveraging on personnel motivation. Optimal use of the appraisal system is extremely important when it comes to achieving this. For these reasons, this year, I am looking forward to receiving your full commitment to the management of the process, which is divided into two phases:

Phase 1: evaluations related to the previous year must be finished by no later than April 15th, 2011.

Phase 2: you are asked to define the 2011 objectives for your subordinates by no later than April 30th, 2011.

Regarding Phase 1, I have to stress the importance of the evaluation, which must be based on fair and realistic criteria, while also respecting deadlines.

I look forward to receiving your full commitment to the appraisal process.

It was January 2011 when Telespazio's CEO, Carlo Gualdaroni, sent this letter to all of the company's managers in order to strengthen their commitment to the appraisal programme. Gualdaroni considered the performance management system to be crucial to the organizational change process undertaken by the company. As a matter of fact, the top management team had been renewed and a new organizational matrix model had been introduced in the fall of 2010. This reorganization also involved the HR function. With the change in top management, the entire HR Management and Development System had been redesigned by the new Organizational Development, Management and Training function. Marta di Santo was in charge of this, and it had been validated by the senior management team. Gualdaroni stated:

For the very first time, all of the components of the HR System (development, organization, HR management and training) fall under a single coordinating structure in the HR Department; this can only provide a new momentum to Telespazio, which will be even more market-driven, international and based on a matrix model (Fig. 2.1).

Figure 2.1 **New Telespazio matrix model**

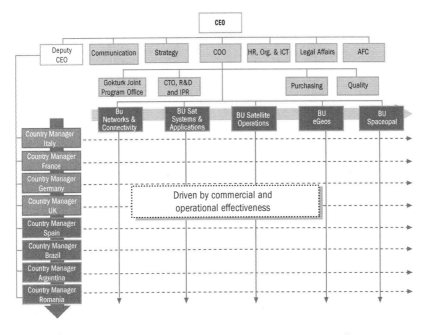

The company had become increasingly present on foreign markets, which required a more articulated structure to manage its global dimension. For this reason, Telespazio undertook a major reshaping of the group model, adopting a matrix approach in order to produce a transnational organization that focused on both geographic markets and business lines.

The new organizational model was characterized by:

- Double reporting, both regional and business, with a strong controlling model

- Responsibilities allocated on a dual basis (central and local)

- Simultaneous control of market and business strategies

- The opportunity to take advantage of synergies

This new model had several advantages, but also introduced a new challenge, especially related to HR management, because of the dual line of authority.

This organizational model was complicated by the fact that, since 2000, Telespazio had focused on project teams in an attempt to deal with the constant and rapid innovation required by the business environment. For example, the company was involved in major international space programmes, including: Galileo, EGNOS, GMES, COSMO-SkyMed, SICRAL and Göktürk. These programmes involved employees from different business units and departments, who would be temporarily assigned to a project on a full-time basis.

The appraisal system could play a strategic role for this organizational change. However, the HR department had to make important decisions about how to manage the ambiguity and potential conflict inherent in the matrix model. Should responsibility for employees' evaluations be shared between two managers, with different views and competences, or should the responsibility be allocated to a single supervisor (the business unit manager or the country manager)?

Giorgio Dettori, Director of Human Resources, was aware that the time had come to review the appraisal system, taking into account the complexity of this new organizational model.

2.1 Telespazio: from its origins to its development into a leading global company in the space industry

Telespazio, a space services company headquartered in Rome (Italy), has roots dating back to 1961, when Italcable and RAI founded the business under the auspices of the CNR (National Research Council) and the Ministry of Posts and Telecommunications.

From the very beginning, the heart of the firm's activities was telecommunications using artificial satellites, and it quickly partnered with NASA. The creation of the company opened the horizons of space to Italy, and enabled the country to take part in experiments with new forms of telecommunication.

In just a few years, Telespazio expanded by way of its successful technological developments, achieving important goals that marked the history of telecommunications, such as the live television broadcast of the moon landing on 20 July 1969, which was made possible by the parabolic antennas at Fucino, the Space Centre inaugurated by Telespazio in 1967. The Fucino Space Centre was, at that time, one of only four such stations on the continent (the others were Plemeur Bodou in France, Goonhilly in the UK and Raisting in West Germany) that were capable of receiving TV signals via satellite from anywhere in the world.

Over the course of 50 years, Telespazio quickly became a point of reference in the space industry, expanding its operations from the design and development of space systems to the management of launch services and in-orbit satellite control, and from Earth observation services, integrated communications, satellite navigation and localization to scientific programmes.

The company's growth and diversification was accompanied by important changes in its governance structure through subsequent mergers and acquisitions. The most important transition occurred in 2002, when Telespazio became part of the Finmeccanica Group, the leading Italian manufacturer of advanced technology, which was ranked among the top 10 global players in the aerospace, defence and security industries.

In 2007, Telespazio, along with Thales Alenia Space, was transformed into a joint venture between Finmeccanica (67%) and the French company Thales (33%) as a result of the new Space Alliance signed by these two giants of the European aerospace industry.

In 2010, Telespazio was ranked among the leading global companies in satellite management and Earth observation, satellite navigation, integrated connectivity and added value services. With €437 million in annual revenues and approximately 2,500 people employed in 25 sites worldwide, the company managed a network of four space centres, including the Fucino Space Centre, the world's largest civilian telecommunication centre. In Europe, the company was now present in France, Germany, the United Kingdom, Spain, Hungary and Romania. Worldwide, Telespazio operated in the US via Telespazio North America and had consolidated its presence in South America with Telespazio Brazil and Telespazio Argentina.

2.2 Performance appraisal at Telespazio (PAT)

A performance appraisal system (PAT) was designed in 2005 to align employees' efforts with the organizational and the group's challenging goals, both locally and in the international arena. The system was conceived as a means to support decisions regarding employee management, such as rewards, compensation, career advancement, mobility, and training. Its aim was to promote the following values:

- Transparency
- Sharing
- Joint definition of objectives
- Reference to observable behaviours
- Focus on roles and competences

The evaluation system covers all employees and managers, with the only exception being executives, who are part of the Finmeccanica management review process.

The last, but by no means least important advantage of this system is the fact that it is totally paperless.

2.2.1 What is assessed?

The aim of the system is twofold: 1) to ensure that the company achieves positive results; and 2) to promote the professional development of employees. Accordingly, it focuses on two aspects of employee performance: goals/objectives and competences/skills (Fig. 2.2).

Figure 2.2 **The PAT program**

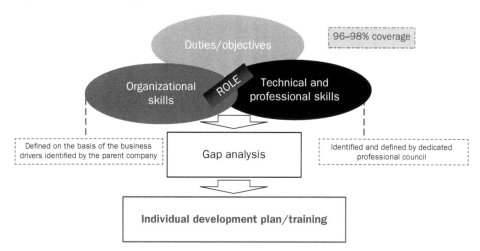

2.2.2 Goals/objectives

The identification of objectives is a crucial phase, as it is considered to be the basis on which each employee focuses his or her efforts throughout the year. Each objective should: be related to an individual department's budget plan, be coherent with the activities planned for an employee's team, and cover an employee's development needs. Along with business-related objectives, attention should also be paid to the definition of goals that are geared towards an employee's professional development, such as the attainment of an advanced proficiency in English, or the acquisition of the technical knowledge needed to operate a specific application.

Importantly, in order to ensure joint ownership of, and involvement in, this process, the system allows middle managers, professionals and specialists to set their own objectives and enter them directly into the system. Their supervisor can then modify them or add new ones with the approval of the employee.

Objectives should be set and assessed as far as possible on the basis of measurable factors, such as facts, deadlines and figures. For the system to be effective, it is important not only to achieve results, but also to reach them in the right way. An objective accomplished using inappropriate or inconsistent conduct is considered to be more harmful to the organization than an unmet goal. The achievement of each objective is then evaluated through an appropriate rating scale with three levels:

For middle managers, professionals and specialists:

1. Not achieved

2. Achieved

3. Exceeded

and, for employees and operators:

1. To be improved

2. Standard

3. Outstanding

2.2.3 Skills and competences

All of the skills and competences related to each organizational role have been identified and included in the competency management system, and managers are asked to communicate with their staff about their role. This enables a thorough communication of the organization's expectations for each role in terms of skills and competences.

The competency management system includes both organizational and technical/professional skills, which are derived from the business drivers. Organizational skills include behaviours and methods adopted by an employee to deal with specific situations and achieve set objectives. Examples of organizational skills for middle managers, professionals and specialists include: "value creation" and "market and customer orientation" (Figure 2.3).

Figure 2.3 **Organizational skills for middle managers, professionals and specialists**

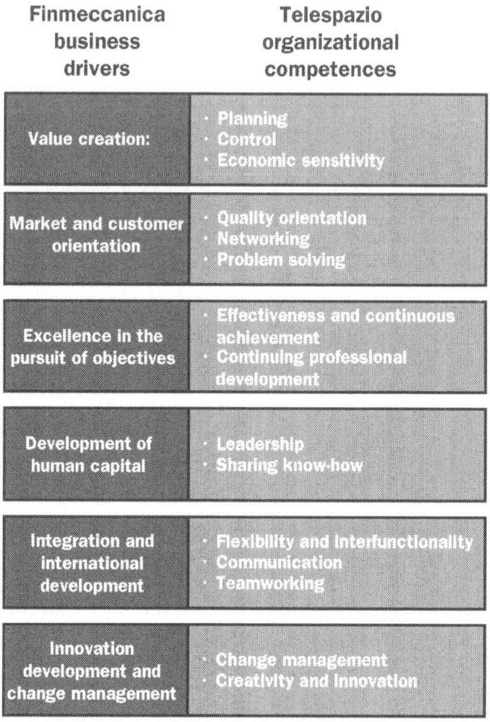

Finmeccanica business drivers	Telespazio organizational competences
Value creation:	· Planning · Control · Economic sensitivity
Market and customer orientation	· Quality orientation · Networking · Problem solving
Excellence in the pursuit of objectives	· Effectiveness and continuous achievement · Continuing professional development
Development of human capital	· Leadership · Sharing know-how
Integration and international development	· Flexibility and interfunctionality · Communication · Teamworking
Innovation development and change management	· Change management · Creativity and innovation

Examples of organizational skills for employees and operators include: "flexibility and interfunctionality" and "customer service orientation" (Fig. 2.4). Technical and professional skills refer to specific knowledge and competences required for a particular role.

Moreover, each manager can add specific skills or professional experience to the role-specific skills, selecting them to be included in the list of competences in the competency management system. These additional skills are not assessed, but can provide useful information on an employee's experience.

For the system to be really effective, managers are asked to focus on performance and the behaviour exhibited by an employee during the assessment period. They are also required to base the evaluation of competences/skills on the observation of concrete facts, adopting a three-level scale: to be improved, standard, outstanding.

Figure 2.4 **Skills for employees and operators**

2.2.4 Basic steps for effective performance management

The appraisal process must be completed by the first quarter of each new year, as employees must have enough time to plan the activities required to meet their objectives. To set the goals half way through the year or, even worse, at the end, is considered to be ineffectual or, in many cases, harmful.

2.2.4.1 *The interview as the core of the appraisal process*

The evaluation process has several steps, which are described in Figure 2.5. The interview is the key part of the process. Indeed, it is so central to the process that it should be regarded as the performance appraisal. Accordingly, particular attention must be paid to preparing for the interview; both managers and employees need to carefully gather all of the information available to support their discussions with concrete evidence. During the meeting, the manager should focus on the results achieved and the gaps between the expected level of skills for the role and those exhibited by the employee. The manager must see the interview as an opportunity to both fully explore areas of performance and skills that require improvement and define the appropriate training.

For their part, the employees should make a list of their achievements and skills, and are invited to suggest training activities that could be useful for improving weaknesses. Employees should not regard the meeting as an "exam", but as a relevant and constructive opportunity to get feedback on both strengths and areas that could be improved.

According to the HR development team, the PAT system should be used as a management tool, and is designed to motivate and develop employees, rather than simply "reward" or "punish" them. In this regard, negative feedback is also relevant, as it should encourage employees to recognize their weaknesses, face their problems and take appropriate action to improve their skills.

Figure 2.5 **PAT process**

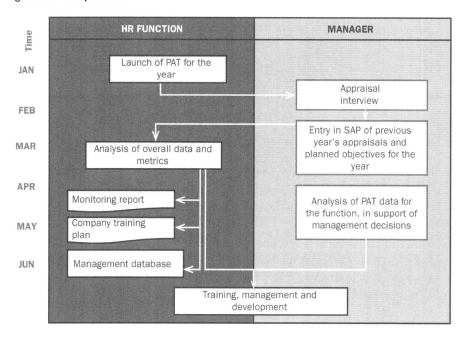

2.2.4.2 A paperless appraisal

The appraisal process is completely electronic. In order to ensure standardized and comparable analyses, all of the information about employee objectives and skills are gathered on specific forms made available by SAP-HR, one for middle managers, professionals and specialists, and another for employees/operators.

The forms also serve to collect all of the data related to training needs and improve the information available with which to evaluate the company's quality and return on investment in training. The SAP system collects the information required to prepare specific training plans for each individual that are coherent with the company's strategies. The effectiveness of an employee's training, in terms of the impact on work performance, during the year is evaluated by the manager and included in the appraisal.

Employees are expected to take an active part in the performance evaluation, writing their comments in the appropriate section, which includes several questions aimed at encouraging them to explain their points of view on key aspects of the appraisal. Both managers and employees are asked to complete this section. If the sections are blank, the appraisal process is considered incomplete and the system does not accept it.

The adoption of the SAP tool enables the HR function and all managers to have real-time access to specific and aggregate data that is valuable for managing and developing employees.

2.2.4.3 Overall appraisal

The evaluation of objectives and competences flows into an overall assessment of employees and uses a three-level scale: to be improved, standard and outstanding. The system itself, on the basis of all of the information obtained, suggests the most appropriate level. The supervisor can modify this value if an employee's professional track record suggests a different evaluation.

2.2.4.4 Who is in charge of the appraisal?

The performance appraisal at Telespazio is based on the views of one evaluator, the direct supervisor. Evaluation is a primary responsibility of each manager, which ensures the appropriate visibility of results by the management level immediately above. An exception to this rule occurs when employees are assigned to project teams on a regular basis, with a mix of line and project responsibilities. In these cases, the performance appraisal is completed by both the project manager and the line manager. More specifically, definition of the objectives for each new year is the project manager's role, as he or she is responsible for the project's budget and timing. The line manager is responsible for the performance interview, as this is the core of the appraisal process. This approach has two objectives: 1) the attainment of the team's project goals; and 2) ensuring the employee's long-term professional growth (Fig. 2.6).

The planning and coordination of the entire appraisal process is the responsibility of the HR department, which is also in charge of analysing and preparing monitoring reports on the overall results.

Figure 2.6 **Dual line of authority and appraisal**

ACTIVITY	PROJECT MANAGER	LINE MANAGER
Identification of objectives	R	JR(*)
Assessment of objectives	R	JR
Assessment of skills	JR	R
Summary assessment		R
Strengths and areas of improvement	JR	R
Assessment of training effectiveness	JR	R
Proposed training	JR(**)	R

R: primary responsibility – JR: joint responsibility

(*) Line manager may set additional objectives, especially those relating to employee development. In this case, the manager must indicate the relevant level of achievement.

(**) Functional manager may propose and discuss with the Line manager training activities related to the achievement of the assigned objectives.

2.2.5 Supporting implementation of PAT through ongoing communication

Each year, several means of communication are used to ensure that important information and the values associated with the programme go out to all employees. Indeed, both the managers who are in charge of evaluating their staff and the workers who will be appraised must be fully aware of the rules of the game. As stated by the HR team: "transparency and equity are essential to guaranteeing that the program is successfully implemented."

At the start of each year, the CEO sends out a letter as a way of engaging all of the company's managers in the process. This letter is accompanied by the setting-up of a management forum for all of the managers involved in the appraisal process, and by a more detailed communication from the Director of Human Resources, Giorgio Dettori, to all employees. Moreover, a section of the company's intranet is dedicated to a PAT description and timeline. There also exists a PAT brochure which explains the evaluation objectives and process.

2.2.6 Assessing the PAT system

On 14 April 2011, Giorgio Dettori and Marta Di Santo met the HR staff to determine the programme for the upcoming management forum, the annual workshop where the Human Resources department presents the overall results of the performance appraisal process to Telespazio's management. The Development Unit had prepared a detailed presentation for the meeting in which it planned to highlight positive aspects of the PAT programme as well as critical issues, with the aim of making recommendations with respect to potential changes.

Marta Di Santo said:

> After six full years since PAT's introduction, we have several reasons to be satisfied. We have gone from a context in which it was necessary to demonstrate the value of a formal performance appraisal process, to an organizational environment that has finally understood its importance. Today, most supervisors acknowledge that PAT is a useful tool that allows them to manage structured feedback with their subordinates. Moreover, employees have begun to appreciate PAT as a tool that ensures a transparent and consensual evaluation process.

Stefania Tomassi added:

> Initially we had to 'chase down' supervisors to get them to complete PAT; now, employees themselves pressure their boss to complete the evaluation process. I realized that we were finally able to bring about a real cultural change when the trade unions came to ask for our intervention with respect to the supervisors who were not completing the appraisal process, as they thought that this wasn't in line with the best practices set by the company.

Marta Di Santo continued her presentation by illustrating the results of the competence gap analysis for all of Telespazio's organizational roles (Fig. 2.7). As she noted, the PAT programme provides valuable data when it comes to assessing average competence levels and evaluating their appropriateness against role requirements. This data was crucial for planning targeted training programmes.

Although these results were considered to be extremely positive, Di Santo did have some concerns about the programme:

- **The timing of the performance appraisal process**. Although the PAT process was deemed an essential responsibility for managers, delays against the planned schedule were still a problem; pressing budget deadlines took precedence over performance appraisal.

- **Equity and selectivity**. Although the company made significant investments in targeted training and coaching for assessors, the analysis of the data generated from the human resources management system showed that the rating distributions were often biased towards positive performance and uneven between different business units and departments (Fig. 2.8).

- Some remarks were made regarding the system's alleged **rigidity**.

Figure 2.7 **Example of a competence gap analysis**

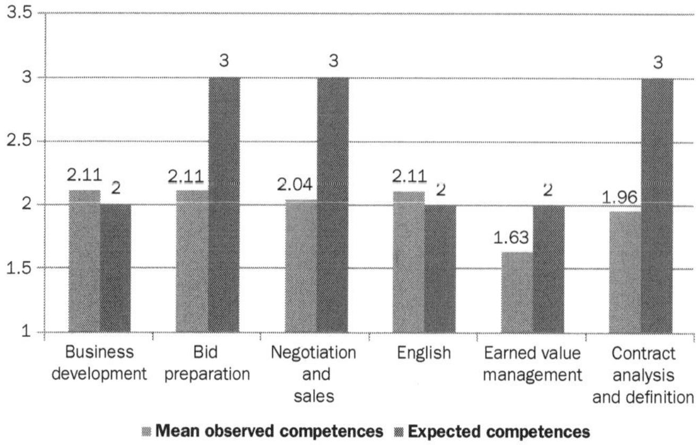

Dettori considered the equity and selectivity issue to be the most critical: "After several years devoted to developing a culture of appraisal, I don't see many steps forward in the ranking distribution." Marta Di Santo added: "Most ratings are inflated, others are not differentiated...some managers award superior ratings to all of their staff!" Dettori continued:

> These kinds of appraisal risk having a demotivating effect on those employees who have been correctly evaluated by their boss, and who come out below the average. Last year, we were in the same situation and decided that more effort was required in terms of communication and training. But this wasn't enough! It's time to make some changes. Our managers have to be aware that differentiation among their employees is essential to the system's effectiveness. We have to evaluate carefully every possible action that goes in this direction. The revision of PAT should also address the important organizational change we're facing. The new organizational model needs to be assimilated by our colleagues; they still need to feel confident with this new way of working. We must attain a stronger integration of our operations across the world and adjust to a multicultural context. The worldwide implementation of the performance appraisal program will be crucial to communicating the new organizational requirements and sustaining the process of global integration.

Figure 2.8 **Comparing evaluator rating distributions (2011)**

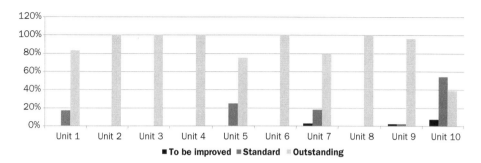

2.3 T-PAD: the revised appraisal programme

At the end of April 2011, the HR development team decided on how to improve the PAT programme. The major revisions included:

- **Revised rating categories.** The old numerical, three-level rating scale for the evaluation of both objectives and competences was replaced by a new four-level rating scale that is consistent with the one used for the overall evaluation. This expansion was made at the request of a number of different evaluators, who expressed the need to have a better opportunity to differentiate between different performance levels. Figures 2.9 and 2.10 set out the new four-level rating scale introduced for both objectives and competences.

Figure 2.9 **New rating scale for objectives**

Managers, professionals, specialists	Employees, operators
Not achieved, Partially achieved, Achieved, Exceeded	To be improved, Adequate, High, Excellent

Figure 2.10 **New rating scale for competences**

Organizational competences	Technical professional competences
To be improved, Adequate, High, Excellent	Aware, Familiar, Skilled, Master

- **More selectivity in the appraisal process**. All company managers were advised that in every department/function, the number of employees with an outstanding performance should not exceed 15% of the overall number of people working in the unit.

- **Assessment of new competences**. Two competences were added to support the implementation of the new model (i.e. international orientation and business orientation).

These revisions were communicated to all managers and employees through an email sent by the CEO during the launch phase of the new appraisal process for 2012. Furthermore, a meeting with all supervisors was planned, with the objectives of sharing the previous year's evaluation results and explaining how to handle the new programme. The revised PAT, now named T-PAD (Telespazio Performance Appraisal for Development), was illustrated in an article published on the intranet. A new brochure was also distributed to all employees.

As 50% of Telespazio's employees work outside Italy, the goal set for the 2012–2014 period was to "export" the roles and competences system and the updated T-PAD to all of the countries where the company's subsidiaries operated. The HR team defined the schedule of the operational plan for the introduction of the T-PAD programme to the company's sites abroad. The pilot country would be Telespazio Argentina in 2012, with the objective of extending the appraisal programme to all of the other foreign subsidiaries by the end of 2014.

2.3.1 The situation in 2012

On 24 September 2012, Giorgio Dettori met the HR team to take stock of the situation and asked Marta Di Santo to report on the goals achieved during the year. Di Santo started her presentation by illustrating the partial results of the 2012 rating distribution among different organizational units (Fig. 2.11):

> I think we've made some steps forward. The introduction of a four-level scale together with the supervisors' training and coaching activities have paid off. Four evaluators used the outstanding level for less than 20% of their staff and no one rated his/her entire staff as outstanding. The assessments now definitely have a more normal distribution compared to those from 2011. The best cases are represented by units 7, 8 and 10, where the managers used the entire rating scale. But we are still some ways from having a really selective evaluation approach.

Figure 2.11 **Comparing evaluator rating distributions (2012)**

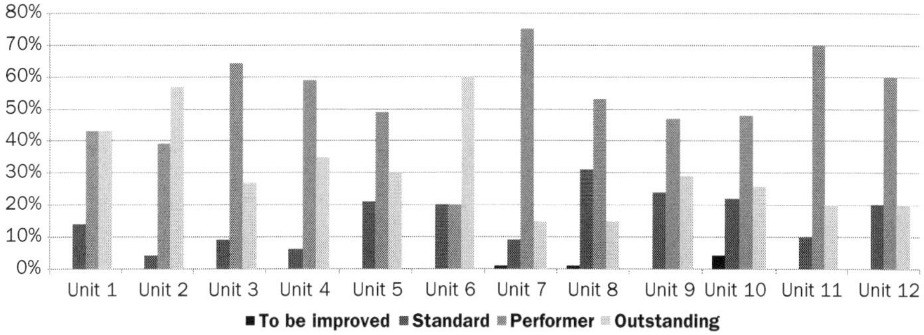

■ To be improved ■ Standard ■ Performer ▨ Outstanding

According to Di Santo, the T-PAD had other positive outcomes:

> These figures are very important, but we need to go beyond them. We've been able to bring about a real cultural shift among our line managers. Most of them are now fully aware that the T-PAD is a powerful tool with which to manage their staff effectively and achieve their unit's goals. All the decisions regarding employee development (training and career advancement) and economic incentives are taken exclusively on the basis of the evaluation results.

Stefania Tomassi added:

> Last week I met Francesco Rossi, who has recently been appointed as Operations Manager of the Network Division, and he told me: "It's a good thing we have the T-PAD! Thanks to this system, I had the chance to conduct structured interviews with my new staff and to get to know each of them in greater depth. Moreover, the SAP forms allowed me to easily reconstruct the personal history of each employee. . . until a few days ago, I didn't even know them, but today I feel like I've been working with them for the last 20 years!" He was very enthusiastic about the appraisal system and its potential.

Marta Di Santo took the floor again:

> We all know that the most important task set by our team in 2012, in line with the company's expectations, is the extension of the T-PAD to all of the foreign subsidiaries by the end of 2014. The program's worldwide extension will be crucial to sustaining the company's global integration. We started this year by implementing the system in Telespazio Argentina, the pilot country, and we didn't have any problems; we worked well with the local HR Department. The local HR Manager, Camila Beliera, was conscious that the subsidiary really needed a structured appraisal system and worked hard to bring all 10 of the local supervisors on board, making them aware of the appraisal system's strategic role. Moreover, I know Camila, as she used to work for a big Italian company in Rome and we have the same people management philosophy. . .working with her was easy.

Stefania Tomassi added:

> By the end of September 2013, we have to complete the implementation process in Germany and France. These countries' subsidiaries have very different managerial systems and leadership styles. . . Telespazio France has nearly 400 employees, a very strong national culture and a well-established local evaluation system. This will make the transfer of our T-PAD not easy at all. . .I don't think that French managers will simply accept our program!

The HR team was aware that the international implementation needed to be carefully planned.

3

UniQuest at UniManagement
Driving innovation through executive development[*]

Corey Billington
University of Wyoming, USA

Rhoda Davidson
Surrey University, UK

Carmela La Cava
UniCredit Group, Italy

Atul Pahwa
Independent consultant, Switzerland

This teaching case documents how UniCredit Group, a major financial services company, used a talent development programme to
innovate throughout the organization and change the corporate
culture. It follows the journey of Anna Simioni, Corporate Learning
and Executive Vice President, who succeeded in embedding open
innovation of business processes into executive development. The
UniQuest programme centred the experience of the participants on
real strategic projects, which were proposed and sponsored by top
executives and endorsed by the CEO. The programme was expertly
supported by organizational talent development processes and an
innovative working environment that was created at the corporate
learning centre, UniManagement, based in Turin, Italy. The case illustrates the opportunity of combining strategic problem solving with
effective talent development processes. It also demonstrates how
to fully engage executive stakeholders in a centrally led executive
leadership programme.

* Printed with permission from Bocconi University.

Anna Simioni, CEO of UniManagement and Executive Vice President of the Uni-Credit Group, reflected back over the past five years with parental pride. Uni-Management had successfully met its initial goals of providing cross-cultural integration and leadership development during a phase of rapid company growth. During 2009, 8,000 employees had walked through the doors of UniManagement's awe-inspiring facility in a historic building in downtown Torino. In this monument dedicated to inspiration and creative thinking, the participants had experienced a total of 18,000 days of innovative training and development. This collaborative environment had been the platform for instilling common values across the 22 countries represented in the UniCredit Group and participation had spanned from UniCredit's senior executives to the aspiring set of next generation managers.

Additionally, Simioni had established UniQuest, an esteemed flagship programme used to develop young talent across the organization. UniCredit CEO, Alessandro Profumo, had personally championed UniQuest and his support was a testament to his belief in the programme's value to the organization. As he commented, "Uni-Quest participants are the ones who are going to make this company one company, with a global mind-set and local roots and connections – a young company".

The previous month had been a tumultuous one for UniCredit. After over 13 years at the helm, Profumo suddenly left the bank. The announcement was made that he would be replaced by one of the four internal deputy CEOs, Federico Ghiz-zoni. Ghizzoni was known to be a supporter of UniManagement and had attended several programmes at the learning facility in Torino. However, with the financial crisis in the banking industry Simioni worried that Ghizzoni may be forced to focus his attention on other more pressing priorities. She would have to impress on him the value created by programmes such as UniQuest to secure continued top management support and their active participation in programmes.

3.1 Company background

UniCredit Group's origins date back over five centuries to the establishment of Rolo Banca in 1473, when Monte di Pietà, a public financial institution providing secured loans, was created in Bologna. During the late 1990s a multitude of acquisition possibilities opened up resulting from a combination of liberalized banking regulations, the introduction of the euro, and the opening up of Central and Eastern Europe. Under the ambitious drive of Profumo, the bank spent $65 billion on takeovers during 1997–2007. In the rapidly consolidating finance industry, UniCredit resulted from the merger of nine of Italy's largest banks and subsequent mergers with the German HVB Group and the Italian Capitalia Group. By 2007 the group had a solid base in Western, Central and Eastern Europe and had pushed further into Central Asia with acquisitions in Ukraine and Kazakhstan.

UniCredit successfully weathered the banking crisis in 2008 and, by 2009, Uni-Credit was truly a pan-European bank with strong roots in 22 European countries and with an international network presence in approximately 50 markets (refer to

Figs. 3.1 and 3.2, Box 3.1 and Table 3.1). The statistics were impressive: 40 million customers, 165,000 employees and 9,800 branches. Revenues in 2009 were €27.57 billion and profits €1.7 billion. In Central and Eastern Europe UniCredit operated the largest international banking network with approximately 4,000 branches and outlets.

Figure 3.1 Organizational structure

Source: UniCredit

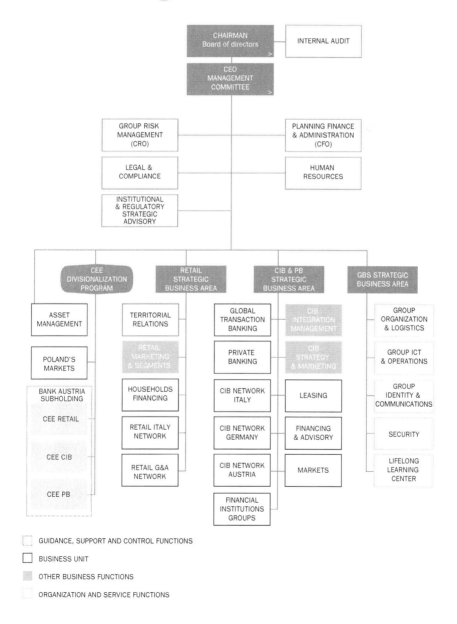

Figure 3.2 **Historical perspective of UniCredit**
Source: UniCredit

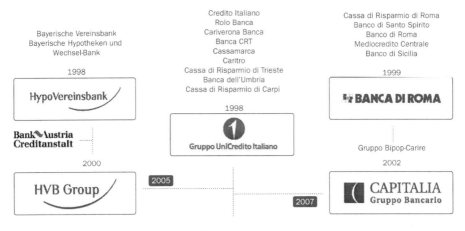

1998   UniCredito Italiano created: merger of Credito Italiano, Rolo Banca, Cariverona, Cassa di Risparmio di Torino, Cassamarca, Cassa di Risparmio di Trento e Rovereto, Cassa di Risparmio di Trieste.

1999   Expansion in growth markets: acquisition of the Polish bank, Bank Pekao.

2000   Creation of the Global Investment Management Division. acquisition of Pioneer Investment, USA. Expansion in growth markets: acquisition of Bulbank (Bulgaria) and Pol'nobanca – then Unibanka (Slovakia).

2001   Focus on three business divisions: retail, corporate, and private banking and asset management.

2002   Expansion in growth markets: acquisition of Zagrebacka Banka (Croatia), Demirbank Romania – then UniCredit Romania – and Živnostenskå Banka (Czech Republic). Agreement with Koç (Turkey) acquisition of Momentum – global leader in hedge funds.

2003   Customer segmentation model: UniCredit Banca, UniCredit Banca d'Impresa, UniCredit Private Banking.

2004   Global Banking Services Division: creation of the Global Banking Services Division, responsible for the optimization of the cost structure and the group's internal process.

2005   Expansion in growth markets: acquisition of Yapi Kredi by koç (Turkey)
Merger with HVB Group: UniCredit merged with the German HVB Group/Bank Austria.

2006   Markets & Investment Banking Division: unification of investment banking activities into a single, global division.

2007   Expansion in growth markets: spreading presence in CEE with its expansion into Ukraine, in Central Asia with acquisitions in Kazakhstan, Tajikistan and Kyrgyzstan.
Merger with Capitalia. Banco di Sicilia, MCC and Fineco are also part of the group.

Box 3.1 **UniCredit business model**

Source: UniCredit

UniCredit business model based on four pillars:

Customer centricity: delivering specialized customer coverage to maximize long-term value and customer satisfaction

A multi-local approach: empowering the Group's local banks to oversee distribution networks and customer relationships

Global product lines: leveraging the Group's significant in-house expertise

Global service lines: supplying network coverage functions and product factories with specialized services, including banking back office, ICT, credit collection, procurement services, real estate and shared service centres

Table 3.1 **Financial results**

Source: UniCredit 2009 Highlights

	2009	2008	2007	2006	2005
Income statement (€ million)					
Operating income	27,572	26,866	25,893	23,464	11,024
Net interest income	17,616	19,385	14,843	12,860	5,645
Net non-interest income	9,956	7,481	11,050	10,604	5,379
Operating costs	−15,324	−16,692	−14,081	−13,248	−6,045
Operating profits	12,248	10,174	11,812	10,206	4,979
Profit before income tax	3,300	5,458	9,355	8,210	4,068
Net profit	2,291	4,831	6,678	6,128	2,731
Net profit attributable to group	1,702	4,012	5,961	5,448	2,470
Balance sheet (€ million)					
Total assets	928,760	1,045,612	1,021,758	823,284	787,284
Loans and receivables to customers	564,986	612,480	574,206	441,320	425,277
Deposits from customers and debt securities in issue	596,396	591,290	630,533	495,255	462,226
Shareholders' equity	59,689	54,999	57,724	38,468	35,199
Profitability ratios %					
Return on equity	3.8	9.5	15.6	16.7	15.6
Operating profits/total assets	1.32	0.97	1.16	1.24	0.63
Cost/income ratio	55.6	62.1	54.4	56.5	54.8

3.2 The origins of a corporate learning centre

At the end of 2005, Profumo recognized the need to create and embrace a common corporate culture to accelerate the integration of the different acquired banks. To accomplish this he envisioned a learning centre that would serve as a way for the bank to channel this cultural integration and to create a common understanding of the global banking strategy. He believed that the bank should leverage the diversity across the organization so that the whole was more than just the sum of the parts. While he recognized the value of local cultural expression, he also believed in developing cooperative platforms to create, support and circulate new ideas between countries. He also wanted to leverage standard best practices where appropriate. The learning centre, named UniManagement, would accomplish this cultural integration through training and leadership development programmes.

Profumo selected Simioni to head up UniManagement. Simioni had spent the past ten years within the UniCredit organization, building up credibility through various roles. She was known in the bank for managing UniCredit through the transition to off-shoring its first service processes outside Italy. Prior to the offer of heading up the new corporate learning centre Simioni had risen through the HR organization. Previously she had been the Head of Organizational and Professional Development as well as the Head of HR Policies and Development and at this point was the HR Director. Intrigued and motivated by the challenge, she accepted the new assignment with one caveat: that she would have *carte blanche* in designing the learning system for developing the next generation of leaders within the organization.

Simioni set out to create a very different type of learning centre. Her major insight was that physical infrastructure and the use of space was critically important to create an environment where executives could learn effectively. She teamed up with a US-based architect, Matt Taylor, to help her design a flexible open workspace that would foster interaction and collaboration. Taylor was renowned for applying the principles of organic architecture, cybernetics and complex adaptive systems to address individual and group creativity. He had designed working environments for clients such as NASA, Vanderbilt University, Ernst & Young and the World Economic Forum. Together Simioni and Taylor set out to create a physical space that would look and feel very different from traditional office space. This space would erase all notions that learning was the same as "business as usual".

UniManagement[2] opened in Torino in January 2006. Torino had been carefully selected as it was considered "neutral ground". The location was close enough to provide easy accessibility to get to and from UniCredit's headquarters in Milan, but it was a new setting for everybody. UniManagement was housed in a historic building within Torino's business district that had previously been the municipal tax office. Simioni had succeeded in transforming this old and dusty government

2 www.unimanagement.eu

building into a state-of-the-art learning environment, a space that now strongly resembled a Silicon Valley design studio.

Simioni deliberately staffed UniManagement with people who were highly knowledgeable about banking rather than with people with only training experience. These people were drawn from a wide range of the company's locations (e.g. Poland, Germany, Bosnia, Austria, as well as Italy). Many of them had held senior positions before moving to UniManagement. Simioni was convinced that to be able to effectively design learning and development events her staff should have banking experience. She was not looking for banking specialists but rather people with a solid grasp of the logic of the banking business. She actively tried to recruit people who could share her passion for collaborative learning and delivering transformational experiences. UniManagement should embody the new "UniCredit working style" – flexible, collaborative, cross-cultural, cross-divisional and innovative.

3.3 UniQuest: grooming the next generation of leadership

The UniQuest programme was launched in 2006, a few months after the merger with HVB-Bank Austria. The programme would be run on an annual basis and it was the first programme of its kind to target a specific group of people.

The goals of the programme were threefold. First, it was intended to identify and develop future leaders from across the organization. These were the "high potentials" that the company felt would rise to senior management positions within Uni-Credit. It was believed that UniQuestors were the next generation of leaders and change agents who would take the bank to a new level of performance. Second, it provided a forum for cultural integration and sharing of UniCredit's values: fairness, transparency, respect, reciprocity, freedom to act and trust. Third, the programme was focused on creating a quantifiable return on investment for UniCredit.

Creating measurable value for UniCredit was achieved through the incorporation of business challenges that would be solved by the participants during the programme (refer to Figs. 3.3–3.5). These business projects and challenges served as the core vehicle for learning. Teams worked on the projects for six months. This time was broken into four main phases: discovery, challenge, delivery and development. Each of these project phases was punctuated by three sessions of three-day, face-to-face learning and teamwork modules at the UniManagement location in Torino.

Figure 3.3 Goal and participant profiles for the UniQuest programme

Source: UniCredit

UNIQUEST AT A GLANCE

UniQuest has been designed to **identify and develop talented young professionals from all across the Group** who are likely to succeed **in an international, cross-cultural working environment** and who might be promoted to **managerial positions in their career with UniCredit Group**

UniQuest participants profile

- Young professionals: 3-6 years of professional experience
- High command of English
- Max. 100 participants (ca. 50% from CEE & Poland Division, ca. 50% from Italy, Germany, Austria, other countries)
- Participants coming from all divisions and competence lines

UNIQUEST AT A GLANCE

UniQuest is far from being a traditional training /"MBA-style" academic program.
It is a **different kind of learning experience!**

Business-driven projects at the core of the programme

- Projects sponsored by Heads of Competence Line/Division
- Projects identified among key business issues
- UniQuest participants remain on their jobs during project phase, but dedicate ca. 25% of monthly work-time to UniQuest projects
- UniQuest participants collaborate in cross-cultural, cross-divisional project groups (virtual, remote project work + "physical" gatherings)
- All 100 UniQuest participants attend 3 events in UniManagement in Turin for a full time learning experience on leadership development and project development

Figure 3.4 **Business-driven projects details for the UniQuest programme**

Source: UniCredit

DETAILED ROADMAP

Listed below, a summary of activities that UniQuest participants do during the 4 phases of the program.

DISCOVERY	■ During the first 3 months, participants select projects, form teams, begin to define roles and responsibilities and start working on their projects to create an intermediate presentation to the sponsors. ■ *Participants get to know each other in their teams and share their experiences (i.e. competencies), contribution to the team, personal traits (i.e. behaviors, learning style).*
CHALLENGE	■ Next, the teams work together on the feedbacks provided by their sponsors to go ahead with their project implementation. They are stimulated to develop an innovative approach for their projects. ■ *Participants reflect on the team experience and the contribution they are giving and can give to the team, especially facing unexpected and complex situations.*
DELIVERY	■ In the third quarter, teams finalize and present their finished projects to their sponsors and reflect on their project experience. ■ *During the graduation, participants take time to reflect on their learning and the way they worked within the team.*
DEVELOPMENT	■ *After the graduation, UniQuest participants update their CVs. Direct Managers and Tutors prepare feedback for participants. TMR collect data and create a profile for each participant. Local HR and direct managers discuss profiles with participants and create their individual development plans. This is an important stage as it is the first step on the path to international career growth in UniCredit Group.*

Project activities *Development activities*

CALENDAR OF UNIQUEST 5 SELECTION

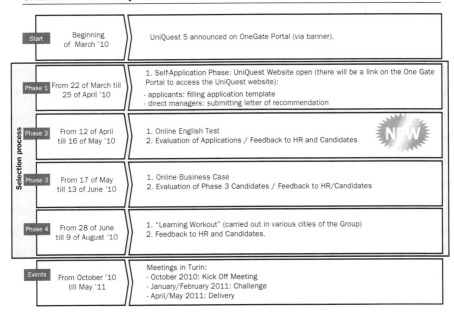

Figure 3.5 **Roadmap and calendar for the UniQuest programme**

Source: UniCredit

KEY ROLES FOR THE PROJECT IMPLEMENTATION

SPONSORS

■ are members of UniCredit Group's senior management team. They propose projects to be developed during the UniQuest program.

TUTORS

■ are identified by the sponsors to support the project's implementation

■ are the CONTENT EXPERTS and the only persons working in the division / competence line to which the project belongs and are the KEY RESOURCE for providing suggestions, guidelines, advice

■ attend periodic meetings with the team (remote or not) to assure that the team stays on target and makes reasonable choices on what issues are key to study and to solve

■ are the LINK with the Sponsor / Head of Division: ensure periodic feedback from the Sponsor; facilitate the organization of the meetings with the Sponsor

■ Provide final FEEDBACK ON EACH TEAM MEMBER as input into the UniQuest participants' development plans

DEVELOPMENT ADVISORS

■ Conduct the project team through the activities focused on team development

■ Offer various tools and support for learning activities while also facilitating the process itself

The pedagogical philosophy at UniManagement was that learning occurred when participants shared their ideas and experiences. Simioni liked to emphasize the difference between this way of learning and more traditional training. She saw the goal of training as passing on knowledge from the mind of the trainer to the participants. But in her view training did not necessarily lead to an increase in productive leadership behaviour. She believed that changes in leadership behaviour were more likely to result from participants working on ambiguous, open-ended business problems. These problems had no right or wrong answer and the team needed to learn to work together to share and build ideas that would create a solution. Feedback between team members and personal reflection would be the catalyst for behavioural changes.

This learning method was also very different from highly academic MBA programmes run by some business schools. The sessions at UniManagement were not intended as a showcase for professors to expound their knowledge to the participants. Instead the goal of these sessions was to provide the real-time pedagogical input that the participants needed to plan out and implement their projects. Participants could draw from this input as they chose. In one sense this was an instructorless environment.

Besides the business projects UniQuest also emphasized a participant-centred approach to learning. Simioni's intention was that each participant should be empowered to create their own learning agenda, individually tailored to their own needs and reflections. While the business projects were a key part of the programme, participants should not feel that their sole purpose for being in the programme was to resolve UniCredit's business issues. Each participant needed to be provided opportunities to work on their own leadership strengths and development needs.

In addition, the UniQuest programme allowed for the development of participants' social skills and multicultural management abilities. Evenings were filled with dinners and discos, providing plenty of social and networking opportunities. Despite the hard work, UniQuest was constructed to be a fun and memorable experience for its participants.

As part of creating a safe place to learn, Simioni eliminated formal assessments during the programme. This was a bold move. In many multinational companies HR directors were encouraged to attend executive programmes and to provide subjective assessments of individuals' capabilities, acting as "talent spotters". Simioni was careful to avoid this at UniQuest because she wanted to provide the participants with a secure and "free" environment where they could test out new ways of working and behaving without constraints.

When designing the UniQuest programme Simioni paid special attention to how components of the programme such as participant selection, project identification, involvement of senior management, project support, and the physical environment were defined and how they linked to the UniCredit talent management process.

3.4 Participant selection

Thanks to a carefully designed self-nomination process, anyone in the organization could apply to the UniQuest programme. In March of each year, UniQuest was announced on the group's OneGate portal. Applicants had to pass through four selection phases. First, applicants completed a formal application and asked their direct line managers to submit a letter of recommendation. Second, participants took an online test to verify that they had advanced English skills. Third, the applicants completed a business competence test that included the evaluation of a business case. In the fourth phase the remaining applicants participated in a "learning workout" session in which they had to demonstrate their learning agility and team work attitude. By the end of July the successful applicants were invited to join the UniQuest programme starting in October.

Applying to UniQuest demanded a high degree of self-motivation. Simioni commented: "Getting in and being in UniQuest is hard work. You choose. You need to be active. If you want to peek over the horizon of your daily job, here is your opportunity to draw attention and gain visibility."

The participant's direct line manager was essential to support the UniQuest application. In addition to writing a letter of recommendation the line manager had to work with the participant to fill out a learning and development agreement and to sign to say that he or she would review these learning objectives until the desired objectives had been met. In addition the line manager was further expected to contribute by releasing the participant to spend 25% of their time on UniQuest during the year of the programme.

Typically, UniQuestors were young professionals with 3–7 years of experience and an average age of 30. There was a maximum of 100 participants in any one Uni-Quest programme. Participants were selected from all functions and business lines. The split of men to women was 60:40. Approximately 50% of the participants were drawn from Italy, Germany and Austria and 50% from Central and Eastern Europe. Some countries tended to send more participants than others. For example, Uni-Quest was very popular in Romania but less so in Poland. The degree of popularity in any one country could be traced to the amount of enthusiasm of the local HR director in marketing the programme and also from the degree of positive feedback from programme alumni.

Figure 3.6 **Participants experiencing the UniQuest Programme**

3.5 Project identification

A significant amount of time and effort was spent by senior managers working together with UniManagement to identify projects that would create good learning experiences.

To be included, projects had to meet several criteria. First, they had to be core to a division's current or future strategy. Second, they had to have the potential to create new and innovative business approaches. And finally they needed to meet some practical limitations of being feasible within 6 months with 25% time commitment by the UniQuestors.

Examples of projects included: identify key drivers influencing an employee's ability to increase customer satisfaction; implement a governance model for Central and Eastern European operations; and develop sales support components that contribute to customer satisfaction.

Simioni had to perform a delicate balancing act of encouraging senior managers to describe and acknowledge their challenges without incurring political consequences. On the one hand it was essential that she find projects which were truly mission-critical for UniCredit. If not, participants would sense that they were only involved in make-work projects and would rapidly become disinterested. On the other hand, acknowledging that the project was both urgent and important might leave the senior manager open to criticism for not yet resolving the issue.

3.6 Project sponsorship

Projects were proposed and sponsored by the top managers in the company. These sponsors were either the heads of competence lines or divisions. They typically viewed the UniQuest projects as the opportunity to quickly and cheaply generate new ideas and potential solutions. It was also a good way to speed up important projects where there were limited available resources.

Simioni created real competition to offer the most exciting project in the programme. Each sponsor was required to create a one-pager that described their project. Given the active involvement of Profumo in the programme, there was no shortage of project proposals. These descriptions were then circulated to the UniQuestors during the first meeting at UniManagement.

During the first 3-day meeting, sponsors actively competed to attract the best talents to their project. Each sponsor was required to attend the meeting and personally present and sell their project directly to the UniQuestors. The participants were then asked to self-organize into project teams around the projects that they found attractive. The rules for this project selection process were simple: no more than two people from the same country on any project, participants could not work on any project that originated within their chain of command, and participants could not work on projects where they had any specific competences. This self-selection process could last anywhere from one to four hours with participants actively negotiating to find a constructive solution.

Right from the start of the programme the participants knew that they would be required to present their ideas to the CEO and the other senior management project sponsors. While this knowledge created a certain level of delivery-anxiety it kept the ambitious young executives focused on the ultimate project deliverables.

Profumo had a reputation for being extremely interactive during the final project reviews. He had a remarkable ability to focus in on each of the projects and quickly cut to the core of the business issue. UniQuestors often marvelled about how he could move from project to project with ease and quiz each team with incisive and highly pertinent questions.

3.7 Project support

3.7.1 Tutors

Sponsors were asked to identify and contribute a content-expert tutor for each project. These content tutors were working in the division or competence line where the project originated and were frequently already taking a leading role in resolving the issues encapsulated in the project.

The tutors typically worked to provide suggestions, guidelines and advice. They were required to attend periodic meetings with the team and to ensure that the team stayed on track. They also provided the link between the team and the sponsor and could represent the view of the sponsor if he or she could not attend a progress review. At the end of UniQuest the tutor gave final feedback on each team member as an input into the UniQuest participant's development plan.

Most often tutors were seen as being helpful and constructive and at the same time providing space for creativity from the team. However in some cases tutors seemed to already know "the right answer" before the teams started to work and as a result stifled the team's learning experience.

3.7.2 Development advisers

During the first years of UniQuest the tutor was the only "responsible adult" working with the team. Over time Simioni recognized that the teams needed additional assistance to learn how to work together productively. She introduced the concept of development advisers. These development advisers worked as process facilitators with the team during the programme modules at UniManagement. They also helped the team to reflect on their team learning experiences and the contributions of each individual to the team task.

3.7.3 Budget

Event expenses for travel and accommodation in Torino were funded by participants' business lines. UniCredit corporate learning covered the fees for attending the sessions at UniManagement. To help develop cooperative skills, each participant was given a budget of €2,500 to use for the project. Project expenses included travel, accommodation, books, and special training courses. The teams were highly inventive with the ways in which they used this money. Some teams used budget airlines to fly to destinations where they could work together cost-effectively. At the end of the project each person was accountable for how they had used their budget.

3.7.4 Project phases and process

During the first UniQuest event at UniManagement, participants selected projects, formed teams, and defined roles and responsibilities before starting to work on their projects. The focus was on building group cohesion and developing a group process.

Over the next three months, groups worked to design an innovative approach for project implementation. Each team was closely followed in this process by the project sponsor, tutor and development advisers. Time was also dedicated to personal leadership reflections as well as team reflections and conflict management.

In the final three months of the programme, the groups completed their assignments, presented their results to Profumo and reflected on their respective individual and group project experiences.

The UniQuest programme used a carefully laid out process over the course of the year that included the physical space at UniManagement, tutors and coaches. In addition, Simioni brought talents from all over the organization – geographies, departments and companies. They were not allowed to work on problems that came from their immediate chain of command or on problems where they had specific functional competences. The teams could suggest pilots but were not responsible for implementation. Instead there was a hand-off to the sponsors to take the project into implementation.

3.8 Linking UniQuest to UniCredit talent management processes

At the end of the programme all participants were given feedback. Tutors were asked to complete a feedback form, containing competences from the UniCredit competency model. The evaluation was aimed at identifying strengths and areas of development for each team member from what the tutor had observed during the UniQuest project. Direct line managers also completed a competency assessment aimed at highlighting important changes in competences and behaviours over the course of the UniQuest programme. Local HR managers together with the direct line managers then discussed how best to define an individual development plan with the UniQuest participants.

Participants entered the UniCredit talent pool, known as the Talent Management Review (TMR). This HR structure was based in Milan and was dedicated to group talent development including developing and managing the talent pipeline for senior positions across the group. Following a UniQuest programme the TMR collected the participant evaluations and created a profile in the system to be used by HR managers.

Alumni could expect accelerated career progression and significant movement within the group. Even after three or four years, UniQuest alumni had risen to influential positions within the group. For instance, at the 5th UniQuest the global talent manager who came to UniManagement to explain the TMR had himself already been through the programme.

These accelerated cross-boundary movements of alumni created challenges for direct line managers who were expected to find replacements. The programme also created turnover issues for local HR managers when local talents were recruited away from UniCredit. However the programme was strongly supported by global HR and senior management.

Upon graduating, alumni were included in the official alumni community. During the first years this alumni community did not have an official structure but met at a yearly ball held in Vienna. By the end of the 4th UniQuest programme an official governance body was set up and regular meetings started in different countries.

Alumni praised the programme primarily for providing them with opportunities to create stronger networks and build friendships across the group. They also valued the chance for best practice sharing, better organizational understanding, and enhanced visibility with senior managers. Many alumni felt that the alumni group could play a stronger role. Some suggestions included formalizing the role of the network as a "think-tank" or leveraging the network more effectively so that individual managers could source answers for various business or career issues.

3.9 UniManagement physical environment

The UniManagement physical environment was designed to support learning experiences such as UniQuest. The layout of the building and the décor addressed issues of power and hierarchy while accelerating the flow of ideas and making the learning environment fun and exciting.

3.9.1 Ground floor

The main auditorium formed the central point of the ground floor of the building and was constructed in a circular shape. This area was termed the "Agora" which is the Greek word for an open place of assembly. This area embraced a mix of traditional and natural lighting that flooded the space with a warm welcome and radiant energy. Presenters spoke from the centre of this area with the UniQuestors grouped in four sections around the outside. The Agora was all on one level with no place in the circle higher than another. The layout kept the presenters and participants at an easy eye level.

The Agora was situated under an open wooden structure. This circular structure was used to house lighting and also artwork created by local artists to depict the theme of the learning event. For instance, an innovation theme resulted in posters with light bulbs, rainbows, brains and many famous quotes to inspire the participants.

Figure 3.7 **Main auditorium known as the "Agora" at UniManagement**

The audio-visual system played a significant role. The Agora was surrounded by a circle of plasma screens that reflected back images of the people within the auditorium during the sessions. The screens were also used to display photographs of individuals and teams at work and for streaming high impact videos – all part of the learning experience. The entire ground floor was equipped with a high quality sound system that could be used to signal the start or end of any single session. Simioni used music to reflect and create different moods. For example, heavy rock to catch people's attention, frenetic music to indicate that people needed to move around the building to their team area, and slow ballads to encourage personal or team reflection.

Surrounding the Agora were outlying areas for group work. These small, open-plan areas were outfitted with circular tables and large wave-shaped panels on wheels. The panelled wall space was perfect for team design work where each team member could use marker pens to write directly on the furniture. Team members captured their output on their mobile phones or digital cameras. The layout of the working areas was more typical of product design studios found in California.

Figure 3.8 **Small open plan areas for group work with furniture on wheels**

The ambience of the ground floor was enhanced by the widespread use of glass, including transparent stairs and walkways. This allowed a maximum amount of natural light to penetrate into the group working areas below. The heavy use of glass suggested that individuals were connected not isolated and that transparency existed rather than opaqueness.

Figure 3.9 **Transparent stairs and walkways allow natural light**

3.9.2 Upper floors

On the upper floor were further experiments with room design. One type of room was designed to foster teambuilding. These rooms had a large round table in the centre and high chairs without back support. These chairs forced participants to lean forward onto the table and engage in the dialogue rather than leaning back and disengaging. In addition each room was equipped with a kitchenette where bonding could take place over group cooking exercises or a shared meal.

Figure 3.10 **Kitchenette for encouraging teambuilding over a jointly cooked meal**

There were several brainstorming rooms. These were white and every square inch of the room, every chair, and every small surface could be used as a whiteboard. Participants were encouraged to brainstorm, write down ideas and prototype solutions for the tasks at hand.

Figure 3.11 **Brainstorming rooms with whiteboard walls**

Three large rooms were designed as quiet places for people to read, think and reflect. These rooms were outfitted with jute fabric panelling, instilling a cosy atmosphere, plush comfortable seating and warm lighting.

Figure 3.12 **Quiet room for learning reflection**

The archive of a former bank was transformed into a flexible room with all the wall surfaces painted in a rich red. This room was often the scene of lively dinner parties where up to 100 people could eat and socialize together.

Even the UniManagement hallways were made visually interesting and were littered with comfortable couches, painted in vibrant colours and covered with nice bookshelves holding an array of books. The content of these collections was not just business books but art, history, travel and philosophy literature. Simioni asked programme participants to bring their favourite books to share with colleagues and this helped add to the collection. Leaving no details unattended, even the administrative offices were transparent, providing participants with an invitation to feel welcome to enter at any time.

3.9.3 Other features

Food stations were located on both floors. Long tables were filled with breakfast items and coffee starting early in the morning. At lunch time these items were swiftly replaced by an amazing selection of food that formed a substantial self-service buffet. Snacks and drinks remained available throughout the day.

Figure 3.13 **Self-service buffet serving food throughout the day**

The building was filled with many pieces of visual art and sculpture. Some of the art was borrowed from the private collection of UniCredit. Progressively much of this art has been replaced with co-created art resulting from programmes that were run at UniManagement over the years. The overwhelming atmosphere was that this was a highly creative place.

3.10 Looking ahead

As Simioni reflected on the last five years she felt proud of her successes. She had succeeded in creating a novel form of instructorless training that fostered the desire of the participants to create their own learning agenda. She had developed a highly innovative space that could be further used and reused for a wealth of other UniCredit programmes. UniQuest was delivering value at three levels. At a company level the business projects were delivering a steady, although largely unquantified, return on investment. At a team level the participants had learned how to work together constructively on open-ended, hard-to-solve problems. At a personal level a large majority of the participants were satisfied with their own personal leadership development. Finally, she had succeeded in more or less aligning the interests of all the stakeholders involved in the programme and in getting the stakeholder system to operate effectively.

At the same time the UniQuest programme had not stood still. Each year new aspects had been added to the programme. For instance, one year they had added presentation skills and another year, individual and team coaching development.

However, she also had her concerns. The banking crisis had left all major financial institutions with rising levels of bad debts. The industry as a whole was suffering from declining revenues per transactions, and eroding margins. The introduction of new standards for regulatory capital and liquidity meant increasing governmental control and the risk of capital shortages. Ghizzoni, the new CEO, would have many urgent issues competing for his time and attention. Would he find time to dedicate to the UniQuest programme? Would he appreciate and recognize the value to the group created by UniManagement?

4

Designing a PPP beyond legal procedures

The case of Fahrenheit Resort*,**

Niccolò Cusumano
SDA Bocconi School of Management, Italy

Giacomo Morri
SDA Bocconi School of Management, Italy

Veronica Vecchi
SDA Bocconi School of Management, Italy

What makes a successful public–private partnership (PPP)? The case deals with the failure of a project to reverse the decline of an old tourist destination on the northern shore of the Adriatic Sea. Through a PPP the local and regional public authority and private market attempt to work together to revamp the thermal complex into a wellness centre. Carlo Martone, a regional authority manager, tried to help special commissioner, Mr Celsius, in his task to implement a public tender and select a private partner.

Venice wasn't the only city built on a lagoon island in the northern part of the Adriatic Sea. Not far away, just 125 km, there was another small, insular resort at the edge of a lagoon: Fahrenheit.

Dating back to the Roman Empire, this small town shared common roots with its well-known neighbour, even if it didn't enjoy its economic and cultural

---

* This case is based on a true story of a public–private partnership based in Italy. All the information and figures are true. However, Fahrenheit and the characters' names are fictitious because the project is currently under competitive tender.

** Printed with permission from Bocconi University.

development. Fahrenheit had a thermal tradition dating back to the 19th century, when it was included in the official list of health resorts in the Austrian Empire.

The healing characteristics of the island were due to the south-facing beach (one of the few in the whole Adriatic Sea), the purity of seawater and the special microclimate generated by the thick vegetation immediately behind the shoreline.

However the city was facing some challenges:

- The renewal of its customer base

- The trend towards shorter holidays

- The concentration of visits only during the summer season

- The competition from emerging destinations on the Balkan shores of the Adriatic Sea

The old thermal complex at the centre of the city, if revamped, could represent an opportunity for growth. For this reason the FVG (Friuli-Venezia Giulia) Regional Authority and the Municipality of Fahrenheit signed a memorandum of understanding and appointed Commissioner Celsius to implement a €100 million renovation project.

Public resources, however, were not sufficient to cover all investment costs; moreover local public authorities lacked the competences to implement and manage such a complex project. So they decided to launch a call for tender in order to find a private partner.

Political stakes were high. Commissioner Celsius alone was not able to carry out the call for tender. Carlo Martone, of FVG Region, would try to help him and build a successful public–private partnership (PPP).

4.1 The new resort

In order to boost tourism activities and upgrade their offers, in 2007 the region had the idea to renovate the whole thermal complex of Fahrenheit. Regional Law 30/2007 conferred to the municipality all regional land properties and rights on the target area.

In 2008, the region and the municipality signed a memorandum of understanding and a special appointed commissioner, Mr Celsius, was appointed as head of a special project unit, in charge of managing the administrative procedures and technical activities required to sign a contract with a special purpose vehicle (SPV), selected through an open and competitive tender (see Annex 1). Notably, the tender notice specified that the shareholders of the SPV could not be changed across the contract life.

Due to the complexity of the project, one of the biggest ever in Europe, and the lack of public funds to finance the development, the region decided to use a public–private partnership (PPP) scheme, notably a build, operate and transfer (BOT) scheme.

The special project unit was equipped with two part-time regional officers – an engineer, Mr Celsius, and a lawyer – both with a deep knowledge of administrative procedures and Public Contracts Code.

The commissioner, retired after a long career spent within different regional departments, was selected because of his experience in the coordination of complex projects requiring the involvement of different experts and consultants, and his knowledge of complicated regional procedures and bureaucracy.

Within a 50-year PPP contract, the private partner (formed by a pool of operators), selected through a public tender, would have received an area of 100,000 m² to develop the following investments:

- Renovate and manage the spa facility with annual wellness-recreational-curative services

- Build and manage a 4* hotel with up to 160 rooms

- Demolish and redesign integrated facility buildings of high quality and low environmental impact, reducing the total surface area

- Realize a functional building for logistics services to the beach

- Create synergies between the spa facilities, beach services and other attractions in order to enhance tourists' experience in Fahrenheit

- Develop the accommodation and service structures to ensure the necessary assistance to swimmers during the summer

- Renovate and manage the existing congress centre

In order to "heat up" the project and improve its profitability, the commissioner decided to include the realization of an underground parking garage with a minimum capacity of 500 cars, going up to a maximum of 1,000. The region also decided to grant €22.623 million, earmarked for the development of Fahrenheit, over 15 years from the completion of works.

The commissioner was in charge of finding agreements with all of the tenants prior to the beginning of the project in order to free up the area.

The existing real estate was in fact made up of land, municipal properties and other facilities leased to GIT Spa (Fahrenheit Tourism Services), a company owned by the Municipality and Region. GIT managed beaches and spas, and conceded to other private operators the management of nine bars, one kiosk, one miniature golf course, and tennis courts (all these contracts ending between 2011 and 2020).

The feasibility study, prepared by Mr Celsius with the support of the Regional Financial Agency for the financial plan, estimated total costs of works at €89.596 million, to be completed within 3 years after the award of the contract.

Annex 2 reports the features of the project outlined in the investment memorandum made available to the market.

4.2 Looking for a partner

In June 2010, Fahrenheit's Mayor was forced to quit after the resignation of more than 50% of the Municipal Council. A special appointed commissioner replaced the mayor until the elections, which were due to be held at the beginning of 2011.

This led to a political vacuum during a key stage of the project's design, depriving it of a link with local stakeholders. Furthermore, the original regional commitment disappeared, as a result of changes in the political environment and consequently among the top management board.

Not everybody in Fahrenheit in fact agreed with the project design: some local associations reported the project as a huge speculation, depriving the town of public spaces. The hoteliers' association complained that many hotels weren't ready to welcome tourists out of the summer season since they hadn't any heating systems.

Mr Celsius and Carlo Martone first met during an Executive Master session they were both attending in Milan. During a work group, when Carlo asked about his current position, he illustrated the PPP project and all the bureaucratic and planning problems he was facing:

> . . . Making financial assumptions is difficult, I'm not an expert in the field and finding information about the wellness sector is a puzzle, it's pretty fragmented and made up mostly by private companies that do not disclose information properly . . .

It would have been a real challenge to publish the tender notice by the beginning of 2011 in order to get it awarded by the beginning of 2012, as previously planned. With regional elections due in 2013, there was mounting political pressure to start works before the end of the term of legislature. "And you know how long it takes in Italy to complete a tender procedure: there are always problems, and for projects of that dimension it is almost inevitable to end up in front of the administrative court".

The Italian Authority for Public Contracts (2010) estimated, in effect, that in the 2008–2010 period, projects above €15 million took 1,600 days from the design to the contract signature, with a tender procedure length of 400 days.

Carlo Martone expressed some doubts about the choice of an open procedure to select the private partner. Probably a restricted or a negotiated procedure (see Annex 1) would have allowed a better engagement with the market.

He knew, however, that these more flexible procedures were viewed with suspicion by civil servants and politicians since they were perceived as longer, complicated and less "transparent" compared with an open procedure, where everybody interested could submit an offer.

Carlo Martone then asked Mr Celsius about market reactions and feelings about the project. The latter gave only a vague answer, because the decision of the Special Project Unit was not to communicate with the market, in order to avoid any pressure or leak, which would have made the procedure and the assessment more complicated.

Nevertheless Mr Celsius was confident of the success of the operation: the feasibility study was detailed and the project in equilibrium, thanks to the regional grant of €22 million.

Back in Fahrenheit, Mr Celsius reported the discussion to the Commissioner and they both agreed that Carlo Martone could be involved in the team, especially to manage relations with the potential investors, once the notice was published.

As the publication deadline was approaching, the two started to be worried about market reactions: the financial crisis and political turmoil were profoundly changing the market conditions they used to conceive the project and its financial plan.

When Carlo Martone took a closer look at the feasibility study and began to investigate the market, he acknowledged that there were three major issues at stake:

- The market was fragmented, companies were small and not used to working with public authorities, at least not in PPP schemes

- There were two prevailing business models: a self-standing spa, or a spa resort where the wellness centre was coupled to a hotel

- Project developers considered the requirement of a stable governance within the SPV for the overall length of the contract an unusual request

From these first considerations he then suggested that the Commissioner start broad project promotion as the project was complex and capital intensive. There was a risk that there would be no responses to the tender.

First of all, he decided to attend the real estate exhibition in Milan, to "smell" the market, which was brand new to him. There, he met some private players, and among them Mr Giorgi, CEO of a company working in the field of tourism promotion and development.

Once back home, he made some phone calls in order to check the reliability of Giorgi's company and after a couple of days he fixed a meeting with him to obtain his consultancy, promote the PPP initiative in targeted fairs and public events, and to stimulate private partners to prepare a bid.

Giorgi was quick to understand that it was compelling to "convert" the 300 page, bureaucratically written feasibility study into a smart memorandum of information that was easy to read and to present to potential investors (mainly investment funds and thermal and wellness operators).

Three road shows were organized with the objective of presenting the project and providing the opportunity to talk privately with some players in order to understand their points of view.

After a few meetings, it emerged that the project was too big (medium-sized companies could not shoulder such a big leverage) and perceived as too risky. It was particularly difficult to forecast demand, thus revenues, because Fahrenheit wasn't positioned as a wellness tourism destination in Europe, despite its past fame.

The other two biggest weaknesses spotted by private operators were the underground garage and the congress centre: they were perceived as adding no value, only risks and costs. The immediate conclusion was that the risk-adjusted return of the project, as estimated in the feasibility study, was too low.

Private builders were mainly interested in building facilities to maximize their margins; investment funds required a 15–20% rate of return to invest and spa-thermal-wellness operators seemed to be interested only in the management phase without any involvement in the project equity financing.

Not all requests made by the market players could be accepted, such as the profitability enhancement through a permit to build flats and villas, but their contributions confirmed that an open dialogue with the market would be useful to anticipate and prevent some issues before the publication of the tender notice.

The only new element that was added to make the project more profitable and to reduce bankability risk was a regional subsidized loan (€20 million with an annual interest rate fixed at Euribor reduced by 60%), to be used only to fund the hotel development.

4.3 Epilogue

The tender notice was published in May 2011; offers were to be submitted by November. Talks continued between the project team and the market. The deadline was extended to 7 March 2012 in order to give more time to private operators to finalize their offers. Nevertheless, no applications were submitted.

After a long political discussion among the regional board, a second chance was given to the project. As soon as the special project unit was asked to activate a second tender, they decided to open a formal dialogue with the market, in order to collect ideas and inputs to make the project more appealing and feasible. The dialogue was conducted during summer 2012 and these are the main suggestions received:

- Smaller investment: approximately €60 million

- Possibility to change the SPV's shareholder structure after the end of the building/development phase

- Removal from the project of the underground car park

To prepare the economic and financial assessment for the new feasibility study, the commissioner appointed two experts with a strong background on PPPs and real estate investments.

On 30 November 2012 a new call for tender was launched. Offers were to be submitted by 29 March 2013, a deadline later extended to 28 May, but this time, too, the call was ignored. In the meantime new regional elections were held and the political majority changed.

The project of building a new spa resort in Fahrenheit could be considered dead. However not everybody in town complained: on 28 May, a local entrepreneur, owner of a supermarket chain and premiere league football teams, presented a €800 million real estate project to start-up Fahrenheit again through a high-level spa resort.

Annex 1 Extracts of EU Directive 2004/18/EC

Article 1: Definitions

- 'Open procedures' means those procedures whereby any interested economic operator may submit a tender.

- 'Restricted procedures' means those procedures in which any economic operator may request to participate and whereby only those economic operators invited by the contracting authority may submit a tender.

- 'Negotiated procedures' means those procedures whereby the contracting authorities consult the economic operators of their choice and negotiate the terms of contract with one or more of these.

Article 31: Cases justifying use of the negotiated procedure without publication of a contract notice

Contracting authorities may award public contracts by a negotiated procedure without prior publication of a contract notice in the following cases:

(1) For public works contracts, public supply contracts and public service contracts:

> (a) When no tenders or no suitable tenders or no applications have been submitted in response to an open procedure or a restricted procedure, provided that the initial conditions of contract are not substantially altered and on condition that a report is sent to the Commission if it so requests;

> (b) When, for technical or artistic reasons, or for reasons connected with the protection of exclusive rights, the contract may be awarded only to a particular economic operator;

> (c) Insofar as is strictly necessary when, for reasons of extreme urgency brought about by events unforeseeable by the contracting authorities in question, the time limit for the open, restricted or negotiated procedures with publication of a contract notice as referred to in Article 30 cannot be complied with. The circumstances invoked to justify extreme urgency must not in any event be attributable to the contracting authority;

8th Considerandum

Before launching a procedure for the award of a contract, contracting authorities may, using a technical dialogue, seek or accept advice, which may be used in the preparation of the specifications provided, however, that such advice does not have the effect of precluding competition.

Annex 2 Project details

The features of the project area are described in Table 4.1. Financial information is provided in Tables 4.2–4.5.

Table 4.1

Field I: Square and Garden (Management: Municipality)	Interventions
Construction of a square connected with the sea for events Redevelopment of the former Marine Spa building Park redevelopment Uses: public entertainment and refreshment	Demolition of former medical building Marine spa and urban renewal
Field II: Spa and Park (Management: Private)	**Interventions**
Spa building: health-wellness-fun-shops, indoor area min. 8,000 m² including 2,000 m² of water; outdoor area min. 2,500 m² of water Luxury hotel up to 160 rooms Outdoor play area and water park Underground parking (from 500 to 1,000 parking spaces) Convention centre (up to 1,000 seats) with modular rooms Five refreshment services include each of two groups of toilets. The Spa/hotel/conference will be integrated into a single architectural identity in continuity with the Park, creating a connection between the complex and the beach	Demolition of existing: sandblasting facility, solarium, tennis equipment, football field, go-cart track, swimming pool, spa facility, indoor pool and possibly a water park
Field III: Sport and Beach (Management: Municipality)	**Interventions**
Clay tennis facility: 3 outdoor, 1 with a grandstand with 400 seats and 1 indoor Green play area equipped for dining and play area Storage area, offices and logistics services Accommodations including two groups each of two bathrooms and changing rooms for bathers Re-fertilization of the ground and planting of a garden	Demolition of existing: Parking at grade and toilets

Table 4.2 **Detailed costs of works**

	Old Project first tender (€)	New project after the formal dialogue with the market (€)
Hotel (with up to 160 rooms)	21,230,000	~ 21,000,000
Congress centre (modular technology for small, medium and large meetings)	4,410,000	–
Spa plants	30,285,000	~ 25,000,000
Demolitions	850,944	~ 800,000
External work	6,883,500	~ 400,000
Underground parking (2 levels for total 1,000 spaces)	23,926,946	~ 7,000,000
Sporting centre	1,225,000	~ 1,000,000
Refreshment facilities	245,000	–
Technical and design costs	5,644,000	~ 3,500,000
Other costs	6,005,420	~ 1,000,000
Rolled up interests	8,929,000	~ 3,600,000
Total	**109,634,810**	

Table 4.3 **Capital structure**

	Old project	New project
Equity	16,038,000	22,549,653
Debt capital	70,973,000	37,145,785
Public Grant	22,623,420	22,623,954
TOTAL	109,634,420	82,319,392

Table 4.4 **Income statement (at year 4), old project**

Facility	Costs (€M/y)	Revenues (€M/y)	Earnings from parking sales (€M/y)	EBITDA
Spa	4,150	6,687		38%
Hotel	3,150	6,300		50%
Congress Centre	467	683		32%
Parking	632	1,680	20	62%
Total	8,399	15,350	20	

Facility	Costs (€M/y)	Revenues (€M/y)	Earnings	EBITDA	Notes
Spa	3,874,545	4,432,569		11%	
Hotel	1,905,281	4,124,457		52%	
Parking		20,000			Rent only Triple Net

Note: EBITDA, earnings before interest, taxes, depreciation and amortization

Table 4.5 **Financial ratios**

	Old project		New project	
	Min	Max	Min	Max
Ke	10.00%	11.50%	11.00%	13.50%
Kd	6.50%	6.50%	6.50%	6.50%
IRR project	7.94%	8.71%	8.02%	9.32%
NPV project	€1,190.05	€267.99	–	–
IRR equity	12.13%	13.68%	13.10%	14.25%
NPV equity	€5,253.56	€4,950.62	45,857	78,956
WACC	7.81%	8.68%	–	–
ADSCR	€1.32	€1.49	1.51	1.76

Ke, cost of equity; Kd, cost of debt; IRR, internal rate of return; NPV, net present value; WACC, weighted average cost of capital; ADSCR, annual debt service cover ratio

Annex 3

Fahrenheit, with just 8,000 permanent residents, attracts almost 1.4 million tourists stays per year (47% foreigners, 73% of which were from Austria and Germany) representing 17% of regional tourism (see Fig. 4.1). However, demand in the 1998–2012 period was almost flat and the total length of stays slightly declined, while yearly turnover (€160–200 million in 2010) experienced a 30% drop over the same period.

Figure 4.1 **Arrivals and stays in Fahrenheit**

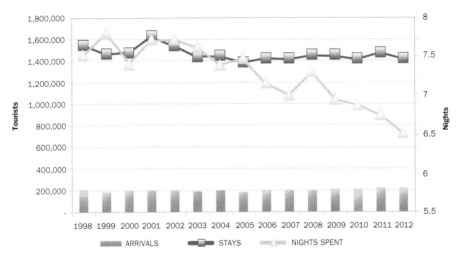

Fahrenheit Spa was active mainly during the summer. In 2009, the overall wellness activities (spa, sand, sun, water park) registered a turnover of €2.140 million and an average spending unit of €7 per visitor. Spa activities were mainly associated with the conventional medically oriented approach; half of the demand was made by services covered through the National Health Service. The wellness centre registered only 7,816 guests, but revenues averaged around €22 per visitor.

This state of affairs was in stark contrast to other countries such as Austria, where the average expenditure in their spa resorts was €328.57 per person in 2010 and thermal activities were carried out all year round (ABA-Invest in Austria, 2010).

Wellness tourism, thanks to its holistic approach, is growing beyond the traditional thermal market niche. The global wellness industry expanded worldwide from $200 billion in 2002 to $500 billion in 2007; the spa segment accounting for an estimated $60 billion alone according to a 2010 study presented at the Global Spa Summit (GSS, 2010).

References

ABA-Invest in Austria (2010). *Austria: Invest in World-Class Tourism and Wellness.* Retrieved from http://ukrexport.gov.ua/i/imgsupload/file/ABA_Tourism_Austria_2010_10703_EN .pdf

GSS (Global Spa Summit) (2010). Spas and the global wellness market: synergies and opportunities. Retrieved from http://www.wellpeople.com/pdf/Spas_Global_Wellness_Market_ SRI_May_2010.pdf.

Italian Authority for Public Contracts (2010). *Annual Report.* Rome: AVCP.

5

Social business plan simulation
The case of Dynamo Camp

Clodia Vurro and Francesco Perrini
Università Commerciale "L. Bocconi" and SDA Bocconi School of Management, Italy

This chapter tells the story of Vincenzo Manes whose goal was to create a holding of non-profits with the aim of playing a more active role as a philanthropist targeting high-potential social enterprises. The philosophy rested on the premise that the best investments in solving social problems required more than money. Rather, combinations of financial and non-financial resources, active involvement, strategic assistance at different levels, and visible endorsements could make the difference in terms of the ability of a social entrepreneurial venture to attain expected social change objectives. Fondazione Dynamo was created explicitly to apply the venture capital model to the non-profit sector. This chapter describes the foundation's project to establish Dynamo Camp, that is, the Italian branch of the "Hole in the Wall Camps" Association. This Association is a non-profit umbrella organization with a family of camps for children with serious and life-threatening medical conditions.

5.1 The beginnings

Having had a successful career in the private equity sector as President and Chief Executive Officer of Intek Group – one of the top ten industrial groups in Italy – Vincenzo Manes became interested in the non-profit sector (i.e. the third sector) in 1997, when he was asked to be the administrator of the first think-tank on the state of the Italian third sector. Despite many best practices, the Italian third sector was mainly based on a few large, very visible non-profit organizations, and a myriad of small actors with good intentions but little entrepreneurial spirit. These first experiences with non-profits nurtured a sense of dissatisfaction with the prevailing operating models.

Manes found his experience similar to that encountered by several other leaders of traditional venture capital and private equity funds he had met during his travelling in the US and throughout Europe. They were all fascinated by the rise of a new breed of entrepreneurs challenging the status quo through the launch of entrepreneurial processes aimed at exploiting social innovations. Named as social entrepreneurs, they shared the firm belief that social change using innovative, business-like methods was possible and worth pursuing. Manes noted that the first social entrepreneurial ventures were quite different from traditional non-profit organizations, because of their obsession with efficiency and innovativeness, and tendency toward measurable, tangible results. At the same time, they were not just businesses with a social addendum; actually, social entrepreneurs were motivated by the possibility of mending a social gap, relying on business models as means to that end.

However, after speaking with peers and with his growing knowledge of dynamics in the non-profit sector, Manes had become aware of the inadequacy of existing infrastructures to shore up these innovative, individual enterprises and enable widespread social impact. Though typically devoted to supporting organizations with a social purpose, most of the national foundations saw their role as funding a large number of small programmes for a short time, hoping that at least a few would enjoy initial success. Sometimes, foundations were expecting government to take over or emulate successful social programmes while they moved on to other initiatives. Foundation programme officers often expressed concern about non-profits becoming too dependent on a single funding source, and this philosophy also set limits on their support to any single organization. As a consequence, foundations were mainly acting as passive fund providers with limited intervention in the funded programmes or organizations. There was a clear need for innovation even on the funding side, in order for more effective social enterprises to be launched, grow and maximize their social impact.

5.2 The logic of "doing well while doing good"

His background and profound knowledge of the **holding company** model made Manes excited about the possibility of creating a holding of non-profits with the aim of playing a more active role as a philanthropist targeting high-potential social enterprises. He was closer than expected to the venture philanthropy model, which was creating excitement through its potential to bridge the competence and funding gaps in the social sector all over the world.

In July 2000, while flipping through *Time* magazine, Manes was attracted by its cover story on the "New Philanthropists" focused on the "multi-millionaires of the technology boom" (Greenfeld, 2000). According to the article:

> Many of today's tech millionaires and billionaires are applying to philanthropy the lessons they have learned as entrepreneurs [. . .] One solution has been the founding of venture philanthropies which use the same aggressive methods as venture capital firms, whose money typically comes with technological expertise and experience at running lean, efficient organizations. This new breed of philanthropist scrutinizes each charitable cause like a potential business investment, seeking maximum return in terms of social impact – for example, by counting the number of children taught to read or the number inoculated against malaria.

Since the Roberts Enterprise Development Fund (San Francisco, USA), the Robin Hood Foundation (New York, USA), Ashoka (Arlington, USA), and Social Venture Partners (Seattle, Washington) – the earliest and most successful pioneers of a new wave of philanthropy – appeared in the early 1990s, venture philanthropy has developed rapidly. Such a new approach to philanthropy was characterized by an impatient disdain for cautious and unimaginative cheque writing that had dominated traditional approaches to charity for decades. In contrast, it distinguished itself by its ambition and strategic orientation, based on the same systematic approach used to compete in business and on a boundary-spanning logic: *doing well while doing good*.

Broadly speaking, the venture philanthropy approach borrowed principles from the practice of venture capitalists in the business world, with a primary focus on increasing the organizational capacity within those innovative social ventures showing entrepreneurial attitudes and high growth potential. Putting together the risk-taking characteristics of the business sectors and the innovative fostering of social change intrinsic to the social entrepreneurship concept, venture philanthropists were resting on the premise that the best investments in solving social problems required more than money. Rather, combinations of financial and non-financial resources, active involvement, strategic assistance at different levels, and visible endorsements could make the difference in terms of the ability of a social entrepreneurial venture to attain expected social change objectives.

Vincenzo Manes was so intellectually attracted by the possibility of uniting his profound business knowledge with social sector peculiarities that he started a restless search for details on venture philanthropy experiments all over the world. He encountered a survey conducted by Morino Institute, Venture Philanthropy Partners and Community Wealth Ventures (2001) on the practices of the major venture philanthropy organizations in the US. A number of areas of contribution to grant recipients emerged as typical in describing the role of active philanthropists. They were engaged in:

- Providing a diversified set of resources, from seed capital to managerial competences

- Addressing organizational issues

- Helping to attract and retain key management and board members

- Assisting in the development of product and distribution channels

- Helping leverage partnerships through their strategic relationships with other organizations

- Creating and executing development expansion strategies

- Developing financial plans, improving funds development, helping to establish new revenue sources, and creating syndicated funding by bringing together other venture philanthropy investors and foundations

- Providing access to industry experts and knowledgeable advisers, as well as networks of peers

Venture philanthropy was poles apart from traditional philanthropic giving. It represented a renewed approach to financing the social sector, applying strategic investment management practices to support *strong* social entrepreneurial organizations in need of help to be launched and grow. Time was definitely up for traditional, weak, non-profit organizations to be rescued.

5.3 The first step into the new philanthropic wave

Fascinated by the venture philanthropy approach, Vincenzo Manes conceived the idea of doing something similar in Italy, with the aim of attracting the attention of successful business executives interested in contributing to the third sector in a way that was more than just giving money.

Thanks to the support of a small number of friends sharing similar views, Manes decided to launch a corporate foundation based on the endorsement, funds, and competences of his holding company, Intek SpA, but operating as a holding of non-profits (see Table 5.1). Fondazione Dynamo – Philanthropy Engine (Dynamo Foundation – Philanthropy Engine) was founded on 9 April 2003, formally as a recognized Partnership Foundation, with the aim of contributing to philanthropic development in Italy through the financial, technical and managerial support and promotion of innovative social ventures able to operate according to efficiency, autonomy and sustainability criteria.

Table 5.1 **Intek SpA and Dynamo Foundation**

	Intek	**Fondazione Dynamo**
Who	A diversified industrial and financial holding company with over €4 billion in revenues and more than 8,000 staff worldwide	A venture philanthropy foundation that provides financial, technical and managerial support to new social ventures
What	Identify and invest in financial and industrial companies with large growth opportunities · Investment company · Long history · Core management team with the best talents in the history of the company · Focus on building an outstanding track record · Listed in the Milan Stock Exchange	Identify and implement in Italy successful, complex and international non-profit projects · Run as an investment company · Based on the venture philanthropy approach · Employing professionals from business · Independent from the founding company · Accountable by releasing quarterly reporting and audited balance sheets · Based on pro bono professional agreements · With a structured governance
How	**Financial capital** · Guarantees the seed capital for its investments · Investments are realized through management and financial resources · The control on the business is maintained	**Financial capital** · Intek Group guarantees the seed capital for Dynamo Foundation's projects · Investment is realized through management and financial resources · Dynamo Foundation is active in professional fundraising for its projects and in making them sustainable in the long term
	Intellectual capital · Use of external business professionals in due diligence, legal advisory, strategic planning, and results accountability · Creation of a network of Italian and international professionals around the initiative · Provision of non-financial support during the lifetime of the investment	**Intellectual capital** · Use of business competences in project evaluation and start-up management, innovative finance and governance, measurement and results accountability · Creation of a network of Italian and international professionals around the initiative · Provision of non-financial support during the lifetime of the investment
	Social capital · Leverage on several competences from professional and corporate partners	**Social capital** · Leverage on several competences from pro bono, professional and corporate partners

Fondazione Dynamo was created explicitly to apply the venture capital model to the non-profit sector. Accordingly, its intervention model was similar to that of a for-profit venture capital firm and based on the following key principles to guide the foundation's investment strategy:

- **High-potential project identification**. The screening criteria to identify potential projects rested mainly on the innovative attributes of the project, on the measurability of expected outcomes, and on the expected social impacts in terms of changing patterns of interaction within a specific field of intervention, as well as possibilities to scale up the innovation.

- **Long-term financial partnerships**. Dynamo granted long-term financial support aimed at guaranteeing financial autonomy and continuity for long-term plans and project development.

- **Continual tutoring**. Dynamo guaranteed a systematic transfer of managerial and entrepreneurial skills such as strategic and financial planning, positioning analysis, organization and internal process analysis, and performance monitoring.

- **Result assessment and performance monitoring**. The foundation paid great attention to the shared identification of key performance indicators allowing both the supported organization and the foundation itself to monitor and assess results in terms of social and economic impact, value creation and achieved goals.

In order for Dynamo to be able to transform entrepreneurial ideas into self-sufficient projects aimed at either initiating or contributing to social change, its structure was conceived as extremely flexible, built around the following principles:

- Streamlined structure with only coordination and guarantee functions

- Systematic outsourcing of all activities aimed at creating and managing social entrepreneurial ventures through partnerships with companies with high professional standing

- Pro bono volunteering to enlarge the project teams when necessary to encompass field-specific competences

Between 2003 and 2005, Dynamo Foundation started to engage with concrete projects in order to explore the basis for the feasibility of the venture philanthropy model in the Italian context. Despite their relevance in terms of expected social change objectives, initial projects were more attempts to infuse entrepreneurial and managerial attitudes into established non-profit organizations than the *de novo* creation of a purely social entrepreneurial venture. Manes was still in search of a project incorporating all those characteristics that he had identified while reading stories about new social entrepreneurs and enlightened venture philanthropists.

5.4 Fortuitous encounters

It took a gala dinner to radically change the future of Dynamo Foundation in December 2004. Vincenzo Manes encountered with a mother who told him the story of her ill son who participated in the summer programmes at one of the camps run by the Association of Hole in The Wall Camps. This fortuitous meeting set the basis for the identification of an unfulfilled gap in the Italian National Health System.

Impressed by the mother's appreciation of the beneficial impacts of the Camp experience on the quality of her son's life, Manes asked his team at Dynamo Foundation to start searching for further details regarding the Association. He soon discovered that, orchestrated by its founder (Paul Newman) since 1988, the Association of Hole in the Wall Camps was one of the most successful global non-profits, run as a business but attaining incredible social impacts. Formally a non-profit umbrella organization, leading the world's largest family of camps for children with serious and life-threatening medical conditions, the Association's mission was quite unusual among the mainstream non-profit panorama: based on therapeutic recreation, the Hole in the Wall Camp experience was explicitly designed to: "Foster self-confidence and independence, and enhance coping and resilience [. . .]. To empower children to reach beyond the limits of their illnesses and to create lasting and positive behavioural impacts on their lives."

As of 2004, over 16 years of experience had gone into the realization of five camps in the US alone, one each in France, Ireland and Israel, in addition to plans for other camps in the United States, South Africa, Jordan, Canada and Costa Rica. Since then, Hole in the Wall Camps have provided more than 50,000 days of service to campers and their families, with over 15,000 people having participated in various camp activities each year. Children from more than 27 countries and 34 states had attended camp programmes, with camps serving children from more than 30 different disease groups. Collectively, camps had received donations from more than 15,500 individuals, foundations and corporations, as well as about 4,500 individuals volunteering their time annually to the camps. The model was self-sustaining at that time and in a stage of replication.

There was no doubt about the innovativeness of the project. It would have been the first project of that kind in Italy. For its completion, careful planning and organization at different levels was required, leveraging a set of competences that were partially present in the Dynamo Foundation network of partners and friends. The development of the project would set the basis for cross-boundary partnerships between public and private actors, bringing with it the opportunity to collaborate with an international network at a high level. Of course, embarking on this project would have been a replication of an existing entrepreneurial model, yet in an entirely different context, characterized by both the prominent role of the public sector in dealing with health problems and needs, as well as low experience in dealing successfully with large-scale social projects. In this situation, in spite of the advantages of learning from the existing camps' experience and expertise, of having a clear idea of the potential target for the project, and of successful track records to be quoted while selling the project to potential investors, the risks of not being able to find the local unique selling points of the project were high. Moreover, a number of standards had to be respected in order for a camp to be part of Paul Newman's Association.

After a preliminary balancing of pros and cons associated with the creation of an Italian camp compared with continued searching for a project to be started from scratch, Dynamo Foundation and its creator decided that the camp project was in line with their objectives. They had to prove to the third sector and themselves not only that it was possible to launch a large-scale social project, but also that professionalism in planning was key to success in making that project sustainable in the long run.

To this end, careful planning was needed for a number of related reasons. The project team needed an action plan to coordinate itself and to evaluate the breadth and depth of resources and competences required and challenges they would encounter during the implementation of the project. Moreover, the scale of the project was so large that further external investors would be necessary. They would have to be convinced about the potential feasibility of the project, without tangible proofs, at least at the beginning. A detailed plan would improve the project's credibility, making it easier to gain access to alternative sources of financing. Moreover, a plan would force the team to define clear objectives, detailed timelines, and the basis for economic and social impact assessment. As a consequence, they started thinking about the areas and themes that would be critical over the project life-cycle – from set-up to sustainability – in order to develop a social business plan.

5.5 The project set-up

Early analysis of the experiences of the Association of Hole in the Wall Camps all over the world showed that there would be an uphill struggle on the road to realizing the dream of an Italian camp. The camps' mission was to empower children suffering from life-threatening and chronic illnesses through providing an opportunity for childlike recreation; as expected, translating this into reality was complex, especially in terms of competences and funds needed. In fact, in order to allow children to socialize freely in a protected environment and learn how to deal better with the challenges of their day-to-day lives, medical assistance was first needed, together with educational and psychological support, entertainment, and comprehensive managerial and financial capacity.

Figure 5.1 **Key values underlying the camp intervention model**

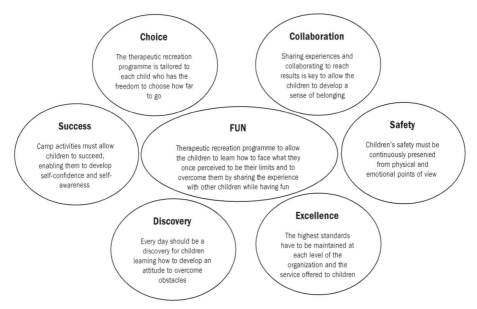

As for the mission, the key values underlying the camp's intervention model were fairly clear in that they had to be common to all the camps belonging to the Association (see Fig. 5.1). The challenge was to translate that mission and related values into an operating model that was able to satisfy the requirements to become a formal member of the Association of Hole in the Wall Camps and get their endorsement (see Fig. 5.2). It was estimated that it would take at least two years to get full membership from the Association of Hole in the Wall Camps. The camp could only be opened after getting the official certification. As a consequence, three years were quite a credible estimate of the time required to plan and launch the Italian camp, at least on the assumption that an existing location could be found and "simply" redecorated.

Figure 5.2 **Becoming a member of the Association of Hole in the Wall Camps**

	Starting the certification process	Getting a temporary membership		Getting a full membership
	STAGE 1	STAGE 2.A	STAGE 2.B	STAGE 3
CRITERIA	Quality, credibility and long-term commitment of the project's proponents Credibility and feasibility of the business plan Availability of a team to be devoted to resource collection Exsistence of a real, unfulfilled niche in the market Commitment and engagement of the medical community locally	Presence of a credible, feasible fundraising plan Identification of a proprietary/donated location consistent with the aim of the Camp Partnerships with local hospitals and scientific partners Availability of the Camp proponents to personally meet the Association	Approval by the Directors of the Association Proofs of solid partnerships with the scientific community at the local level Detailed plan for the building/redecoration of the physical infrastructures where to locate the Camp Definition of an industrial plan with 3- to 5-year projections Proof of the capacity to collect 75% of the capital and operating costs needed to operate in the first 3 years, before the Camp's start-up	Defined recreative therapeutic programmes Availability of resources to open the Camp Full-time medical director hired

Based on such preliminary considerations, the Dynamo Foundation's permanent team, composed of Manes, the managing director (Maria Serena Porcari), the Director of Development, the Communication Director, and a few other assistants, started to set up an action plan in late 2004, identifying the critical challenges to be faced in order to be ready to begin the membership process a year and a half later.

First of all it was necessary to convince the Board of Directors of the Association of Hole in the Wall Camps of Dynamo's trustworthiness, credibility and commitment to the project, in order to at least be taken into consideration for inclusion in the camps' network. Commitment and trustworthiness were the easiest part. On the one hand, proper legal status was necessary to give substance to the project. According to the Italian legal system, Dynamo Foundation had created an Association – the *Dynamo Camp Association* – operating in the health-based field of intervention and having a formal governance structure with Maria Serena Porcari as CEO. Having a strong international business background, with experience spanning from corporate intrapreneurship to customer relationship management in companies such as IBM and FIAT, combined with passion for and profound commitment to non-profits, she was the right person to lead such a complex process. On the other hand, Dynamo decided that a strong signal of commitment and trustworthiness would be its alignment with a well-established Anglo-Saxon tradition;

that is, the **board contribution** practice. The board of directors of both Dynamo Foundation and the Dynamo Camp Association should be the leaders in terms of resource commitment, and frequency and average value of the grants to the camp. This practice was widely recognized as the main indicator of the excellence of a social project.

Showing the commitment of the promoters was not enough to convince the Association of Hole in the Wall Camps. A physical location to set up the camp was necessary in order to give the whole project a certain level of credibility to start with. According to the basic characteristics of the services to be offered by the camp – recreational periods during which to perform a wide variety of group activities in a protected environment – the place to be selected should have a strategic location in terms of proximity to hospitals and general accessibility. Moreover, the location should be characterized by a favourable climate in order to perform outdoor activities, in a green area, and potentially in a natural protected environment. Indoor space would be required to allow children to spend holiday periods living at the camp, with areas to be transformed into theatres, restaurants, and so on. Accordingly, locations should be compared in size and occupancy capability relative to the target population number; that is, for example, the number of children relative to the population of children with unmet needs, the number of children per activity session, and the total number of people to be hosted in the camp (children and staff). Administration and local community support would be welcome. Finally, the camp's cost should be minimized as much as possible. It was quite unreasonable to expect to be able to buy land and build the camp starting from scratch. This would have incurred multiple delays and set back the opening of the camp indefinitely.

There was no doubt that the decision regarding the location had to come out of a clearer identification of the target population for the camp. It was even clearer that this was a much harder task to be performed, since official, national databases of children affected by life-threatening, chronic illnesses were non-existent at that time. The easiest and most affordable way to proceed was to strategically involve leading Italian paediatric hospitals. This would enable definition of the target market, in terms of typology and number of admissible diseases, as well as numbers of children affected by those diseases. At the same time, consultations with hospitals would represent the first step to developing those solid relationships with the local medical community that were required to become an endorsed camp. The project team thought that it would be a good idea to involve leading members of the *Conferenza Permanente degli Ospedali Pediatrici Italiani* (Permanent Conference of Italian Paediatric Hospitals). This would have guaranteed the excellence of paediatric care, openness to the project and innovativeness in contributing to it, as well as the opportunity to raise awareness of the project throughout Italy by communicating through a capillary organization. Thanks to his previous experience on the Board of Vita, Vincenzo Manes had good personal relationships with the Gaslini

Institute in Genova and Meyer Hospital in Florence. Each had all those characteristics the Dynamo team was looking for, and both hospitals decided to buy into the project, giving initial support in identifying the target population.

The paediatricians of the two hospitals estimated that about 10,000 Italian children were affected each year by the kinds of diseases the camps were targeting all over the world.[1] The problem was real and needed attention. Moreover, despite the existence of scientific studies having proved the benefits of play and sports for children in psychological and emotional terms, the doctors confirmed that there was a lack of facilities in Italy, specifically designed to meet the needs of those children whose lives had been so dramatically altered by such illnesses.

Hole in the Wall Camps' activities were the same as those of a traditional summer camp, such as diving, soccer and basketball, rope courses, arts and crafts, dancing and drama nights, pinewood camping or horse-riding, and many other activities for children to succeed in and have a lot of fun. Activities had to be safely structured in order to allow campers to achieve and succeed, regardless of their specific disease or disability. Given the need to adequately protect children, guaranteeing excellence in each and every aspect, and given the newness of the project at the Italian level, the project team and the paediatricians agreed that, at least at the beginning, a limited number of diseases and children would be preferable (see Table 5.2).

1 The following is a representative list of the disease groups and conditions served by the Hole in the Wall Camps: anaemia, asthma, cancer, congenital immunodeficiency, cystic fibrosis, diabetes, Crohn's disease, epilepsy, heart/cardiovascular diseases, haemophilia, nephropathies, leukaemia, metabolic disease, neuromuscular disorders, Prader-Willi syndrome, renal-related diseases, solid tumours, spina bifida, thalassaemia, and disorders requiring ventilator assistance.

Table 5.2 **Four-year projection of the target market**

	2007	2008	2009	2010*
No. of sessions offered	2	4	5	6
Average no. of children/ session	30	33	60	80
Total no. of children in sessions	*60*	*129*	*300*	*480*
No. of family weekends	0	3	3	4
Average no. of families/ family weekend	0	6	15	20
Total no. of children in family weekends	*0*	*35*	*90*	*160*
Total no. of children in special events	*0*	*54*	*120*	*120*
Total no. of campers	60	230	510	760
Nationality of children	Italian and non-Italian (under treatment in Italy, speaking Italian)	Italian and non-Italian (under treatment in Italy, speaking Italian)	Italian and non-Italian (under treatment in Italy, speaking Italian) German children	Italian and non-Italian (under treatment in Italy, and Europe)
Age of children	7–16	7–16	7–16	7–16
No. of different hospitals	7	14	20	25
No. of diseases admitted	4	5	5 Yearly defined diseases based on medical consultation	5 Yearly defined diseases based on medical consultation

	2007	2008	2009	2010*
Activities available during sessions	Ropes courses	Ropes courses	Ropes courses	Ropes courses
	Farming	Farming	Farming	Farming
	Outdoor role plays and sports	Outdoor role plays and sports	Outdoor role plays and sports	Outdoor role plays and sports
	Indoor role plays and sports	Indoor role plays and sports	Indoor role plays and sports	Indoor role plays and sports
	Theatre	Theatre	Theatre	Theatre
	Horse-riding	Horse-riding	Horse-riding	Horse-riding
	Archery	Archery	Archery	Archery
	Outdoor camping	Outdoor camping	Outdoor camping	Outdoor camping
	Arts and crafts	Arts and crafts	Arts and crafts	Arts and crafts
	Disco dance	Disco dance	Disco dance	Disco dance
	Carnival	Carnival	Carnival	Carnival
	Astronomy	Astronomy	Astronomy	Astronomy
	Bonfire nights	Bonfire nights	Bonfire nights	Bonfire nights
	Stage nights	Stage nights	Stage nights	Stage nights
	Casino-games	Casino-games	Casino-games	Casino-games
	Treasure hunt	Treasure hunt	Treasure hunt	Treasure hunt
	Award night	Award night	Award night	Award night
	Cabin night	Cabin night	Cabin night	Cabin night
		Digital photography	Digital photography	Digital photography
		Dynamo radio	Dynamo radio	Dynamo radio
			Swimming pool	Swimming pool

* 2010 is estimated as the year of full operation

In particular, it was decided that, at least for the first three years of operation, the criteria to select children for the camp's programmes (campers, hereafter) had to be:

- Age between 7 and 16 years, divided in two groups (7–12 years old; 13–16 years old)

- Suffering from chronic diseases or not under treatment for at least 4 years

- Potential to fully participate in the activities of the camp

- Not at risk of severe neutropenia (low level of white blood cells) or blood platelets $< 20,000/\mu L$

Moreover, explicit consent from the children's parents would be necessary together with the consent of the serving medical director of the Dynamo Camp. The project team was extremely committed to reaching a total of 1,000 campers housed in the camp when in full operation. No children and their families would have to pay for the camp. Participation would be completely free of charge.

At that stage, the time was definitely right to select an appropriate location. After considering the possibility of establishing formal partnerships with other Italian non-profit institutions, the project team decided that having its own location would be more in line with the autonomy and entrepreneurial orientation that they had always considered as basic values for Dynamo Foundation's model of intervention. An opportunity emerged from the strict relationships that linked Dynamo Foundation with its formal founder, Intek SpA.

There was an abandoned farm estate among the properties of KME, an Intek SpA controlled company. KME was the world's largest manufacturer of semi-finished copper and copper alloy products. The land was situated in Tuscany – Limestre, very close to the province of Pistoia. The buildings had the potential to be refurbished as a holiday village. Moreover they were surrounded by more than 360 hectares of mountainous, pristine landscape. A perfect place for sports, camping and all the activities the project team had in mind. They could have even requested an endorsement by the World Wide Fund for Nature in order to preserve the area and maintain it for the public.

At that time, early 2005, KME began to be interested in implementing a more sustainable strategy, aligned with recent advances in the field of corporate social responsibility. Managers in charge were in search of a concrete project to strengthen their participation in and contribution to a group of stakeholders they considered key: the local community. This set the pace for a stronger collaboration with Dynamo Foundation. In fact, KME agreed with Manes to actively participate in the project, offering the farm estate for rent below the market level. In exchange for this, KME committed itself to cover the costs of landscaping under the supervision of the Dynamo project team. The architectural project was offered pro bono by another company whose president was part of the Dynamo Foundation Board. It was estimated that almost 15 months were necessary for the infrastructure, buildings and landscaping to be completed. Dynamo Camp would cover the yearly maintenance costs of the structure equal to 20% of the annual rent.

After collecting all this initial information in a preliminary business plan, the Dynamo project team submitted it to the Association of Hole in the Wall Camps in order to get their initial approval to start a membership process and their conditional fund commitment. In case of approval the Association would donate €1 million to cover the camp's initial operating costs.

5.6 The pre-launch: planning, planning, planning!

After one and a half months, in mid-February, the project team received this response from the Association of Hole in the Wall Camps:

> The promoters' commitment to and engagement in the initiative is extremely valuable. The preliminary plan is commendable, especially with regard to the credibility of the project team and the targets they defined. Based on these elements, the Association has decided to give a conditional acceptance to the Dynamo Camp Project.

More detailed plans had to be promptly developed, covering every aspect of the launch. This was a necessary precondition to start thinking about a consistent fund-raising plan.

Ideas were clear on both the services to be offered and the target market. Regarding the former, the idea was to offer holiday weeks (7–10 days long), during which children would experience fun and team working, participating in many different activities. Moreover, starting from the second year of operation, children's sessions would have been complemented with the offering of family sessions, aimed at normalizing the life of the whole family and strengthening emotional relationships among family members in a comfortable, protected context. Given the aim of the camp, summer would be the perfect period for the sessions to be conducted. Summer sessions would be organized as follows:

- A ratio of one adult to two children would be constantly maintained (staff and volunteers) in order for the children to feel protected during the stay

- Nurses would administer medicines in the least possible invasive way

- Excellence, attention to detail and aesthetic care in designing spaces would make every place in the camp accessible to the children regardless of their condition

- Rest areas would be provided throughout the camp for those children having particular problems, though designed in a way to enable them to constantly feel part of the groups

- Specialized consultants would be provided to assist children with specific behavioural or emotional problems

- A medical centre would assist the camp 24 hours a day, yet designed in a way to be dissimilar from a medical centre. Nurses and doctors would spend their days with the children, as friends

Since the camp would operate as a traditional holiday camp, it was quite important to identify the main costs related to the children and family programmes. In fact, the project team decided to compare the experience of summer schools and holiday camps weighted by the expected number of guests to be hosted during sessions and family programmes. Moreover, given the peculiarity of the Dynamo Camp, the team added medical expenses (Table 5.3).

Table 5.3 **Estimated costs (four-year projection, €)**

	2007	**2008**	**2009**	**2010**
Total programme-related costs	181,000	348,000	465,000	679,000
Catering	30,000	75,000	120,000	250,000
Services (e.g. laundry, consulting services)	50,000	60,000	70,000	90,000
Transportation costs	15,000	25,000	30,000	40,000
Camp material (e.g. T-shirts, play equipment)	40,000	45,000	50,000	60,000
Cleaning	35,000	70,000	90,000	130,000
Utilities	10,000	70,000	100,000	100,000
Medical tests	1,000	3,000	5,000	9,000
Total permanent staff	481,600	540,063	567,063	567,063
Seasonal staff members (number)	10	23	36	63
Seasonal members average cost (per staff member)	2,175	3,176	3,796	3,734

Yet, the camp would have been the first facility of that kind, with no track-record or visibility in the health sector, a problem that was evident in the search for "target clients". A shortcut was at the team's disposal in the relationships with paediatric hospitals and their associations; their involvement should be deeper, with a permanent medical advisory board to stand over the camp's activities, guaranteeing the medical and scientific competences necessary to protect children at the highest possible level. Moreover, paediatricians could contribute to the camp in both attracting and selecting potential campers, creating awareness among families.

Together with a medical director, the CEO and the camp director, the following professional profiles were needed to permanently manage the structure:

- **Director of development**. Supervising all activities to develop the camp and its sustainability over time (e.g. fundraising, commercial activities, and so on)

- **Medical director**. Supervising all the medical activities of the camp, the definition of the admitted diseases, and specific cases, the maintenance and development of the partnerships and collaboration with hospitals

- **Communications director**. Supervising all those activities aimed at improving the visibility and existence of the camp

- **Quality director**. In charge of supervising both the quality at every level in the camp and the security during the sessions and programmes

- **Recruiters**. Supervising the recruitment process for both staff and volunteers

- **Administrative staff**. Working on control and the administration of the camp

- **Nursing director**. Coordinating the seasonal nursing activities under the supervision of the medical board

- **Food director**

- **Assistant camp director** under the supervision of the camp director to assist in the coordination of activities and programmes

Based on market level salaries for those positions, yearly costs were estimated for the necessary permanent staff (see Table 5.3). Moreover, given the seasonal character of the camp, temporary staff were needed to assist in the planned sessions. They would be estimated on the basis of the expected number of campers (see Table 5.3). A typical problem shared by almost all non-profit organizations was to be solved at that point: the profile of volunteers to be recruited to support the camp activities during both the summer sessions and family sessions. The competence gap between expectations and actual behaviours was a common trait among volunteers, in that their motivation to *do good* was often considered enough by itself to justify their participation in an initiative. In the Dynamo Camp, children would be vulnerable and needed to be constantly protected. A professional recruitment process was necessary even for volunteers, with specific training programmes months before the camp's sessions. The cost of staff training was estimated at €15,000 each year.

5.7 Professionalizing fundraising and searching for sustainability

It was clear at that point how costly the whole project was, and how tough the shift from set-up to early growth and full sustainability would be. €10 million would have been enough to support the first five years of operation; €5 million to cover the launch and the first three years of operation and the remaining €5 million to support the search for long-run sustainability.

If definitive approval was granted, the Association of Hole in the Wall Camps would contribute to cover the project's costs, donating €1 million. Similarly, Dynamo Foundation was committed to providing €1 million as seed capital for the project start-up.

Funds had to be supplemented through a fundraising plan consistent as much as possible with the basic values underlying the Dynamo investment-like approach and leveraged on the existing network of relationships surrounding Dynamo Foundation and its corporate founder. In other words, asking for money was not enough. The project team should develop an ability to inspire donors to take part in an ongoing project. There was no track-record of the effectiveness of the camp model, or proof of the satisfaction of the target clients to motivate donors. Their attention should be mobilized around a project with a clearly defined social mission. Professionalism was both a core competence and a key objective for the Dynamo team. They would have to show donors their ability to foresee future challenges and future targets even more effectively than for a business project. The investment they would have to propose was a high-potential social project aimed at changing children's lives. They had to find ways to communicate this with as much credibility as possible, together with the expected effectiveness of the service. A list of indicators to track expected social impacts could even have been proposed to show interested donors the attention paid by Dynamo to quality monitoring.

However, to be run as a business aiming at sustainability and self-sufficiency it was certainly not enough to ask for generic support from potentially interested donors, as their commitment should have been more than a one-off, money-based contribution. They had to work on a comprehensive action plan with alternative fundraising vehicles (e.g. campaigns, events, grants) and different options to motivate donors to give their support (see Table 5.4).

Table 5.4 **Standard fundraising vehicles**

Annual campaign	Major gifts	Capital campaign	Planned gifts
A yearly fundraising campaign to raise support for operating expenses May include direct-mail campaigns, telephone solicitation, individual or corporate donations, special events	May be either a one-off gift or repeated large gifts given to support a particular programme, project or improvement	Increases the assets of the organization's holding Is an extensive fundraising programme that calls for high-level gifts, often paid over a number of years	Add to the endowment of the organization These gifts are usually made from a donor's estate Large and carefully planned

Relying on a single funding source was too risky; their business mind-set was continuing to emphasize this point, especially if the camp's objective was sustainability after 2010, the year of full operation. Innovative efforts were needed to find ways to support growth in conjunction with the fundraising. The camp facilities represented an incredible asset, only partially used during the summer months or for special events. On the other hand, progress could be made at the organizational level in order to optimize and systematize processes.

There were also emerging trends at the national and international levels that had to be taken into account, with regard to the relationship between profit and non-profit organizations. Spreading rapidly across contexts and intervention areas, partnerships crossing sector boundaries between profit and non-profit were starting to be considered as the forefront of creative organizational models to offer innovative solutions to increasingly complex and persistent social problems, balancing non-profit attitudes to social service with business entrepreneurial orientation (see Table 5.5). Such innovative partnerships would provide further access to resources, competences and networks that could be functional to the attainment of the camp's goals and sustainability.

Table 5.5 **Cross-sector social partnerships: basic classification**

Agreement type	Description	Goals integration among partners	Power sharing among partners
		Low	Low
Corporate philanthropy	Episodic, informal corporate giving		
Corporate foundation	Systematically managed philanthropic activity		
Licensing	Use of non-profit logo in exchange for fees/royalties		
Sponsorship	Company/brand logo association to non-profit in exchange for sponsorship fees		
Transaction-based promotions	Business contribution to non-profit proportional to sales		
Joint issue promotion	Business involvement in activities to jointly support a social cause		
Joint venture	Creation of a new formal entity to achieve mutually desirable objectives		
		High	High

Time was running out fast and decisions had to be taken. Everyone on the team was firmly striving for the attainment of final approval from the Association of Hole in the Wall Camps.

References

Greenfeld, K.T. (2000). A new way of giving. *Time*, 156(4), 24.

Morino Institute, Venture Philanthropy Partners & Community Wealth Ventures (2001). *Venture Philanthropy: The Changing Landscape*. Washington, DC: Community Wealth Ventures.

6

Strategy execution at Mediolanum Bank

A role play case study[*][**]

Olga E. Annushkina
SDA Bocconi School of Management, Italy

Giorgio Invernizzi
Università L. Bocconi, Italy

Mediolanum Bank, one of the leading retail asset management financial institutions in Italy, aims to boost its growth during the recession years by offering a new financial product – a high-return deposit account. A team of bank managers must solve multiple issues regarding the new strategy implementation. How will the new online product be taken by more than 5,000 of the bank's independent financial consultants, the Family Bankers, who are the bank's

* This case study was prepared on the basis of publicly available resources and face-to-face interviews with the management team of Mediolanum Bank Srl (Milan, October–January 2013). The case is designed to serve as a basis for class discussion rather than to illustrate either the efficient or inefficient handling of a company situation. The individual "roles" of managers participating in the role play were created ad hoc by the case authors to facilitate the class discussion. The financial data contained in the case is disguised for confidentiality reasons and to facilitate the case discussion. The case authors sincerely thank Mediolanum Bank CEO, Massimo Doris, and Mediolanum Bank managers, in particular Gianmarco Gessi, William Giribaldi, Antonio Zaffaroni and Lamberto Mencarelli, for the support and attention given to this case study. The case authors are also grateful to the SDA Bocconi School of Management Strategy and Entrepreneurial Management Departments for the support and useful insights provided during the preparation of the case and of the teaching notes.

** Printed with permission from Bocconi University.

main gateway to its clients? Will the existing bank clients be irritated by not being offered the opportunity to access the high-return online deposit account? Should the bank launch the new project with a completely new brand and with a new legal entity?

Teams of six class participants each aim to solve these and other issues and prepare a master plan for the new strategy deployment and implementation. There appears to be a clash between the interests of the financial, marketing, sales, IT, HR and operations departments. The role play exercise, based on the case, will aim to explore the main challenges of the strategy implementation in a complex organization. Also, the role play may represent an excellent basis on which to test in practice the various facets of team dynamics and decision-making.

At 9.30 am the atmosphere in a meeting room overlooking the lake was tense. By 12.30 pm the team of six Mediolanum managers was supposed to communicate their joint vision on the new product implementation to the Mediolanum Bank founder, Mr Ennio Doris. Yet one hour into the meeting the managers' opposing opinions seem irreconcilable. The team have to produce a common vision for the new online banking product that potentially could create important discontinuities within the bank's strategy based on the one-to-one relationships between Family Bankers and retail clients. Despite the remarkable growth results, Ennio Doris believes Mediolanum Bank's growth potential has not yet been realized. Introducing the high interest rate online deposit account, he thinks, would be one way to achieve this potential.

6.1 Entrepreneurial strategy at Mediolanum Bank

Long before the arrival of the Internet, Ennio Doris, an Italian entrepreneur and the founder of Mediolanum Group (see Box 1), introduced an innovative concept in the Italian banking system: "a bank without bank offices and queues". Mediolanum clients were served via telephone, via a dedicated TV channel, later via the Internet and, of course, via visits by "global financial consultants" for more complex value-adding operations. This allowed clients to access financial services according to their needs, time and place preferences. The absence of traditional bank offices allowed Mediolanum to avoid important fixed costs incurred by traditional banks and to share the advantages of its strategy with its clients by competitive pricing of financial services fees. The mass diffusion of the Internet in the 2000s allowed Mediolanum to reinforce its strategy by offering services requiring human interaction (with global financial consultants and, for routine banking operations, via phone) and the best of the online banking (speed and convenience).

The growth of Mediolanum Bank was related to three main factors, all leading to an increase in the total amount of assets managed: the number of global financial consultants, the number of clients and the new products launch. The new clients were acquired primarily via personal networks of the global financial consultants, including by word of mouth from existing clients. In addition, Mediolanum Bank invested in traditional advertising and, starting from mid-2000, in events for existing and prospective clients (such as wine-tasting, art gallery openings) during which the global financial consultants had a chance to meet new potential affluent clients and introduce themselves.

In the 2000s Mediolanum started taking up possibilities abroad by acquiring niche players in Spain, Germany and Austria. In 2006 Mediolanum Bank launched the concept of a "Family Banker" who, with its human touch and impeccable professionalism, would substitute a "global financial consultant", and become a symbol of the final transition for Mediolanum from a financial services company to a retail bank.

The assets were managed through a "5D" strategy: duration diversification; geographical diversification; stock diversification; growth potential and risk diversification; and financial instruments diversification.

6.2 The growth imperative

Ennio Doris, the Bank's CEO and founder, believed Mediolanum Bank's growth potential had not yet been realized, and wanted it to become the leading player in Italy in retail asset management (Table 6.1). The analysis of the past nine years of the bank's performance showed an average 3.6% annual growth rate in client numbers (Fig. 6.1).

Table 6.1 **Mediolanum Bank ranking vs. other asset management players in Italy**
Source: company data

	July 2007	Dec 2007	Dec 2008	Dec 2009	Dec 2010E
1	Eurizon	Intesa Sanpaolo	Intesa Sanpaolo	Intesa Sanpaolo	Intesa Sanpaolo
2	Pioneer	Pioneer	Pioneer	Pioneer	Pioneer
3	Crédit Agricole/ Intesa	UBI Banca	UBI Banca	UBI Banca	UBI Banca
4	UBI Banca	Arca	Arca	Bipiemme/Anima	Mediolanum
5	Capitalia	Banco Popolare	MPS	Arca	Bipiemme/Anima
6	Arca	MPS	Mediolanum	Mediolanum	Arca
7	MPS	Crédit Agricole	BNP Paribas	Prima	BNP Paribas
8	JPMorgan	BNP Paribas	Generali	BNP Paribas	Prima
9	BNP Paribas	JPMorgan	Azimut	Azimut	Generali
10	BPVe-No	Mediolanum	Banco Popolare	Generali	Azimut

	July 2007	Dec 2007	Dec 2008	Dec 2009	Dec 2010E
11	Mediolanum	Azimut	JPMorgan	JPMorgan	Amundi
12	Generali	Generali	Bipiemme	Crédit Agricole	JPMorgan
13	Azimut	Bipiemme	Crédit Agricole	Credem	Credem
14	RAS	Allianz	Allianz	Banco Popolare	Banco Popolare
15	Bipiemme	Anima	Credem	Allianz	Allianz
16	Deutsche Bank	Credem	Anima	Kairos Partners	Banca Carige
17	Credem	Deutsche Bank	Polaris	Banca Carige	Fondaco
18	Kairos Partners	Kairos Partners	C.R. Firenze	Ersel	Deutsche Bank
19	C.R. Firenze	C.R. Firenze	Kairos Partners	Deutsche Bank	Kairos Partners
20	Anima	Polaris	Deutsche Bank	Fondaco	Ersel
Market share	2.73%	2.79%	3.81%	4.44%	4.83%
Mediolanum					
Assets (€ billions)	16.6	15.9	12.0	16.4	20.1

Figure 6.1 **Mediolanum Bank: number of clients vs. number of agents**

Source: company data

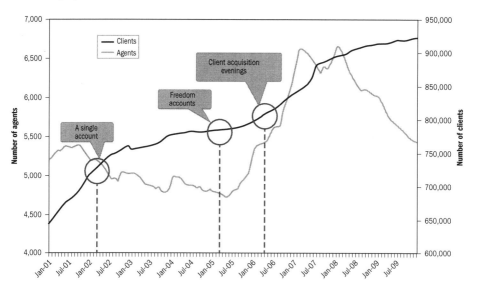

For Mediolanum, the main growth factors were the number of agents (Family Bankers) and the new product initiatives. The new agents' recruitment activities were conducted constantly throughout the year, but each new entrant required three months of training and some time to start working to their full potential. Moreover, circa 50% of new entrants left within one year, while the remaining half had much a lower turnover rate. Another growth option was the introduction of innovative financial instruments. For instance, "Freedom" launched in 2009 combined characteristics of a current account and of life insurance for savings exceeding €15,000. The bank chose organic growth, without acquisitions, but the growth rates were still too slow, even when the financial markets were growing.

Box 1 **Ennio Doris and Mediolanum Bank**

Born in a village close to Padua, Ennio Doris spent his twenties as a bank clerk. At the age of 28 he became the general manager of an engineering company owned by one of the bank's directors. As the young man's ambitions grew, he decided to quit the job and to become a salesman for insurance and financial products, paid in commission, rather than a salary. This invaluable "field" experience allowed him to formulate his business idea of selling a wide spectrum of financial customized products with a high level of service and of customization. The start-up capital was provided by Silvio Berlusconi, at that time busy building his real estate empire. Doris offered his idea, implementation skills, some capital and the possibility to add real estate products to the newly born financial group's portfolio. The 50/50% partnership started in 1982 with the name "Programma Italia". By 1984 Programma Italia achieved its business plan forecasts and acquired Mediolanum Vita and Mediolanum Assicurazione, providing customers with the possibility of real one-stop shopping for all the basic financial services. In 1985, with Fininvest (a financial holding majority owned by Berlusconi), Programma Italia started offering investment trust products and other asset management services.

In the 1990s Programma Italia became one of the fastest growing players in the financial services industry. The product offering was very clear and simple. Since its foundation Programma Italia has worked exclusively in the retail segment of asset management, offering 360° ("global") financial services (saving, asset management, life insurance and retirement plans) to its clients: families, entrepreneurs and wealthy individuals. Its success was also based on the company's sales force, a network of global financial consultants, trained and groomed in-house with the utmost care and dedication. In 1995 Programma Italia changed its name to Mediolanum SpA, maintaining the original ownership structure. In 1996 Mediolanum SpA started offering traditional banking services to its retail clients and listed its shares at the Milan Stock Exchange.

6.3 Growth idea: an online deposit account

In 2009 competition in the retail online banking sector in Italy was heating up, as the share of online accounts was strongly growing (Fig. 6.2). In the late 2000s, most of the traditional banks were suffering from the reduction in interbank loans and therefore were looking for new sources of cash. Online deposits offering high interest rates became a new emerging market sector in retail banking.

Figure 6.2 **Retail bank accounts in Italy (millions)**

Source: company data

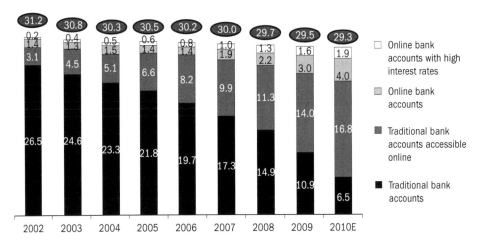

For Mediolanum, online deposits could become a way to accelerate the clients' acquisition rate, boost the bank's growth and fuel the customer base for the Family Bankers during the years of economic recession, by helping them to "open the door" of the new retail clients' "financial houses".

The idea to offer a current account was discarded from the very beginning. From the business point of view, an online current account with possibilities to access other online saving instruments (an online deposit account, for instance), would have been perceived by Family Bankers as an alternative to their services. Moreover, an online current account would have been too complex to manage, would have required a number of completely new internal processes, and would have brought much higher operative risks. An online deposit account, on the contrary, was characterized by a reduced number of operations (no credit cards, no bills, no charges, and no frequent payment orders). Mediolanum did not consider offering any other financial service online, as the online deposit account served to attract new clients to transfer them to the Family Bankers, rather than to substitute Family Bankers or to become a new sales channel for the bank.

The decision to offer a new online account was taken by the bank's board in late 2009. The online deposit account could be opened by prospective clients autonomously, using a "self-service" approach, with the possibility to use a banking call centre ("banking centre") operator's assistance. To open an account, a prospective client had to make a bank transfer from another account. If the transfer arrived from a "traditional" bank, the client's request to open an account was approved on the assumption that the traditional bank should have collected all the necessary personal data on the client before opening the account. If the transfer arrived from another online bank, to assure compliance with money laundering legislation, the client was asked to contact a Family Banker in order to provide Mediolanum with additional information. A new "online" client would be contacted at the first interest rate accrual expiry date to be offered the option of being contacted by a Family Banker, to discuss other possible investment options. The online clients also had the possibility to navigate around various investment products and to eventually request extra information or a contact from a Family Banker. Mediolanum Group identified a dedicated "elite" group of Family Bankers for the first, precious contacts sought by the online clients.

The telephone assistance was an important component of the new service. Initially, the idea was to put the effort into minimizing telephone assistance costs. Traditionally, the Mediolanum Banking centre answered clients' phone calls within 5 seconds and the same level of service was to be offered for the new product. However, the simplicity of the new product did not require a full three month training to be offered to the "traditional" banking centre operators: the assumption was that a week-long training would suffice and the "new online" telephone operators would have an opportunity to switch the clients to their more experienced colleagues for more complex requests. The role of the telephone operators that supported the online deposit account turned out later to be an important factor, as it distinguished Mediolanum from other online banks, and not only when the client was about to decide which online bank to choose. Several days would pass between the initial bank transfer, the internal authentication and confirmation of a new client's personal data, and the moment when a new client saw the money appear on the new, fully functioning account. That waiting period, lasting on average 5 days, would usually lead new clients to follow-up with the bank via a telephone call, to which a five-second response was very reassuring.

At the time of launch, it was decided that the online deposit account would offer gross annual interest of 3.5%, 0.5% more than the competition. A major concern was the cannibalization of existing deposit and current accounts: if the possibility was offered, existing clients might move all their cash and assets to the new online products, thereby deteriorating the bank's financial position and destroying the key asset of the bank: the face-to-face, trustworthy relationships between clients and Family Bankers.

6.4 The team's decision

The implementation of a new online product by 2010 was entrusted to a group of the bank's managers[1]:

- Federico Soldini, a deputy to vice-president for finance

- Marco Mazzini, a deputy to vice-president for marketing

- Anna Gentile, a deputy to vice-president for human resources

- Elisa Netti, a deputy to vice-president for sales network management

- Carlo Itti, a deputy to vice-president for IT

- Sara Tuttofare, a deputy to vice-president for operations

After some weeks of intense work, the team met for the final meeting before the informal presentation to the CEO. Twenty minutes before the deadline, the new information arrived via email to all the meeting members: the project's financial plan (Table 6.3). The team had to find consensus on the following issues:

- **Question 1**. How to manage the online deposit introduction without damaging the cohesive relationship between Mediolanum Bank and its major asset, the network of Family Bankers. What are the expected benefits for the Family Bankers from the new product introduction and is there any extra work for them?

- **Question 2**. How to deal with the existing "traditional" clients. Should they be offered the possibility to benefit from the new online deposit product?

- **Question 3**. How to brand the new product. Should Mediolanum follow the other banks' example and use a completely different brand, to distinguish the online deposit account from the rest of the bank's products?

- **Question 4**. Is there a need for a new legal entity, to isolate the new business processes and, consequently, the eventual operative risks?

6.5 Role play profiles

The following personal profiles were distributed individually to the six team members. Each team member had to read the role description autonomously and to act according to the indications received, without disclosing the profile information to the other participants.

---

1 The team members' profiles and names were invented by the authors of the case to facilitate and to stimulate the case discussion and are not related to the actual managers who worked on the project.

6.5.1 Federico Soldini, deputy to the vice-president for finance

(this is your initial point of view which can be modified during the discussion, but only if you find other colleagues' arguments convincing)

Your major concern: To make sure that the financial factors are taken into account during the discussion, otherwise it will be your and your department's fault if the attention of the team is driven towards qualitative and intangible reasoning. During the discussion you repeatedly call the attention of the team to the "numbers" (project financials; Table 6.2). The qualitative reasoning about organizational culture and the Family Bankers' attitude by other colleagues tend to make you feel uncomfortable and, if prolonged, irritate you.

Table 6.2 **Online deposit account: project financial plan (estimates)**

Source: company data

	year 1	year 2	year 3	year 4	year 5	
Euribor, 12 months	1.7%	2.5%	3.0%	3.5%	3.5%	
Online deposit interest rate, 12 months	3.5%	3.75%	4.25%	4.75%	4.85%	
Treasury income yield, 12 months	3.3%	3.3%	3.8%	4.3%	4.4%	
New clients (no.)	63,000	75,000	93,000	110,000	130,000	
New online clients "independent"	39,000	45,000	55,000	64,000	74,000	(A)
New online clients introduced by Family Bankers	24,000	30,000	38,000	46,000	56,000	(B)
New clients switching to other asset management products, including:	0	10,440	29,872	51,936	76,716	
New online clients "independent"	0	5,760	15,886	27,795	41,464	(A)
New online clients introduced by Family Bankers	0	4,680	13,985	24,140	35,252	(B)
New assets under management	**year 1**	**year 2**	**year 3**	**year 4**	**year 5**	
New online clients (all)	1,260,000	2,329,977	3,388,226	4,548,228	5,871,738	(A) + (B)
New clients switching to other asset management products	0	313,200	981,477	1,816,052	2,824,284	(A) + (B)
Total	1,260,000	2,643,177	4,369,703	6,364,280	8,696,022	

Your position on question 1: From the financial point of view, the new project's profitability depends strongly on two issues. First, with reasonable and prudent assumptions, the project is going to lose money if Family Bankers are not involved. Second, the bank should use the online deposit account to flood the new clients into the pool of clients managed by Family Bankers with "traditional" asset management products. In your view, at the initial stages of the project it would not make any sense to increase the cost side of the project with the remuneration of Family Bankers.

Your position on question 2: Existing clients should not be given access to the new online deposit account, if not for "new cash", to avoid the cannibalization effect on existing financial products and reducing the profitability of the new project.

Your position on question 3: Your position is neutral, even if, from the financial point of view, the investment in a new brand creation might be against any financial logic, given the uncertainty about the new project outcome.

Your position on question 4: You strongly support the idea of a separate legal entity that would simplify the accountability (planning and control of the financial results) of the project and of the managers in charge of the project.

6.5.2 Anna Gentile, deputy to the vice-president for human resources

(this is your initial point of view which can be modified during the discussion, but only if you find other colleagues' arguments convincing)

Your major concern: how to structure the hiring and the training for the new personnel needed to assist new clients on the phone. As a cost centre, the Human Resources department has to define the exact number of new hires needed for the project. Moreover, the introduction of the new product meant a revision of many back office processes and premises. Since the four issues on the agenda do not directly impact your department, you shall try to press the colleagues from Marketing and Sales, to give you more precise data on which to base your own projections.

Your position on question 1: The remuneration of Family Bankers should not be an issue as the online deposit account served to "open the door" to the client for the Family Bankers. The issue was different when Family Bankers went to visit existing or potential clients: those efforts had to be and were remunerated. To clarify the bank's position, you suggest that your department offer a special online tutorial for the Family Bankers on the role of the new product in the overall bank growth strategy. Still, if the matter becomes of concern, you would rather support the idea of giving a small remuneration to Family Bankers, to keep the organizational climate calm and collaborative.

Your position on question 2: Your opinion is neutral: if the existing clients were given the option to access the new online accounts, your department would organize a short training for all telephone operators on the new product.

Your position on question 3. You are strongly against the idea of the marketing department to call the new product "InMediolanum". A special account dedicated to Mediolanum staff promoted by your department was already called an "In" account. Moreover, the new brand should be used not only for external, but also for internal communications. "MediolanumNext", in your opinion, is a good idea, to convey to the whole organization that as times change and the external environment evolves, so also the whole Mediolanum organization, its people, processes and its culture, should follow and adapt.

Your position on question 4. You do not see a separate legal entity as a way to isolate any possible operational risk: most of the operative risks had already been analysed and dealt with. A separate legal entity, although involving extra costs, would allow the bank to create from scratch, a new, more dynamic and flexible organization dedicated to the new online clients. The traditional organization of Mediolanum was structured to serve clients that were not particularly technologically advanced and were not expecting a real-time reaction to their requests. Moreover, responsibility for client satisfaction was completely in the hands of the Family Bankers. The success of the new online deposit account is now entirely the responsibility of headquarters – are they ready to abandon their traditional "support role" and to problem-solve to bring home results?

6.5.3 Marco Mazzini, deputy to the vice-president for marketing

(this is your initial point of view which can be modified during the discussion, but only if you find other colleagues' arguments convincing)

Your major concern: the marketing department at the moment is acting as the agent of change in the creation and potentially implementation of this new project, and is very much concerned about the resistance encountered from other colleagues. So you have to try to guide the meeting and to make your colleagues agree on a common solution. Your "natural" ally is the IT department manager, who is very much concerned about the time spent on the decision-making as it "steals" time from the implementation phase, where the IT department is going to be one of the key process owners.

Your position on question 1: the new online deposit account is not only the way for Mediolanum to grow, but also is a service for the Family Bankers who obtain access to a broader database of real and concrete, not potential, clients. Mediolanum's investments into the new online account are substantial (the IT system and promotion alone account for several million euros). Therefore the Family Bankers should not be remunerated for the new clients' accounts, even if in some cases the Family Bankers' help might be needed for the client's identification and data transcription. If the existing clients are given the option to use the new account, the Family Bankers would receive commission only for the "new cash".

Your position on question 2: The existing clients should not be given access to the new online deposit account, if not for "new cash", to avoid the cannibalization effect on existing financial products and reducing the profitability of the new project.

Your position on question 3. You speak up first: after some weeks of brainstorming inside your department and with a team of external consultants you propose to call the new account "InMediolanum", to transmit the idea, internally and externally, that the project is inside of the Mediolanum group.

Your position on question 4. You advocate a separate legal entity. Even before the implementation phase the organizational resistance you encountered, in particular in your one-to-one meetings with other colleagues, make you think that a minor increment in the project investment for the creation of a new legal entity will speed up the implementation phase significantly.

6.5.4 Elisa Netti, deputy to the vice-president for sales network management

(this is your initial point of view which can be modified during the discussion, but only if you find other colleagues' arguments convincing)

Your major concern: the relationship with the network of Family Bankers, the cornerstone of the Mediolanum Group strategy. In the past, the Family Bankers usually showed themselves to be open to the new products added to the Group's portfolio. Would they react in the same way to the online deposit account?

Your position on question 1: You speak up first and loudly: any change in Mediolanum Bank should not undermine the relationship with the Family Bankers, otherwise the best of these freelance professionals might sense this new initiative as Mediolanum's attempt to avoid intermediaries and leave, taking clients away with them and convincing them to join other financial institutions. In the least dangerous scenario, following the potential "disenchantment" with Mediolanum's strategy, the Family Bankers would concentrate their efforts on developing existing clients, where the fee certainty is high, and would not care about new clients' research and acquisition. Therefore you suggest that a Family Banker has to be assigned a new online client from the very beginning, from day zero, and receive a small commission on each new online client deal, in addition to the option for existing clients to open online accounts (in this case the commission payment is taken for granted).

Your position on question 2: Also for this question, you have to try to convince other colleagues that the option for existing clients to access the new online product is the only way to maintain good and trustworthy relationships with the network of Family Bankers. In addition, Family Bankers should receive a fee for the sales of the new online deposit account, for the existing clients' "new cash" (incremental additional investments by existing clients) and "old cash" (existing clients may decide to move their money from another Mediolanum financial product to the new online deposit account).

Your position on question 3: You strongly agree with the proposed brand: "InMediolanum" transmits the idea that the new online deposit account is one of Mediolanum's products, therefore may contribute to reassure the sales network about their central and important role for the sales of this product.

Your position on question 4: You strongly support the idea of maintaining the single legal entity and not spinning off the new project to another legal entity. Even if the decision is not directly visible to all clients, it will be public (as Mediolanum is a public company) and this piece of news might create some tension with the network of Family Bankers.

6.5.5 Carlo Itti, deputy to the vice-president for IT

(this is your initial point of view which can be modified during the discussion, but only if you find other colleagues' arguments convincing)

Your major concern: since the general decision to launch the online deposit account is already taken, the current lengthy and qualitative discussion by other team members is seen by you as the major obstacle to starting the project as soon as possible. After the implementation plan is cleared by the top management, the major headache about meeting the launch deadline is going to be yours. Therefore you try to act as a moderator, to speed up the discussion and to bring all the parties to a reconciliation.

Your position on question 1: Neutral; your main point is that the rules should be clear and account for all possible situations: Family Bankers working with new clients, Family Bankers working with existing clients, "new cash" (new assets) vs. "old cash" (assets already under management) and so on.

Your position on question 2: Neutral, even though looking at the project financials shown by your colleague from the financial department, you see that the cannibalization effect, even as an estimate, is important.

Your position on question 3: You are against the idea of the marketing department – "InMediolanum" – because according to your personal perception of the current market conditions you strongly believe that a separate brand, not directly identifiable with Mediolanum, would be the best solution, to avoid cannibalization of existing products and sales channels.

Your position on question 4: Strongly against the new organization and a separate legal entity as it might create extra delays in the design of an additional IT architecture.

6.5.6 Sara Tuttofare, deputy to the vice-president for operations

(this is your initial point of view which can be modified during the discussion, but only if you find other colleagues' arguments convincing)

Your major concern: the operations function will have to design several completely new processes, working in strict collaboration with the IT department. You have to make sure that the investments in IT, new personnel and training are sufficient; therefore you strongly support all ideas aimed at reducing the project costs and boosting the project revenues.

Your position on question 1: in your opinion Family Bankers should be actively involved in the promotion of the new online deposit account, but receive the commission fees only when the new clients add other financial products, more lucrative for the bank compared with the online deposit account.

Your position on question 2: here you believe an exception should be made, to preserve the main asset of the bank. By daily ensuring the high quality of customer service you perfectly understand how much the bank invests in client relationships and how much they are valued. Existing clients should be given the option to access the online deposit account for old and new cash. Also, a client may withdraw money from Mediolanum, temporarily store it at another bank and then return and open an online deposit account as though it was "new money". So it is absolutely not worthwhile to distinguish between "old" and "new" cash.

Your position on question 3: You have a neutral position but some negative feelings towards the "InMediolanum" brand. A special account dedicated to Mediolanum staff is already called the "In" account. So if the new account is called "InMediolanum", you would need to slightly alter some procedures regarding the existing "In" account, most probably at zero extra budget.

Your position on question 4: You support the idea of a separate organization, not legal entity. Designing the new process from zero would benefit from the experience of the existing organization. Even before the implementation phase the organizational resistance you encountered, in particular in your one-to-one meetings with other colleagues, make you think that a minor increment in the project investment for the creation of a new legal entity will speed up the implementation phase significantly.

Annex

Table 6.3 **Online deposit account: detailed project financial plan (estimates)**

Source: company data

Profit & loss (P&L) statement for new online clients ("independent")	year 1	year 2	year 3	year 4	year 5	(A)
Net interest income on online deposit	(2.5)	(0.3)	12.1	25.5	29.5	(A)
Net commission income on asset management	0.0	0.3	1.4	3.3	5.8	(A)
Operations costs*	(1.0)	(2.0)	(3.1)	(4.3)	(5.5)	(A)
Full client management costs**	0.0	(0.3)	(0.8)	(1.4)	(2.1)	(A)
Labour costs***	(0.9)	(1.3)	(1.5)	(1.8)	(2.1)	(A)
Advertising	(6.6)	(7.2)	(8.4)	(9.7)	(11.1)	(A)
Depreciation (IT)	(1.3)	(1.3)	(1.3)	0.0	0.0	(A)
Gross profit	(12.2)	(12.0)	(1.6)	11.6	14.4	(A)
Taxes	4.0	4.0	0.5	(3.8)	(4.8)	(A)
Net profit	(8.1)	(8.0)	(1.1)	7.8	9.7	(A)
Cash flow	year 1	year 2	year 3	year 4	year 5	
Net profit	(8.1)	(8.0)	(1.1)	7.8	9.7	(A)
Depreciation (IT)	1.3	1.3	1.3	0.0	0.0	(A)
Investments	(3.8)	0.0	0.0	0.0	0.0	(A)
Cash flow	(10.7)	(6.7)	0.2	7.8	9.7	(A)
Discount rate	7.7%					
Project NPV	(3.1)					(A)
P&L statement for new online clients introduced by Family Bankers	year 1	year 2	year 3	year 4	year 5	(B)
Net interest income on online deposit	(1.5)	(0.2)	7.6	17.1	20.6	(B)
Net commission income on asset management	0.0	0.3	1.6	3.7	6.6	(B)
Operations costs*	(0.6)	(1.3)	(2.0)	(2.9)	(3.9)	(B)
Full client management costs**	(0.3)	(0.7)	(1.4)	(2.2)	(3.1)	(B)
Labour costs***	(0.6)	(0.8)	(1.0)	(1.2)	(1.4)	(B)
Gross profit	(3.0)	(2.7)	4.8	14.4	18.7	(B)
Cannibalization effect (premium lost due to the existing clients switching to the high interest rate online deposit)	(1.4)	(1.4)	(1.4)	(1.4)	(1.4)	
P&L statement for new online clients ("independent" and introduced by Family Bankers)	year 1	year 2	year 3	year 4	year 5	(A)+(B)

Net interest income on online deposit	(4.0)	(0.5)	19.7	42.6	50.0	(A)+(B)
Net commission income on asset management	0.0	0.6	2.9	7.0	12.4	(A)+(B)
Operations costs*	(1.6)	(3.3)	(5.1)	(7.2)	(9.5)	(A)+(B)
Full client management costs**	(0.3)	(1.0)	(2.3)	(3.7)	(5.3)	(A)+(B)
Labour costs***	(1.4)	(2.1)	(2.5)	(2.9)	(3.4)	(A)+(B)
Cannibalization effect (premium lost due to the existing clients switching to the high interest rate online deposit)	(1.4)	(1.4)	(1.4)	(1.4)	(1.4)	(A)+(B)
Advertising	(6.6)	(7.2)	(8.4)	(9.7)	(11.1)	(A)+(B)
Depreciation (IT)	(1.3)	(1.3)	(1.3)	0.0	0.0	(A)+(B)
Gross profit	(16.6)	(16.1)	1.8	24.7	31.8	(A)+(B)
Taxes	5.5	5.3	(0.6)	(8.2)	(10.5)	(A)+(B)
Net profit	(11.1)	(10.8)	1.2	16.5	21.3	(A)+(B)

P&L statement for new online clients ("independent" and introduced by Family Bankers)	**year 1**	**year 2**	**year 3**	**year 4**	**year 5**	**(A)+(B)**
Cash flow	year 1	year 2	year 3	year 4	year 5	(A)+(B)
Net profit	(11.1)	(10.8)	1.2	16.5	21.3	(A)+(B)
Depreciation (IT)	1.3	1.3	1.3	0.0	0.0	(A)+(B)
Investments	(3.8)					
Cash flow	(13.6)	(9.5)	2.5	16.5	21.3	(A)+(B)
Discount rate	7.7%					(A)+(B)
Project NPV	8.1					(A)+(B)

* Operation costs: deposit account taxes payable by a bank, cost of the legally required communication with the client

** Full client management costs: banking centre personnel and telecommunication costs

*** Labour costs: back office and inbound and outbound operations management

7
Ametista

Antonella Moretto and Margherita Pero

Politecnico di Milano, Italy

Ametista is an Italian luxury lingerie company, with over 60 years' experience, which designs, produces and sells its product worldwide to mainly female customers. The company has a turnover of €150 million and 550 employees. After the 2010 economic crisis, the company faced a dramatic fall in turnover, which prompted the company to turn itself around. The owner carried out an in-depth analysis through which it became clear that it was necessary to completely revise the core process of the company, the collection development process. Although this process embodies the real value of the company, it is now too long, too costly and unable to adapt to market change. This case aims to describe the collection development process in depth and pushes students to revise it using a structured approach, without missing the link between design process, operational processes and company strategy.

7.1 The company

Ametista is an Italian brand with over 60 years' experience, specialized in manufacturing luxury lingerie. The company was established in 1940 by Lea Garavaglia, a young seamstress with big, nearly elusive, dreams. Lea set up a small workshop in Florence, calling it Ametista (amethyst) after her favourite gem. Lea's idea was not just to make simple undergarments and corsetry, but to create precious items that would make any woman wearing them feel like a princess in her heart.

Over the years, the company expanded greatly, in terms of both the range of products on offer and its turnover, and, in 1980, Lea handed over the management of her company to her son, Giacomo Mancotti, who, like his mother, had always been captivated by this fascinating business. The company reached its peak in turnover in 2000, and the same year confirmed its place as the world leader in the creation and manufacture of luxury lingerie. Its mission was both to create the best lingerie in the world, by focusing on its Italian traditions and its position within the luxury sector, and to establish itself as a leader for quality and innovation. After many years of strong growth in sales and the number of markets covered, from 2001 onwards, the company felt the first signs of recession. The worst of this downturn came in 2010, compounded by the effects of the financial crisis throughout the entire sector. In 2010, the company's turnover was €150 million, with an overall staff of about 550. Mancotti realized that the business had been making a loss for too many years, and he could no longer make up for it with his own money.

7.2 The luxury and fashion sectors

Ametista's products are both fashion items and luxury products. While companies working in the fashion sector typically manufacture clothing, accessories (belts, bags, hosiery), footwear and lingerie, they are classified as belonging to the fashion sector because their products have a very short life-cycle. Ametista's products reflect this and, in addition, they are of the highest quality and are very expensive, which means that they are also luxury products.

The luxury and fashion sectors have very specific characteristics, which are defined below.

7.2.1 The luxury sector

The concept of luxury originated in the ancient world, and was already then associated with exclusivity, power and wellbeing, as well as satisfying non-essential needs. Internationally, luxury is a multi-million euro business, and Italy alone accounts for around 30% of the total world turnover for luxury brands, with a turnover of over €60 billion.

Companies belonging to various industrial sectors (including the boat, jewellery, clothing and furnishing industries, catering and restaurants, hotels, personal and professional services, etc.) can, at the same time, be defined as luxury companies. Luxury companies can be more readily compared with each other (e.g. Ferrari, Louis Vuitton, and the luxury kitchen manufacturer Boffi) rather than with companies belonging to the same sector, but in a lower band (e.g. Fiat, Ikea and the luggage manufacturer Carpisa).

Luxury companies also have similar key success factors:

- **Product quality**. By quality, we mean that the product must respect the specifications set out during the design phase and that the quality of manufacturing is above average. Luxury brands are defined as such because they are far superior in terms of their quality than other brands, justifying the premium price they ask from their customers.

- **Uniqueness and exclusivity**. People who buy a luxury item want to feel that they are acquiring something unique, that their purchase is something that few others can afford or share with them. In addition, they want a sense of exclusivity, and relish genuinely exclusive aspects, such as precious stones, prized materials or top design.

- **Style and design**. It is not enough to use materials of the highest quality in order to operate in this sector. A product must also give that something extra to the person buying it. Its design and its look are elements that make it unique, transmitting all sorts of emotions and sensations to its buyer.

- **Country of origin**. In most cases, the value placed on a product by a customer is tightly linked to the country where it was made. For example, in the fashion world, a "Made in Italy" or "Made in France" label is an assurance of high quality, something still sought by people who buy luxury products.

- **Technical performance**. People who buy a luxury item also want the technical aspects of the product to be better than for the average product on the market. This factor is important, especially in categories with a highly technical component, such as cars, yachts or home automation.

- **Emotional attractiveness**. People who buy a luxury item want an experience that is unique not only in terms of what they are buying but also because of the surroundings and the people assisting them when making their purchases. Therefore, luxury companies must provide a service that reflects this and fulfils their customers' dreams and expectations.

- **Brand reputation**. When consumers buy a luxury item, they wish, and indeed have the right, to feel special when they make the purchase and when they use the product. They want to feel part of an exclusive group, an elite community of people who share the same passions and aspirations, reflected in the brand.

- **Creating a lifestyle**. Synergy must be created between how the product is perceived by customers, the purchasing experience they encounter and the values conveyed by the brand.

- **Craftsmanship**. Luxury products must have some aspect of traditional craftsmanship, a certain element of artisan legacy in the way the product is made.

The brands belonging to luxury companies can be grouped into three categories – **absolute** luxury, **aspirational** luxury and **accessible** luxury – according to how exclusive they are.

The highest tier is that of *absolute luxury*. Brands in this category are linked to very exclusive products, with a very high price and sold through an extremely selective distribution network. Many brands in this category are only known to a very narrow group of privileged people. In many cases, the products are unique. The brands in this category have become true icons, and their key success factors are often artisanship and country of production.

The second tier is that of *aspirational luxury*. Companies in this category also make products that are highly exclusive and produced to an extremely high standard. In general, these brands are well-known around the world; their name and their distinguishing style and/or design are widely recognized. A critical strength of this luxury category is its emotional attractiveness.

The third tier is that of *accessible luxury*. This is a form of luxury that has made an appearance in recent times as an effect of the current phenomenon of "democratizing luxury". Although it is the "lowest" tier of luxury, exclusivity is still important, but companies will focus more on emotional exclusivity than on technical performance. Brands operating in this segment are also known globally and they tend to concentrate on illustrating their worth. The fundamental strength of this kind of luxury lies in its ability to construct a certain lifestyle that people can identify with.

7.2.2 The fashion sector

The fashion sector is a massive resource for Europe. In 2014, the sector was worth around €165 billion, generated by over 170,000 companies; a total of over 1.6 million people work in the sector in the EU-28 (Euratex estimates, 21 May 2015).[1] It is a very mixed bag with many companies that are completely different from each other in terms of size, processes and technologies. Competition within the fashion industry is based on continuously changing styles and trends, with very short times in which to complete an entire "concept to customer" cycle.

Products made by fashion companies all have the following in common:

- **Short product life-cycle**. Fashion products have an increasingly symbolic and emotional value, which comes from their links to style and design, making them somehow ephemeral. This means that the sales window has to adapt to the continuous changes in consumer choices, becoming shorter and shorter.

- **High volatility**. The final demand is unlikely to be stable or have a linear progression. It easily falls prey to consumers' choices in style, the weather, advertising campaigns and what celebrities prefer.

- **Low predictability**. As a consequence of this volatility, the demand for fashion items is difficult to predict, either in terms of total volumes throughout the season or when making weekly forecasts.[2]

- **Impulse buying**. Often customers decide to buy something on a whim when they are in a shop, rather than for any thought-out reason. This means that it is very important for the products to be available in the shop, to provoke this impulse.

---

1 http://euratex.eu/fileadmin/user_upload/documents/key_data/fact_and_figures_2014. pdf, accessed 11 December 2015.

2 The work rhythms of fashion companies are split into two seasons: autumn/winter (A/W) and spring/summer (S/S).

The products of companies in this sector can be grouped into three generic classes:

- **"Basic" products**, which have a life-cycle that can last for years, so they can be sold season after season. These cover around 20% of the market and, after the initial launch period, have a long mature phase (typically several years) when sales level out, making it relatively easy to predict the demand for the end market.

- **"Seasonal" products,** which are proposed repeatedly in basically the same version every other season and have a life-cycle of about 20 weeks (one season). This type of product covers around 45% of the market.

- **"Fashion" products**, which account for 35% of the market, have an average life-cycle of about ten weeks, and are never proposed for more than one season. Sales to end consumers are concentrated in the first half of a product's life-cycle, which is so short that it never really reaches the mature stage.

Note that the more a product tends towards being a "fashion" item, meaning that its life-cycle is short, the more pressing the company's work rhythms. In particular, as seasonal products and fashion items have a brief life-cycle, there is a need for comprehensive updating at least twice a year; this may involve redefining the bill of materials and the production cycles for the products.

In addition, the products and brands of companies operating in the fashion sector can be classed in terms of the market band they wish to target. There are products and brands in the fashion sector that are also luxury items and so can be classified into the three tiers mentioned previously (*absolute, aspirational* and *accessible* luxury). However, there are also companies that make fashion products for the mass market, offering products in large volumes at low prices. Fashion products can therefore be grouped into the following five tiers, ordered according to their decreasing exclusivity and price: *absolute* luxury, *aspirational* luxury, *accessible* luxury, **mass market-volume** and **mass market-mass**.

Note that mass market-volume and mass market-mass brands concentrate on producing large volumes and target a wide swathe of the population. However, mass market-volume brands are of a slightly better quality and are marginally more expensive than mass market-mass brands.

Every company in the fashion sector can therefore classify its products along two axes in a diagram: length of its cycle-life and its market band, as shown in Table 7.1.

Table 7.1 **Classification of fashion company products**

	Basic	**Seasonal**	**Fashion**
Absolute Luxury			
Aspirational Luxury			
Accessible Luxury			
Mass market-volume			
Mass market-mass			

Clearly, a company may have several brands belonging to different classes. For example, a generic luxury company can own two brands: one an aspirational luxury brand and the other an accessible luxury brand. Moreover, different products for the same brand may be placed in different boxes in the diagram, so that, for example, the company's "traditional" jeans fall at the intersection between aspirational luxury and seasonal products, while jeans in the same collection that reflect the latest craze fall at the intersection between aspirational luxury and fashion products.

7.3 Products and channels

Ametista sells two types of items, lingerie (bras, briefs, slips and bustiers) and nightwear (nightgowns, pyjamas, bed jackets and dressing gowns), exclusively for a female clientele.

Traditionally, the company only sold products of *absolute* luxury but, more recently, its aim has been to create products that bring dreams to everyday life. For this to happen, alongside their products of *absolute* luxury, Ametista introduced items of *accessible* luxury. This meant creating two brands: Ametista Luxury (*absolute* luxury) and Young Diamond (*accessible* luxury).

Ametista Luxury is aimed at mature, sophisticated women; the products are enticing yet refined in design and there is great care for the quality of the materials and finishing touches. The average price of a bra and brief set in this brand is €350, while the average price of an item of nightwear is €400. To date, this brand still represents 90% of the overall company turnover.

Young Diamond is offered to younger consumers, so its designs are clean and fresh, with a preference for soft colours and light fabrics. The average price for a bra and brief set in this brand is €80, and the average price for an item of nightwear is €120.

The method used to determine price, for both brands, is the full cost plus a mark-up, applying two different mark-ups, with that for Ametista Luxury items being significantly higher.

No item (whether of lingerie or nightwear) is ever presented for more than one season, so all Ametista products can be defined – according to the classification described above and based on the product's life-cycle – as "fashion products".

While Ametista Luxury and Young Diamond can both be said to be fashion brands, Ametista decided to introduce a further internal distinction for each brand on the basis of how significant the "fashion" component is. This means that products that follow the vagaries of fashion less closely can be differentiated from those that follow them more:

- *Products with a low fashion content* are items that follow the current tendencies, without going to any extremes. These products reflect the main trends in the market, in terms of colours, patterns and fabrics, but never forgo the classical approach traditionally followed by Ametista.

- *Products with a high fashion content* are products that follow seasonal fashions closely and are sometimes extreme in terms of the models designed or the use of colours, patterns and fabrics. The top priority for these products is to amaze, to create something that does not simply conform to trends and crazes but can even anticipate them.

Table 7.2 illustrates the positioning of Ametista's two brands according to their level of luxury, and also the average distribution of the collection in terms of the fashion content of the items. The table also shows the number of SKUs (stock keeping units) with lower or higher fashion content as a percentage of the total SKUs (see Section 7.6.1 for a definition of SKU) in the collection of each brand.

Table 7.2 **Positioning of the brands and distribution of the collection's SKUs in terms of their fashion content**

Absolute Luxury	Ametista Luxury (60% of the collection)	Ametista Luxury (40% of the collection)
Accessible Luxury	Young Diamond (30% of the collection)	Young Diamond (70% of the collection)
	Products with a low fashion content	**Products with a high fashion content**

As well as the products already mentioned, the company also owns a cosmetic and fragrance brand, Ametista Parfums, produced under licence by a famous perfume house. Alongside its own brand, this company manufactures on behalf of well-known fashion and clothing brands that also want their own line of perfumery.

All products are sold both in Italy and abroad. Currently, Ametista has a presence in most of the European market, in the USA, Russia, the Arab Emirates and the Asian market.

The two main distribution channels for all Ametista's products are "monobrand" company-owned shops or franchises and multibrand shops.[3]

There are Ametista monobrand shops all over the world. Monobrand shops are generally furnished so as to portray an image of luxury and exclusivity. Given the high initial investment to buy and manage a monobrand shop, this channel is mainly used to sell products from the Ametista Luxury brand. The multibrand shops exist only in Italy and other parts of Europe. To date, this channel is used by both brands, which, however, are never sold in the same shop. The choice of which brand to sell in a shop is determined by the other brands on sale there.

3 By monobrand, we mean shops that only sell Ametista products. By multibrand, we mean shops that sell products in a number of makes, including Ametista.

7.4 The Ametista organization

Giacomo Mancotti is the President of the company and Chairman of the Board of Directors. The company is run by the General Director, Alessio Ferrari, and the main company departments reporting directly (hierarchically or as support roles) to him are:

- **Finance and control**, which is responsible for company finances and management control. Personnel administration, specifically the administration of wages, salaries and staff bonuses, reports directly to this department. Overall, 11 people work in finance and control, of which four are in personnel administration.

- **Human resources**, which is responsible for the selection and management of personnel. Four people work full-time in this department.

- **Information systems**, which covers the control and management of all company information systems. The information systems manager works with the help of two newly graduated assistants.

- **Organization**, which is a new department responsible for monitoring company processes and suggesting improvements to them. The department is run by a manager assisted by three other people.

- **Sales**, which manages the sales network. Three people report to the commercial director: the manager for monobrand shops, the manager for domestic multibrand shops and the manager for foreign multibrand shops. In turn, reporting to the manager for monobrand shops are the manager for domestic monobrand shops, who runs the monobrand shops based in Italy – company-owned and franchises – with four assistants, and the manager for foreign monobrand shops, who runs the monobrand shops in Europe and the rest of the world. Staff working for Ametista in these shops are located in the various countries. The manager for domestic multibrand shops, together with his team of six people, runs all the multibrand shops in Italy. The people working with him are in constant contact with the shop managers, keeping an especially close watch during the collection selection phase, which takes place in the showroom at the Ametista main offices. The manager for foreign multibrand shops manages the multibrand shops throughout Europe. Given the intensely complex nature of this work, a dedicated staff of 12 works alongside the manager, with other staff where necessary located in each specific country.

- **Operations**, which manages all the production operations. The following people report to the operations manager :
  - The purchasing manager, with four people who manage the purchasing process, from issuing orders to receiving goods.

- The manager of the time and motion office, where there are five people whose job it is to determine the time-cycle for every manufacturing process required to produce each SKU and therefore the production time for each SKU. Two demonstrators also work in this department.
- The production planning manager and four assistants who manage all operations relative to planning the production.
- The production manager, who manages the manufacturing process of the finished product. He supervises 150 seamstresses, 3 assistants and 50 people controlling the machines.
- The logistics manager, who manages the flow of ingoing and outgoing materials from the plants' warehouses. As regards outgoing logistics, the logistics manager looks after the shipment of goods to the distribution centres of the main logistics operators, from where the products are sent to the multibrand shops as well as to the company-owned shops and those in franchising. Fifteen people report to him.

- **Style department**, which is responsible mainly for the collection development process. This office is headed by the style department manager and the following sections report directly to him or her: the idea generation office, with 20 full-time stylists (although this number can increase significantly at peak times when additional freelance stylists are brought in), the pattern-making department, with 20 paper pattern-designers, and prototyping, with five prototyping operators.

- **Marketing**, which is responsible for image management, communications and product promotion. This is considered a particularly important function in the company, and is headed by a manager with two people reporting to him or her, one for each type of product, lingerie and nightwear. Twenty people work in marketing, split evenly within the department.

All these departments are located at the Ametista Italian headquarters, but there are also several branches in the principal countries in which the company operates (Europe, USA, Russia, Arab Emirates, Asia), with an essentially commercial function.

7.5 The challenge

In January 2011, Giacomo Mancotti, having recognized that the company was in real financial difficulties, decided to ask an external consultancy firm to help him identify the reasons why Ametista was on the brink of bankruptcy. After several months of hard work within the company together with benchmarking exercises on similar companies in the same sector, the consultancy team gave Mancotti a report detailing the results of their work.

On reading their report, Mancotti was clear about three main problems at Ametista:

7.5.1 Long lead-times

The lead-times for company processes are very long, which means that Ametista takes far too long for its products to get to market. Being "late" in reaching the market means not having products in the shops when the shopkeepers want them and when their customers are most inclined to buy new things, at the start of each new season. Taking the winter season as an example, people are most likely to buy new clothes in September and October, to update their wardrobe leading up to the winter. Sales drop in November because people normally start saving for Christmas. In December, customers are keen to buy gifts, but it is very unlikely that Ametista's female clientele would buy an Ametista item as a gift. In January, the sales start, so trade goes up but margins are lower.

Being late has serious repercussions for company turnover. First, customers who are unable to find Ametista products in the shops when they are ready to buy, start to choose competitive brands. This is corroborated by a decrease in loyalty towards the brand on the part of customers.

Second, in Italy there are no penalties for late delivery. The manager of an Italian shop will be selling the products after the normal selling period, and so it is likely that they may have to sell them during the sales (at a lower margin). Currently, the company only sells 35% of its products in the selling period, compared with a target value of 80% of sales during the selling period for the sector in question. Since the company systematically delivers late, product stock-out tends to be excessive. If the products could be delivered sooner, so that 80% of them are sold in the selling period, this problem would be avoided. In Europe and the rest of the world, however, shop managers behave differently. For a late delivery of less than two weeks, they expect large discounts on the purchasing price from Ametista, while if it is over two weeks, they cancel their orders.

7.5.2 High costs

The company has very high costs, linked to internal inefficiencies. It would seem that the most critical process relating to this issue is the company's key procedure: the collection development process.

7.5.3 Inability to adapt to change

The company has been unable to adapt to changes in the market taking place over recent years. In the past, Ametista customers thought so highly of Ametista that they were ready to buy the products whatever their price, fit, the style offered or even when the items reached the market (even two or three months late). Today, this is unfortunately no longer the case. Competition is fierce and consumers are more knowledgeable about what the market offers. In particular, customers have become more demanding in terms of quality/price ratio. They are much less willing to pay a lot for the brand, and prices are sometimes considered excessive despite the high quality of the products. The company must therefore recognize that business needs have become more pressing and must try to adapt its products and processes to this new type of clientele.

After taking note of these considerations, Mancotti was still not convinced that the consultants had truly appreciated the spirit and singularity of his company, which had spent years at the top of the market. Being an old-style businessman, he resolved to find out for himself what was wrong, deciding on two courses of action. First, he wanted to analyse the collection development process thoroughly and understand its dynamics and critical aspects. Mancotti was unable to understand why this procedure should be the main source of the problems and inefficiencies in the company, as the collection development process had always been the jewel in Ametista's crown. Second, he wanted to organize a meeting with all the managers of the main departments, to hear directly from his staff what they thought the problems in the company were.

7.6 Developing the collection

7.6.1 How the collection is structured

The work rhythms in fashion companies are split into two seasons: autumn/winter (A/W) and spring/summer (S/S). Every year, Ametista presents a collection at each new season for both of its two brands, Ametista Luxury and Young Diamond, with a total of four collections a year (Ametista Luxury A/W; Ametista Luxury S/S; Young Diamond A/W; Young Diamond S/S). At Ametista, every collection is managed with the same passion, care for detail and time involved, independently of the brand or the season in question. It makes no difference in terms of the process stages and operations, or the staff dedicated to it, whether a collection belongs to one or other brand: the company does not want its lines to be seen as class A and class B products. In addition, in line with the company philosophy, no model will ever be exactly the same from one season to the next. This implies that, at the end of each collection, work on the new collection (the new collection development process) must start again from scratch, and all the phases of the process must be repeated in full twice a year, in a continuous loop.

Every collection can have between two and n different *moods*, and each mood can involve several colour variations, depending on what the stylist decides (for example, "Living in Nature" came in pastel green and forest green). All standard items must be produced for each colour variation of a particular mood (for example, underwired bras, triangle bras, slips, bustiers, nightgowns, pyjamas, briefs, Brazilian cut briefs, bed jackets, suspender belts, etc.) All these standard items are made in several different models for all the colours of a particular mood (for example: short slip with narrow shoulder straps, short slip with wide shoulder straps, long slip with narrow shoulder straps, long slip with wide shoulder straps). Each model also includes a choice of fabric to be used (for example: short slip with narrow shoulder straps in satin; short slip with narrow shoulder straps in silk). All 15 sizes on offer must be produced for each model (I-30"; II-32"; III-34"; IV-36"; V-38", in the three cup sizes A, B and C). A stock keeping unit (SKU) is defined as one item of a certain model in a particular variation of colour and in a certain size. This is summarized in Figure 7.1.

Figure 7.1 **Structure of the collection**

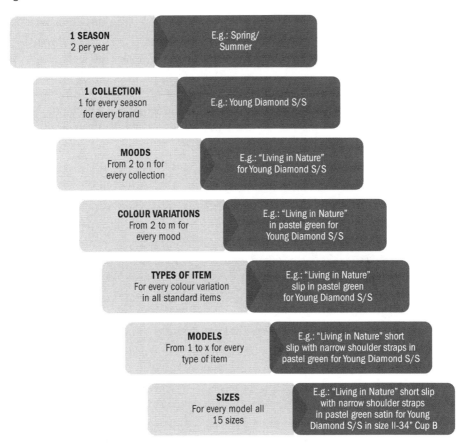

While this is the standard structure, in many cases identical models are proposed in different colour variations for the same mood, or, more rarely, for different moods. The company calculated that, the previous year, using this method meant that a total of 55,000 SKUs were created in one season for the two collections. By offering such a high level of diversity to its clientele, it is unlikely that two people who know each other will both buy the same Ametista item. A customer buying an

Ametista product feels that she has both the benefit of a prestigious name and the exclusivity of an artisan product. The main difference between Ametista and its main competitor, Micol, lies in the number of items sold around the world for each mood. For Ametista, a big selling mood means 45,000 items sold, while for Micol, it means 3 million items sold and a total of 15,000 SKUs every season. At Ametista, they still talk about an infamous case when, in 2011, a total of five items were produced for one particular SKU.

7.6.2 How the style department is structured

The style department is one of the main offices involved in the process of developing the collection. The style department takes up the entire second floor of the company premises, to avoid influence or pressure from other company departments. A total of 46 people work exclusively in the style department, between stylists, pattern-designers and prototyping operators. Additional freelance stylists are also called upon during specific phases in the development of the collection, and external prototyping operators prepare some of the prototypes when necessary during peak periods. The total number of part-time staff during peak periods is at least the same as the number of full-time employees, but can be even higher.

7.6.3 The most important dates

On entering the second floor, there is an immediate sense of urgency and creativity. On the walls, there are posters illustrating the company's cardinal values: luxury, exclusivity, quality and rareness. The poster that has always attracted Mancotti the most shows the only binding do-not-forget dates for the people creating the products: the dates of the textile trade fairs and the fashion shows, and when a collection must be in the shops (Table 7.3).

Table 7.3 **Do-not-forget dates – 2012 collection programming**

	Autumn-Winter (A/W) 2012	**Spring-Summer (S/S) 2012**
Textile trade fairs	Mid-September 2010	Mid-February 2011
Presentation of collection at fairs	End-February 2011	End-September 2011
Collection reaching shops	August 2011	January 2012

7.6.4 The collection development process

The process to develop its collections has always been Ametista's crowning glory: no mistakes may slip into this process and no limitations are allowed to curb creativity, because the creations must not only be beautiful but also "exhilarating".

The process involves the following steps:

- **Idea generation**: this includes all the work to define the moods and their relative colour variations, and to sketch the models of the Ametista products.

- **Product line creation**: this includes all the work to choose the suppliers of the fabrics and all the components, and to create the patterns, define the technical sheets for the products and, lastly, create the prototypes.

- **Market preparation**: this includes all the work, starting from the prototypes, involved in creating the sample collection and choosing the products that will go on the market.

- **Collection engineering**: this includes all the work needed to engineer the production process.

Ametista takes between eight and ten months to complete all the work from the idea generation phase to producing the sample collection.

7.6.4.1 Idea generation

Stylists have total autonomy on how they allocate their work over the year, as long as they respect the dates presented above. This means that some tasks may have to be completed in a hurry, because they have lost their sense of time. Stylists are given the same level of autonomy in deciding how to structure the collections (such as, the number of models, the mood of the collection and the types of items that must be presented at every collection), the choice of fabrics, the number of colour variants for each collection, and so on.

Idea generation starts with a meeting of the creative management team, composed of the manager of the style department and the five senior stylists in the company, which takes place every time the idea generation process begins. The aim of the meeting is to choose the moods that will inspire the styles selected for the collection. Examples of moods chosen in previous years are "Living in Nature", a collection with a fresh, countryside feel in tones of green, and "Life in Paris", provocative and naughty, in a slightly nostalgic vein, and inspired by the film *Moulin Rouge*. For every collection, the creative management team can choose between two and n moods (the average is five). In this phase, the desired colour variants are set out for each mood. The creative management team also decides how many stylists will work on each mood (the average is six internal stylists for each) and, for every mood, the types of item that each stylist will be working on (on average, each stylist is responsible for 1.7 types of item for each mood).

Walking down the corridor, Mancotti goes past the two main open plan spaces forming the second floor: the office reserved for stylists during the "generation of ideas" phase (this is a combination of purely creative operations) and the office reserved for stylists during the "product line creation" phase (a combination of purely practical tasks). These operations take place in open plan spaces because developing a collection is, as Mancotti often says, the grey area of the business, where work often overlaps and can proceed in parallel using internal product development teams, where the various players (stylists, pattern-designers, prototyping operators) frequently interact and can pass on unwritten information. Generating sketches, patterns and prototypes can be repeated a number of times for each model as, at each stage, the stylist may want to go back to a previous phase, in order to achieve the best results. In addition, not all the models that enter the process actually see the light. It is like a steeplechase, with only a small number of the models that enter actually finishing the race.

Stopping in front of the idea generation office, Mancotti looks inside and, as usual, is fascinated by what he sees. Three stylists are working there: currently the company is in between collections, so the pressure on the stylists and their work intensity is relatively low. At peak times, many people can be seen working frenetically alongside each other in the same office, each following the thread of their own thoughts. The three stylists are currently occupied with different models for the same collection and, to be precise, they are sketching out the models they want to create on sheets of card. The sketches show the models actually being prepared for the collection, but at this point there is no reference either to the variations in colour or to the materials that will be used to make them. The model only shows the mood, the type of item and the general look of the model.

This work tends to be very time-consuming, as all the stylists will make dozens and dozens of different sketches, gathering them together in their own, strictly private, folders, and only going ahead creatively with some of them. Stylists are like parents imagining their perfect child: they are full of ideas that may seem wrong the next moment and, above all, they will never be satisfied with anything less than perfection.

Stylists will present their sketches to the creative management team when they feel they are ready. When all the stylists have chosen their sketches and presented them to the creative management team, the team will start generating the collection, which means assembling all the sketches that potentially will make up the collection. In this phase, at the "sketch selection" meeting, the creative management team will look at all the sketches together and decide which really reflect the mood of the collection and, therefore, which will continue to the next stages of development. On average, this meeting will take place about three months after the idea generation phase started.

The stylists will start work on the idea generation process about one to three months before the textile trade fair, which all of the stylists attend. At the fair, they are often thrilled by a particular fabric presented by a supplier, and decide to modify a number of the sketches already prepared and/or presented to the creative management team, or they may be inspired to draw new sketches. In some cases, if one stylist in particular, or possibly the style department manager, is especially struck by a specific fabric, they may even decide to alter the mood of the collection or create a new one to add to the existing ones, going back to the idea generation phase.

7.6.4.2 Product line creation

Once the moods and the variants in colour are identified, and the sketches chosen, then the product line creation phase begins. This involves selecting fabrics and suppliers, and creating patterns and prototypes, to give life and body to the collection. In this phase, the stylist and the pattern-designer must work closely together if the collection is to be a success. Mancotti still remembers when, years previously, a pattern-designer described her work:

> My task is to turn a stylist's creative idea into a technical reality. To do this, I have to interpret the sensations that the stylist wants to transmit with his product, and has tried to convey in his sketch, but sometimes it means doing much more. It means interpreting what he wants the product to express without making it obvious, or what he would have liked to put in his sketch but was not capable of drawing. From the outside, my work only requires me first to prepare paper patterns, and then technical sheets. In reality, it requires a psychological effort to understand the stylist's spirit, it means looking beyond what is there, to see what is not yet there but should be, according to him.

Stylists start thinking about the materials they want to use right from the start of the idea generation phase. However, during the initial stages, they only have a vague idea about the fabrics. Only during the work to create the patterns, with the help of the pattern-designer, will they choose the fabrics and, accordingly, the suppliers.

Searching for fabrics is an important task for the company, and is carried out in a particularly "aggressive" way by the stylists and the pattern-designers, who have no restrictions either in financial terms or in the variety of materials they can use. It often happens that a stylist will ask a supplier for nothing but a hook produced according to Ametista specifications, which will be used for a single model of bra, in only one collection and in only one colour. Moreover, stylists go to the fairs where they expect to see the fabrics they like and will ask suppliers for samples to show the pattern-designers. Finally, stylists may not be satisfied with what they find on the market and ask the pattern-designer to seek out collaboration with a supplier to make a bespoke fabric.

It is, however, the pattern-designer who has the last word on the selection of suppliers. To choose the suppliers, apart from the stylists' suggestions, pattern-designers all make use of their own personal books giving the contact details and distinguishing factors of their favourite suppliers for every technical aspect. This book is considered the personal wealth of each pattern-designer, who will take it with them if ever they leave the company.

Pattern-designers choose specific suppliers to use for each model, selecting them from among those listed in their personal book. Any proposed new supplier, whether on suggestion of a stylist after meeting them at a fair or found by the pattern-designer herself, as long as they comply with all the necessary requirements, will be included as an approved supplier in their personal book. Ametista is very open towards proposals coming from suppliers, in terms of new fabrics or new textures on existing fabrics, meaning that decisions about the fabrics to be used are often changed. Suppliers who introduce themselves must be approved by the stylist and the pattern-designer and must be listed in the pattern-designer's book if they are to be used in the future.

A pattern-designer chooses suppliers for fabrics and components totally independently, without consulting the other pattern-designers and, having identified a supplier, she will contact them to see if they are willing to work with Ametista. Sometimes, pattern-designers will ask suppliers for samples of fabric so that they can see them for themselves before making any such request. Today, the company has a pool of 1,300 suppliers and may buy very little from some of them, but this is because of its strategic decision to make Ametista's products the top priority.

The pattern-designers will also take a leading role in negotiating with suppliers, as they consider themselves to be the only people truly capable of explaining to the supplier what Ametista really needs. Once negotiations are concluded, the pattern-designer sends an email to the sales department stating the contractual terms agreed for that supply. There are no framework agreements or repeat contracts with the suppliers, and specific contracts are stipulated for every supply.

The purchasing department, after gathering the sales orders, will carry out the various operations to draw up the contracts and manage the purchasing orders.

Stylists will all tend to work with a specific pattern-designer, with whom they develop a nearly telepathic relationship of absolute trust and who helps them to create the patterns.

As soon as the sketches have been approved by the creative management team, the stylist and pattern-designer will meet to discuss the sketches. At this meeting, it is not unusual for stylists to see that the product does not correspond to the idea they had in mind and so decide to reject it. When this happens, in 80% of the cases, stylists will feel the need for a new creative phase and will go back to the idea generation phase. This new creative phase can conclude with a totally new sketch or a simple alteration to an existing one. Before going ahead with preparing the patterns of these sketches, the stylist must also obtain the approval of the creative management team.

The relationship created between the pattern-designer and the stylist means that there may be occasions when some pattern-designers are totally oversubscribed, because they work with a very productive stylist who has prepared a large number of sketches in a very short time, and wishes to proceed with them all. Other pattern-designers may be under-occupied because their particular stylist is still at the idea generation phase.

While pattern-designers have a "creative and psychological" role, their function is also highly technical and specialized. After the sketch has been produced, the pattern-designer, in conjunction with preparing the corresponding paper patterns, must also create the technical specifications of the sketch in an Excel spreadsheet. A technical sheet is prepared for each model, giving information about the fabric to be used, the contact details of the supplier selling it, and a description of all the components used in the product, such as small hooks, underwires and shoulder straps. Before inputting the information on the Excel spreadsheet, the pattern-designer must assemble and check it. It is particularly critical to research information on the specific codes used by the supplier for all single fabrics and components, as well as the sales names of these items. In order to carry out these operations, the pattern-designer must have a good knowledge of product terminology, and must also contact all the suppliers identified (if new) to ask for these codes or (for existing ones) to find out whether any codes have been changed.

Once the pattern-designers have all completed their patterns, the creative administration team – at a new meeting to ensure consistency of mood and collection – will choose which patterns to use in the collection development process. At this point, the prototyping phase can start. On average, the two meetings take place 2½ months apart.

For each type of model, the pattern-designers produce a prototype in fabric to give a good impression of the look and feel of the finished product. The phase in which the prototypes are created lasts an average of 1½ months and does not depend on the type of product. The prototypes are only very rarely made up in the materials that will actually be used for the products presented in the shops. This is because the timescales would be too long if the process involved introducing the entire purchasing process for the definitive materials.

In reality, the prototyping operators are often unable to make all the prototypes they are asked to prepare to a sufficiently high standard (to give the best possible representation of the finished product). Given the very specialist expertise involved in making these items, nobody within the company, without suitable training, can in fact help them in this work. In addition, given the highly seasonal nature of the work, the company does not want to employ further staff, as people would be under-employed in off-peak periods of the year. What normally happens is that part of the work is sent out and some of the prototypes for the accessible luxury line are produced by workshops in the area that have been working with Ametista for many years, although in about 25% of the cases they produce inferior prototypes that do not meet the required specifications. Sometimes, new prototypes must then be made by internal staff (for about 10% of the inferior prototypes).

Once a prototype is produced, it is tested in the fitting room (on a flexible mannequin or a model when the stylist requests one) under the supervision of the prototyping operator, the stylist and the pattern-designer, so that all the alterations in terms of fitting can be made (to adapt and adjust the prototype to the shape of the mannequin or the model, and therefore fit the real female body correctly). During this phase, the prototype is inspected by the stylists and the pattern-designers to assess the product's aesthetic look, examine the standards of production and, as a consequence, identify all possible limitations relating to production. This is carried out directly by people working in the style department, because they feel that their long experience in the sector means that they can understand the potential problems that may arise in production, even if they have no specific experience in that area.

In terms of judging aesthetics, after the initial prototype has been made, around 30 to 40% of the models are slightly altered to satisfy the stylist's aesthetic taste and another 20% are rejected. In terms of production problems, normally the prototypes are not rejected, but often the sketches and/or patterns are altered for reasons linked to production standards. This happens in around 30% of cases (and sometimes sketches can be re-worked for either aesthetic or production reasons). In total, 2.7 prototypes are made on average for each model.

At the end of the prototyping phase, the creative management team meets once again to evaluate the consistency of the collection compared to the mood, and to identify the models to be presented at the fashion show. Not all the collection is presented at the show, only a small and very carefully chosen selection. The models to be presented at the fashion show will be made at the same time as the other items in the sample, but they will be the first to be produced, to make sure that they are ready in time for the show.

7.6.4.3 Market preparation and collection engineering

The perception of a separation between the sub-processes of the collection development process described above (idea generation and product line creation) and the subsequent phases of the same process (preparation of the collection for market and collection industrialization) is emphasized in physical terms, by moving from the second to the first floor of the company. This floor also contains the sales department. In this department, they evaluate the collection on the basis of the sample, which is an entire collection made in a single size using the same production process as the finished products that will actually go on sale.

The scope of the sample is to allow the sales people to see for themselves the products that will be offered to the market, and to present the products in the showroom during the sales campaign.

Creating the sample is part of the sub-process called "preparing the collection for market". It is overseen by the pattern-designer and the prototyping operator, who provide basic instructions to the demonstrator to make this limited series. The prototype of each model is given to the demonstrator who has the task of producing the sample with the help of several of the most expert seamstresses.

Producing the sample requires several operations:

Creation of the bill of materials

Creation of the bill of materials starts with the information on the technical sheet prepared previously by the pattern-designer and sent by email to the production department assistants. Preparing the bill of materials involves analysing the finished product and breaking it down into all its components, and establishing the coefficient of use for each. These operations are carried out by the assistants working in production.

The bill of materials is inputted into the company's enterprise resource planning (ERP) software to be ready for use by production and production planning. All the purchased elements must be recorded in the system with the specific code for the supplier and indicating the supply lead-time for each purchased component. The production assistants will then retrieve the supplier's name and contact them to find out whether their official name has changed in any respect from the one registered on the system in previous years. The production lead-times are inputted after the cycle times have been defined.

Generation of the materials requirements

In this phase, the materials requirement (fabric and components) to produce the sample is generated. Production planning defines the latest date by which it must receive the individual components in order to make the sample. The lead-time of production for each model in the sample is estimated by the demonstrator on the basis of her experience and the seamstresses available.

The sample is required by the sales department, but it is also needed by production, as it allows them to understand the problems or limitations that may appear when making the product, before it is manufactured on a greater scale. In fact, many problems, such as creating unexpected seams for all types of bra, like S or Z shaped stitches (which may never be recognized or even noticed by the customer wearing the item), are not considered to be important by the style department (which should highlight them during the prototyping phase). However, they could be significant for the people in production, as they require lengthy sewing times and could actually be very difficult to do. By initially producing the models on a small scale, some of these problems can be identified. At this point, there are two possible options:

- Production contacts the style department which agrees to the proposed changes to the models. The alterations are formalized by each department and production updates the bill of materials on the system while the style department updates the technical sheets.

- The style department does not agree to the changes to the product (in 30% of the cases where there are problems) and so production is forced to find the best way to make the impossible, possible.

Generally, the sample is presented after the fashion show. This is because the sample is often not ready in time for the show and so there is usually never time to show it beforehand. It takes on average two months to complete the entire collection. Therefore, only a selection of the sample is presented at the fashion show, although it is quite a large one.

Once the sample is created, the process goes into the hands of the dreaded director of sales, Dr Zuccotta. She decides which models will actually go to the market, and only the models approved by her will be produced and sold.

Mancotti remembers having a very lively discussion with her several years previously, when he criticized her for not fully appreciating the spirit of their stylists. Dr Zuccotta, totally undaunted, replied:

The reason why you pay me my salary every month is that I have to make sure that someone somewhere is ready to buy stuff from our collection. Sales has the right (and, in my view, the duty, for the good of the company) to approve the collection or ask for changes to it. If the stylists made ghastly products that fitted horribly, forgetting that women have to wear those things, should I just shut up and agree? If I did, then our agents and our boutiques would not touch those products. Must I bring up the subject of the stylist Sir Carlos and his collection "Venus of Botticelli" with the bra shaped like a flower? He proposed it for three years in a row even when none of our retailers ever bought it. And then, to show that the company really believed in a return to Ancient Greece, he made 12 identical items, where the only difference was in the type of flower and nobody bought any of them. What amazes me is that you are getting at me because I am trying to say no to this mayhem before they complete the collection, rather than tackling them, with their ideas that what customers want is something bad to be avoided at all costs. I am well aware that, if I say no sometimes, we will have to throw out work that has reached the sample stage and maybe we will even have to rework part of the process, but it's not my fault if you tell me I can say no when it is nearly too late and the sample has already been completed. And as for the issue of prices! If you can show me women ready to spend €1,500 for bra and briefs, I'll convince the shops to stock them, but it's not that simple, and of course I have to reject them. Is there nobody who can try and work out what the cost of a bra and brief set is coming out as before it's finished?

Mancotti realizes that, from her point of view, Dr Zuccotta is right, but it is really not possible to reject one item in three (at best) when the sample is finished.

After the sample has been produced and when Dr Zuccotta has sieved through the collection, the development process is finalized by industrializing the collection, which takes about a month.

In this phase, every model is analysed by production to define the production cycle and then by the time and motion office to establish the time cycle of every manufacturing process for every SKU. The results of these operations depend very strongly on how the previous operations were carried out, in particular during the creation of the sample and prototyping (especially the alterations to the models due to production requirements). At the industrialization phase, there is no looping back to previous phases and, as the key critical decisions have already been taken, there are no particularly critical issues.

7.7 Inter-departmental meeting

Once the collection development process had been analysed, Mancotti decided to organise an inter-departmental meeting where everybody working in the main areas could express their views. As he saw it, it was impossible to emerge from the crisis unless everyone worked together with the same objective.

Attending the meeting were the manager and an operator from each of the following departments: marketing, purchasing, production planning, production and sales.

Having decided to chair the meeting, Mancotti set out the three main critical factors identified by the consultancy firm.

First, he presented the serious issue of internal lead-times, which result in persistent late arrival on the market. At this statement, the production manager, Dr Festoni, immediately flared up. Festoni knew that production was often late, so he understood that the process he managed was partially responsible for this critical aspect, but he wanted the rest of the company to understand that he was greatly affected by delays generated by other people:

> I would start production sooner, but until I have the components to make the finished products, obviously I cannot begin. We cannot launch production of the products that will go to market, or even assign what workload to which piece of equipment until the sales campaign is over, as we have always made to order. The same can be said about formalizing our orders to the suppliers: we cannot issue orders for materials and fabric to our suppliers with the precise quantities until the sales campaign is over. Also, due to internal policies, we do not launch production of a product until we have all the countless components that make it up and we must take this into account. This means that there is an average delay of about 30 days to the agreed times for a collection to reach the shops, and once we were actually 50 days late with the "Elegant for night" models, but it's not my fault, it's the fault of the company policy.

Festoni was particularly cross with the suppliers, who regularly deliver late:

> ...although I would be surprised if it were not so, as we ask them to deliver in 70 days when their processing cycle is 50 days and, above all, as the people making the decisions don't look at any such silly things like punctuality, level of service or cost.

The purchasing manager immediately answered in kind, stating that he and his team every year, after the collection is closed, carry out an assessment of the suppliers' performance, to see how well they had worked. This information is also sent to the people responsible for choosing the suppliers (the style department) but, more often than not, they do not even get an answer to their emails, which makes it extremely unlikely that the information will be used the following year when selecting the suppliers.

> I have also pointed out to a pattern-designer on more than one occasion that, year in year out, 30% of the models in any one season, for either brand (Ametista Luxury or Young Diamond) are made in the same fabric (say satin) and in the same colour (mainly black or white). I asked her why we don't try and send our requirements to the suppliers early, since we know what they are. I also asked why we don't keep the same supplier from one year to the next, but she answered that it depends on the "feelings" of the stylist in that period. Stylists need new things or they lose their creative vein. Tell me whether this makes any sense.

The second point covered at the meeting was the exceedingly high internal costs. Even this second aspect aroused the indignation of the production planning manager, who immediately uttered the following:

> I for one noticed our high costs and tried to find out why. The first interesting thing is that I tried to discover who in the company has the responsibility of monitoring the costs of a product, and I discovered that it is "nobody". The question of costs is not an isolated one: nobody can give me any information about other aspects, such as the time to develop a product, the costs to produce a prototype, the number of loops in a process, etc. At this point, I wanted to find out where the problem is, so I did some investigations on my own and even had a talk with a friend who works at Micol, and guess what? Ametista takes 60 minutes to make a bra, with a cost per minute (personnel and machine time) of €0.45. Taking the average cost of a metre of lace (a major component for the company) of €7 to 8 and the cost of the other materials, generally a bra has a full costing of €50, and this does not depend on the brand (Ametista Luxury or Young Diamond) and, therefore, neither on the price that it will be sold at on the market. We must clearly add to these costs the costs of development, other variable costs, and so on. If our direct competitor can make a bra in 12 minutes and achieve an average price for lace at €4 to 5/metre, by standardizing processes more and exploiting its contractual power with suppliers better, then maybe we have a problem.

At that point in the conversation, the manager of marketing, Dr Giuseppe Abbondanza, stepped in. He had been quiet up until then, but looked visibly annoyed. Abbondanza stated that

> Festoni is right but he sometimes talks like a classical supply chain man, forgetting where he is. Ametista is Ametista because it is unique, otherwise it wouldn't be luxury, it wouldn't be exclusive and it wouldn't be a product we can sell at our prices. It's all very well to highlight the problems but please remember that Ametista cannot be for everyone, and anyway there are other brands in that category.

This comment set Festoni off again, who reminded people that currently the company takes 10 minutes to sew in a wire because the stylists want very complex seams, just because they look good. This goes for both the top line selling at up to €600 and the less expensive line, with some items at €50. "I would like to interview our customers and see how many of them noticed that this year the seam fixing the hook to the bra is shaped like a Z in the 'Don Diego de la Vega' mood."

Finally, the third point to be analysed was about changes to requirements in Ametista's market of reference. This statement ignites the manager of the domestic multibrand shops:

> I have been saying this for years, thank goodness that we paid some outside consultants to come and agree with me. Talking to some of our most loyal customers, they told me that women often won't buy our products because it takes too long to choose what to buy. As we change the

collection entirely each year, customers are puzzled and every time they want to buy one of our items they have to spend ages in the shop trying on the different models. This means that now our products are seen as something for "special occasions", for when they are prepared to spend time in deciding. You will realise for yourselves that the special occasions in a year are much less than the "normal every day occasions". And the problem of changes to the market is tightly linked to the length of our internal times. Looking at the data we got from the multibrand shops, it seems that we have often lost sales because when a customer arrived and wanted to buy something, we weren't there but our competitor was, so she decided to buy their product instead of ours.

The marketing manager, Dr Abbondanza, who up until the previous year had been working at a prestigious fashion company, made a very interesting comment at this point. He stated that, in the company where he worked before, not only was the pre-collection[4] a must, rather than an opportunity to gain more sales where possible, but in order to accelerate things somewhat and try to understand what shopkeepers thought of their collection, the sample was presented to a small group of selected customers before the fashion show. Old cases were then raked up about very negative opinions on the part of sales that led the company to review entire parts of the collection days or even hours before the fashion show.

At the end of the meeting, Mancotti was dismayed. He had expected a lively discussion and guessed that there might be some tension between the departments, but had not realized just how bad these were. By this point, it had become increasingly clear that something must be done, by overhauling the company entirely and radically reviewing how the company processes work.

Mancotti however gave further thought to the words of the style department manager, reminding him of the importance of creativity in the sector where Ametista operates. Certainly, a greater standardization of processes and products was necessary; however, limiting the creativity of stylists and pattern-designers, with the resulting excessive uniformity, could mean that the brand was no longer recognized by customers. Only the day before, Mancotti had read in the newspaper about a shoe company operating in the *absolute luxury* market that was on the edge of bankruptcy after carrying out a rationalization policy that greatly curtailed the creativity of the stylists and brought about a significant standardization of their products: the new collections made by this company no longer excited their customers.

---

4 Pre-collection is the presentation in preview of some models of a future collection before the entire collection reaches the shops. This is done by using presentation corners in the shop to display the products.

7.8 The assignment

In order to understand whether the consultants were right or not, Giacomo Mancotti needed to investigate the real problems of Ametista more effectively; the following points should be investigated.

- Illustrate the main processes performed within the company using Porter's Value Chain model (Porter, 1985).

- Identify the phases of the collection development process and map the flow of the phases.

- What are the main critical issues of the process? And which of the identified critical issues have an impact on process lead-time?

- How would you redesign the collection development process to reduce lead-time?

Reference

Porter, M.E. (1985). *Competitive Advantage: Creating and Sustaining Superior Performance.* New York: Free Press.

8

Implementing a co-branding decision

The Magneti Marelli and Mopar case

Maria Carmela Ostillio and Chiara Solerio

SDA Bocconi School of Management, Italy

Through the results of market research and long field experience, the Mopar CEO identified a significant market opportunity: 2.6 million non-Chrysler cars visited Chrysler dealerships and more than 80% of the Chrysler dealers have an "all-makes" programme that allows them to offer services to all vehicles (not only Chrysler cars). Mopar aimed to develop a new business, accessing the independent after-market (IAM) through the Magneti Marelli product range. In order to construct a successful co-branding strategy, the two companies had to take several factors into consideration, sometimes not directly connected just to the brands themselves. By carrying out some research focused on dealers, the marketing departments aimed to understand the factors involved in developing customer satisfaction and customer loyalty. The companies had to adopt the appropriate legal form and carefully design the entire process.

From: "Pietro Gorlier"

Sent: Tuesday, March 16, 2010 12:43 pm

To: "Dino Maggioni"

Subject: Business Opportunity in North America

Dino

Let's talk on Saturday March 20th to discuss some ideas that popped up in my mind.

PG

This message was sent by Pietro Gorlier, President and CEO of Mopar Service, Parts & Customer Care at Chrysler Group LLC to Dino Maggioni, CEO of Magneti Marelli After Market Parts and Service. After earning a degree in business from the University of Turin, Pietro Gorlier worked for Fiat and Iveco for several years and for the last six years he worked directly for Sergio Marchionne, CEO of Fiat S.p.A. and Chrysler Group LLC, in different roles for the Fiat-Chrysler Group. Dino Maggioni, after getting a degree in engineering from the Polytechnic of Milan, joined Magneti Marelli in 2001, becoming CEO of the After Market division in 2007.

Saturday, 20 March 2010 – 7:00 am EST
It is a fine spring morning in Detroit. The motor city – the city that put an entire nation on wheels – is slowly waking to its daily rhythm. On the tenth floor of the world headquarters of the Detroit giant, Chrysler, located in Auburn Hills, Pietro Gorlier is sitting in his office while he calls Dino Maggioni in Italy.

Pietro Gorlier starts the conversation:
"Dino, as you know the number of vehicles sold in the US has been decreasing at a gradual yet continuous rate since 1999; most of the cars sold in the US come from the big three: General Motors, Ford, and Chrysler. But, during the last few years, lots of imported cars and other competitive brands, such as Toyota and Honda, have gained an increasing market share. Overall, in 2008, there were more than 255 million registered passenger vehicles. Many Americans own three or more vehicles, because of the low marginal cost of registering and insuring additional older vehicles. In March 2009, R.L. Polk & Co. released a study which showed that, in the US, the average age of cars increased, from 2007 to 2008, to 9.4 years, and that the one for light trucks increased from 7.1 to 7.5 years."

Then, he added:
"I am calling you because of your knowledge and experience in the aftermarket. As you already know, the United States is home to the largest passenger vehicles market all over the world. And I'd like to share some insights from your preferred market: the automotive aftermarket."

8.1 The automotive aftermarket industry

The aftermarket industry consists of the purchase of products and services for vehicles after the original sale: it includes replacement parts, accessories, appearance products, lubricants and service repairs.

Aftermarket parts are usually divided into two categories: replacement parts and accessories.

- **Replacement parts** are automotive parts built or remanufactured to replace OE (original equipment) parts, as they become worn or damaged.

- **Accessories** are parts made for comfort, convenience, performance, safety or customization.

The US automotive aftermarket industry is highly competitive and generally fragmented. Companies compete on a mix of elements: customer service, product selection, price and location. The size and growth rate of the automotive aftermarket depends on a number of different factors (Annex 1).

The automotive aftermarket includes different segments: most significant is the aftermarket parts segment with 54% of the revenue, followed by purchased labour (25%), tyres (15%) and speciality equipment (9%).[1]

For a certain range of automotive products, the aftermarket outweighs the new vehicle market. For example, a new car gets only one battery installed by the vehicle assembler, but during its life it may be necessary to replace the battery five or six times. For some other products, such as oil filters, the ratio can rise up to 35 to 1. These aftermarket products are sold through dealers or auto parts stores and are used by service technicians in garages and speciality service providers.

According to the Automotive Aftermarket Industry Association[2] (AAIA), the US market size is estimated as follows:

- In 2008 the market was valued at $281 billion and employed approximately 4.2 million people.

- In 2009 the market was valued at $274 billion (-2.4% Y/Y) and employed approximately 3.8 million people.

- In 2010 the forecast estimated the market to be worth $284 billion (+3.8% Y/Y).

The aftermarket industry makes use of three main channels: dealers, IAM (independent aftermarket) and retail.

8.1.1 Dealers channel

The OEMs (original equipment manufacturers) – through the so-called OES (original equipment supplier) – strategically try to bind final customers with dealers, by offering them a car warranty valid for two years and by extending the validity for an incremental payment. OEMs prefer the customer to stay loyal to the dealer for services and parts.

---

1 AASA Automotive Aftermarket Status Report. AASA (Automotive Aftermarket Suppliers Association) is a North American association for suppliers of automotive aftermarket, providing data on the US market (http://www.aftermarketsuppliers.org/).

2 AAIA (Automotive Aftermarket Industry Association) is a US association representing members who distribute and sell motor vehicle parts, accessories, service, tool, equipment, materials and supplies. It provides data on the US aftermarket (http://www.aftermarket.org/)

OES sales, for 2009, were $76.21 billion versus the total market of $274 billion with a total gross profit as a percentage of service and part sales of 46.24% and a net profit of 8.38%.

The OES business has been focused on make- and model-specific products; that is, the OEM products. Each manufacturer has to manage, on average, 200,000 parts, essential in order to guarantee the repair and substitution service for all vehicles (those still in production and those out of production). There exists a strong link between OEM and OES for the parent brand that appears in the OES brand: Ford, Toyota, Honda and Nissan are some examples of this kind of branding strategy (Table 8.1). They primarily target new car customers, but also service old cars.

The OES channel is characterized by weak competition. However the market weight of each actor is quite different in terms of characteristics and dimensions: some dealers are large and publicly quoted; others are smaller, structured as family businesses. Some drivers choose exclusively to get their vehicles serviced by a dealer. They represent a consistent, relatively less price sensitive source of demand for dealer networks.

In order to take up the aftermarket opportunity, growing in size and value, some OEMs have recently decided to introduce the so-called "All Makes" concept or "Value Line". This means selling parts and accessories, inside the OES points of sale for competing makes of vehicles, under a new brand (Table 8.1). This explains the launch of ACDelco (General Motors) and Motorcraft (Ford). The Japanese carmakers do not have a value line range of products. Mopar (Chrysler), which fulfilled the all-makes strategy by using its brand, had limited success: probably because Chrysler decided to distribute Ford/Toyota/etc. parts for non-Chrysler vehicles, using the Mopar branding.

Table 8.1 **OES and all makes/value line**

Source: Internal data

OE	OES	All makes/value line
Chrysler	Mopar	Mopar
General Motors	Goodwrench	ACDelco
Ford	Ford Genuine Parts	Motorcraft
Toyota	Toyota Genuine Parts	
Honda	Honda Genuine Parts & Service	
Nissan	Nissan Genuine Parts	

8.1.2 IAM channel

The IAM (independent aftermarket) is the second most important channel and it relates to independent actors purchasing make- or model-specific products. Consequent to the closure of various dealerships in 2009, the aftermarket sales for parts and services have been consistently redirected to independent service outlets, auto parts stores and non-OE auto parts distributors. Together, they form the Independent aftermarket (IAM). Nowadays, the market is structured in a ratio of 37 IAM to 1

OES. In 2009, the IAM estimated that it employed 332,262 individuals; 70% of out-of-warranty vehicles were repaired at independent shops, while 30% went through the OES channel.[3]

The IAM channel targets the owners of older cars that are no longer warranty-protected. Most independent dealerships have a relationship with large independent parts wholesalers, through whom they order most of their stock. The IAM channel is extremely competitive. Consumers who decide to get their vehicle repaired at an independent garage are provided with a wider variety from which to choose. The customers are much more price-sensitive than in the dealer/OES channel.

8.1.3 Retail channel

This channel primarily sells products that are not make- or model-specific, such as cleaning products, motor oil and anti-freeze. People also purchase first-aid kits, emergency flares and warning triangles at retail outlets, as well as less expensive comfort items such as car mats and other items for interior protection and decoration. While independent garages and dealers compete at the same level, the retailers seem to represent almost a separate market.

Pietro shares some additional data with Dino:

"the estimated parts and service penetration (Table 8.2) lets us better work out the low customer loyalty shown to US car-makers, then to understand the huge opportunity to gain additional customers and to obtain additional sales in the aftermarket industry; 2.6 million non-Chrysler cars visited Chrysler dealerships in 2009 and the development of our Express Lane service (Mopar Express Lane is a Check 'n go service: lube, oil, filter change and 26 more point inspections) is going to increasingly attract non-Chrysler vehicles (because of the characteristics of cheapness and quickness in service). Besides, around 80% of our dealers would be happy to also provide a service to the drivers of non-Chrysler cars!"

Table 8.2 **Parts brands, parts penetration and % of US vehicles (2009)**

Source: Internal data

OE	OES	All makes/ Value line	Est. 2009 parts penetration	% of US vehicles*
Chrysler	Mopar	Mopar	TBD	
General Motors	Goodwrench	ACDelco	TBD	
Ford	Ford Genuine Parts	Motorcraft	TBD	
Toyota	Toyota Genuine Parts		TBD	11.2%
Honda	Honda Genuine Parts & Service		TBD	7.9%
Nissan	Nissan Genuine Parts		37%	5.1%

* Includes med/heavy trucks; data as of 10/1/09 (RL Polk)

3 http://www.aftermarketsuppliers.org

Despite the lack of quantitative data, it is possible to state the following: GM has the highest proportion of vehicles in the US vehicle fleet, but a low penetration of parts, compared with the other competitors; Ford is second in the US car ranking, but it shows a better penetration of parts than GM.

"Dino, as an example, I'd like to show some of the key players in the US automotive aftermarket."

Pietro started a meticulous description, shown in Box 8.1.

Box 8.1 **Key players in the US automotive aftermarket**

Advance Auto Parts/AAP. The second largest US retailer of automotive parts and accessories; in 2009, it earned $5.41 billion in total revenues, compared with its 2008 total revenues of $5.14 billion. Founded in 1929, the company operates through 3,420 stores in the United States. The stores have commercial delivery programmes catering for the independent garages and other commercial customers whose end-user "do it for me" (DIFM) customers seek maintenance from them. AAP targets regions in which they estimate there are a large number of old vehicles, given these cars' requirements for repairs and maintenance.

Autozone. A leading chain of automotive replacement parts and accessories. The company has around 3,000 stores in the United States, which use its brand on box-parts and have commercial delivery programmes catering for the independent garages and other commercial customers whose end-user "do it for me" (DIFM) customers seek maintenance from them.

National Automotive Parts Association/NAPA. Founded in 1925, the company has a total of 13,000 service centres in the programme group, 6,000 of them are denominated as "jobbers" and the remainder, warehouses.

"But, we have also to pay attention to the fact that each OEM has more than one brand in their car brand portfolio. Ford has four brands: Ford, Lincoln, Mercury and Mazda; General Motors has eight car brands: GM, Pontiac, GMC, Chevrolet, Buick, Cadillac, Saturn and Oldsmobile. That means that we have to consider a wide range of different parts for each brand and each model".

Pietro Gorlier adds:

"Some customers own Chrysler, others GM or Ford, others imported cars. The car's average age is growing. These data are picking out that US car drivers need care, services, and parts. It could be a big opportunity for us!"

Interested by the business opportunity, Dino Maggioni observed:

"The American car market is huge, especially in comparison with Europe. However there are lots of significant differences in terms of service networks, customer car culture and usage, market competition and, of course, we have long-term experience in the aftermarket sector all over the world. But in the US market we have limited awareness, all linked to the motorsport tradition".

Pietro Gorlier agreed with Dino: "It is true, the European market is really different from the American one" and stressed the fact that: "we have already had lots of strategic changes in our dealership network. The pressure coming from the market is getting higher and higher!" Then, after a pause, he added: "Mopar is Mopar! The company has a long history, always closely linked to the Chrysler brands. I think that we cannot risk blemishing our image. Besides, vehicles different from Chrysler brands need different parts to be replaced. I'm not sure of facing the challenge!"

Pietro and Dino concluded their fruitful conversation and scheduled a follow-up for the next week, with the following order of business:

1. Can we take this business opportunity in the aftermarket?

2. Which are the most important factors to compete in this market?

3. Which asset do the two firms need to join?

4. Which kind of brand strategy do we need to perform?

5. What is the suggested brand marketing programme required in order to fulfil the strategy?

Saturday, 27 March 2010 – 7:00 am EST
At Chrysler Headquarters, both Dino and Pietro were on the Mopar floor of the Chrysler Tower. They were analysing a lot of data and working through different dimensions of the analysis. . .

8.2 The customer: the American "auto culture"

The United States has the largest passenger vehicle market in the world. Overall, in 2008, there were 255,917,664 registered passenger vehicles; this number, along with the average age of vehicles, has increased steadily since 1960, showing a growing number of vehicles per capita.

William Faulkner lamented in 1948, "the American really loves nothing but his automobile" (Shi, 2001). His sardonic observation retains its force over time. The intense love affair with cars began as soon as cars were invented. Since its first appearance in the 1890s, the automobile has embodied deep-seated cultural and emotional values that really became a consistent part of the American Dream.

Americans have always cherished personal freedom and mobility, rugged individualism and masculine force. The automobile was able to materialize those aspirations. It was the symbol of personal democracy, acting as a social levelling force, granting more and more people a wide range of personal choices: where to travel, where to work and live, where to seek personal pleasure and social recreation. As a journalist explains, the automobile is the "handiest tool ever devised for the pursuit of that unholy, unwholesome, all-American trinity of sex, speed and status" (McCall, 1999).

The automobile continues to be a metaphor for what Americans have always prized: the seductive ideal of private freedom, personal mobility and empowered spontaneity.

American drivers are stuck in traffic for 8 billion hours a year. Therefore they are able to transform the automobile into a temporary office, a bank, a restaurant, a bathroom, and stereo system. While people drive, they also talk on the telephone, eat meals, do makeup, cash cheques and listen to music or to audio books (for these reasons, drive-distraction is a topic increasingly debated in the US).

Besides, living without a car can be very difficult, especially in the US, where public transport is frequently missing and where questionable urban planning has caused the average person to live far away from workplaces, schools and supermarkets. A car is, thus, a basic necessity.

In 2001, 70% of Americans drove to work by car. Despite congested traffic, road rage, polluted air and rising fuel prices, Americans have not changed their driving or car ownership patterns over recent years.

People are always happy to talk about their car, essentially because of a widespread car culture. During a focus group, the consultant Bob Schnorbus, chief economist at JD Power & Associates, says: "We've moved further and further away from where we work. You have to have a car to have any chance of generating income." Schnorbus adds: ". . .the cars for the American driver are, also, an indispensable part of their self-image."

This kind of car use and attachment implies that car drivers, over time, have become more and more demanding in terms of high service levels and product availability; the inability to meet customer requirements could undoubtedly result in a vehicle standing still with no work taking place.

Recently, campaigns to prevent "driving distraction" have become more popular and an important discussion topic for the automotive industry.

Evidence, from newspapers, TV and websites illustrates that consumers are keeping their cars longer. The last few years have seen the automotive repair market grow by leaps and bounds. Why? A shift in economic conditions is forcing the average American to limit discretionary funds, therefore minimizing large capital expenditures such as new cars. According to experts from the automotive repair industry:

> Where drivers in the past would scrimp on maintenance and repairs. . .
> they are now looking at the cost of trying to purchase a new vehicle. . .so
> in relative terms that $1,000 repair to keep a $2,500 car running may be an
> attractive alternative (Streitfeld, 2009).

8.3 The industry

Manufacturing represents the backbone of the American economy and the automotive industry can be imagined as its heart. No other industry links as closely to the US manufacturing sector or directly generates as much business and employs as many people.

The auto industry has, historically, contributed around 3–3.5% to the overall gross domestic product (GDP). The industry directly employs over 1.7 million people, engaged in designing, engineering, manufacturing and supplying parts and components to assemble, sell and service new vehicles. Besides, this industry acts as an important customer of goods and services coming from many other sectors, including raw materials, construction, machinery, legal, computers and semi-conductors, financial, advertising and healthcare services.

The auto industry spends $16 to $18 billion, every year, on research and product development; 99% of this amount is funded by the industry itself.

The industry contributes to a net employment impact of nearly 8 million jobs. Approximately 4.5% of all US jobs are supported by the presence of the auto industry. People involved in the automotive sector collectively earn over $500 billion annually in compensation and generate more than $70 billion in tax revenues.

Recently, the auto industry has faced some tough times. The three US-based companies started a shakeout period in order to optimize their operations and to respond to strong competition, mainly from imports.

In the latest restructuring period, the burst of the housing bubble and the collapse of the financial sector led to a tightening of credit, making it nearly impossible for companies and consumers to make investments.

The industry structure has been transformed over the past two decades: domestic automotive assembly firms (Chrysler, Ford and General Motors) have slowly lost market share in favour of international firms ("imports" e.g. Toyota, Honda and Hyundai). For the first time in US history, market share parity occurred; by the end of 2009, the Detroit 3s' market share dropped to 40% (Table 8.3).

For 2010 and 2011, a levelling-off effect is expected. The stark erosion of domestic OEM market share, during recent years, reveals how competitive the US automotive landscape has become from the manufacturer's perspective.

Table 8.3 New-vehicle sales and market share, by manufacturer (1999–2009)

Source: NADA DATA, Industry Analysis Division, 2009

Year	Chrysler	Ford	GM	Toyota	Honda	Nissan	VW	Other import	Total
1999	2,638,600 15.62%	4,115,600 24.36%	4,974,600 29.44%	1,475,000 8.73%	1,076,900 6.37%	677,900 4.01%	381,500 2.26%	1,555,300 9.21%	16,895,800
2000	2,522,700 14.54%	4,147,700 28.31%	4,911,700 28.31%	1,619,200 9.33%	1,158,900 6.68%	752,800 4.34%	435,900 2.51%	1,800,800 10.38%	17,349,700
…	…	…	…	…	…	…	…	…	…
2008	1,444,750 10.97%	1,942,050 14.72%	2,955,900 22.4%	2,217,700 16.81%	1,428,800 10.83%	951,450 7.21%	310,900 2.36%	1,940,050 14.7%	13,194,600
2009	927,200 8.91%	1,656,100 15.92%	2,072,200 19.92%	1,770,200 17.02%	1,150,800 11.06%	770,100 7.4%	296,200 2.85%	1,758,900 16.91%	10,401,700
Avg. 99/09	2,079,259 13.08%	318,091 19.75%	4,209,495 26.49%	1,993,627 12.54%	1,321,686 8.32%	855,500 5.38%	360,636 2.27%	1,934,386 12.17%	15,892,673

8.4 The dealers

Starting from the advent of the mass-market automobile, early in the 20th century, car-makers had employed dealerships to sell their vehicles. Manufacturers require an extensive distribution network with outlets throughout the entire country, not only in order to sell cars but also to service them. Rather than tie up their own capital and administrative resources in those retail and service operations, car-makers left dealership to independent businessmen. This kind of arrangement benefited manufacturers because they could both leverage the capital of private investors and capitalize on the dealers' knowledge of the specific markets they served and in accurately forecasting the demand. Manufacturers distributed their products through a network of franchised dealers. The franchise is a formal legal agreement entitling the dealer to operate a factory-authorized sales and service outlet, for a specific brand of automobile, in a defined geographic area. The contract includes numerous requirements, such as minimum sales levels and service capabilities. Only franchised dealers are entitled to purchase inventory direct from the manufacturer. Car-makers support their dealers through extensive marketing, advertising and promotional campaigns.

Industry observers generally agreed that the auto industry is a push-oriented system of production and distribution (by which manufacturers pumped products into distribution channels based on imperfect measures of demand).

While high-demand vehicles are sold quickly, less popular models require greater sales and promotional effort. Because dealers have to pay interest and insurance on vehicles, they have pressing reasons for moving their inventory as quickly as possible. Dealers often motivate their salespeople to sell lower-demand vehicles by offering higher commissions. Wishing to maximize their profit per vehicle, dealers try to stress as much as possible the potential customer's willingness to pay. These characteristics tend to create an uncomfortable sales environment that typified most US dealerships.

Results from a recent survey corroborate this scenario of the car-buying experience. A 2008 Gallup poll asked people to rank the honesty of various professionals: car dealers scored lowest. Consumers' poor view of the car-buying experience is reflected in dealers' poor customer loyalty performance. While manufacturers enjoy moderate rates of customer loyalty – averaging 56.9% – dealers achieve only 20%. A 2007 study conducted by R.L. Polk & Co. found that the single-most important variable determining customer loyalty is the "attitude of sales staff". Manufacturers have long recognized that dealer sales tactics represent the primary element in turning consumers sour in the car-buying process.

The dealership market is very broad. The abundant supply of dealerships, within very close proximity to one another, provide both choice and variety and permit highly competitive pricing. Over time, this model has become more and more unsustainable, primarily due to the downturn of the industry and to a new topography of dealership locations.

The number of new car dealerships decreased from more than 25,000 units in 1988 to less than 20,000 units on 1 January 2009 (NADA DATA, 2009), before the GM and Chrysler restructuring plan. A NADA review of dealership data (NADA DATA, 2009) suggests that the industry is moving from smaller-volume dealerships (150 new vehicle sales per year) to larger-volume establishments (400-plus new vehicle sales per year).[4] And, based on GM and Chrysler company announcements, researchers estimate that the recent wave of closures (2009–2010) associated with the auto-makers' restructuring plans now fix the number of dealerships in the range of 17,500 to 18,500 (NADA DATA, 2009). For example, Chrysler can count 2,600 dealers of which 500 are also parts wholesalers. In addition to those franchised dealers, more than 36,000 independent actors serve the used-vehicle market (Nada, 2009).

Franchised car dealers earn money from several sources: sales of new and used cars (including revenues from financing, insurance and service contracts), and parts and service. Table 8.4 shows a breakdown of sales, profits and expenses.

Net profit increased by 43.7% from 2008, yielding 1.5% net profit before taxes on total sales or $398,067 in net pre-tax profit for 2009, up from $277,045 in 2008.

Since 2004, the new car department has remained the most significant in terms of revenue generation although it had to face a tough recession period: from 61% of total sales in 2004, to 52.3% in 2009. New-vehicle sales fell to 10.4 million units in 2009 and new-vehicle sales revenues lost 15.4% from 2008.

On the used-vehicles side, dealers' profitability has been significantly better. There has been an increase in yearly sales at around 3.5% with a contribution to the average dealership's sales of 32%. The dealers sold nearly 15 million used vehicles during 2009: 9.1 million vehicles were retailed and 5.8 million were wholesaled. The average selling price of a used unit, retailed in 2009, was $14,976, down slightly from $15,201 in 2008.

Service and parts sales – sold by OES – have increased their weight in total sales from 2004 (11.5%) to 2009 (15.7%).

Aftermarket income (combined gross from finance and insurance and service contracts) reached 25.7% of new- and used-vehicle department gross profit in 2009 from nearly 30% in 2008. In ten years, service contracts income has increased its percentage by almost 12.5% (Fig. 8.1).

Table 8.5 shows the total OES sales of service and parts ($76.21 billion) with an average of $4,128,580 per dealership (15.7% of sales in 2009, up 1.9% from 2008) with a gross profit of 46.24% and net profit of 8.38%. Parts and service (P&S) businesses thus have to face huge pressures.

A car manufacturer has to manage service for vehicles in production and out-of-production, generating the complexity of more than 200,000 part numbers to manage in its portfolio.

The increase in dealer closures created a gap in the market, filled by independent repair shops. In addition to the large number of independent service stations and quick-lube centres, dealers faced increasing competition from regional and national service franchises, focused on a specific service (e.g. oil change, muffler installation, tyres, body repair, tune-ups, transmission repair) and coming from chains of auto-parts speciality stores. Car dealers also had to face competition from the internet, where private market sellers can bypass bricks-and-mortar retail channels. As a result, dealers' share of the P&S market decreased, even if dealers were continuing to attract customers with competitive pricing and upgraded facilities.

---

4 NADA (National Automobile Dealers Association) today represents all dealers – domestic and import franchises. It develops research data on the US retail automobile industry (http://www.nada.org/).

Table 8.4 **Dealership profits (2006–2009)**

	2006 [US$]	2007 [US$]	% change 2006/2007	2008 [US$]	2009 [US$]	% change 2008/2009	% change 2006/2009
Total dealership sales	31,855,768	33,379,501	+4%	28,517,867	26,378,752	- 7.5%	-17%
Total dealership gross	4,338,448	4,546,212	+4%	4,077,497	4,020,028	- 1.4%	-7%
As % of total sales	13.6%	13.6%		14.30%	15.2%		
Total dealership expense	3,848,964	4,038,084	+4%	3,800,451	3,621,961	- 4.7%	-6%
As % of total sales	12.1%	12.1%		13.3%	13.7%		
Net profit before taxes	489,484	508,127	3%	277,045	398,067	43.7%	-19%
As % of total sales	1.5%	1.5%		1.%	1.5%		
(Net pre-tax profit in constant 1982 dollars)	242,799	245,117	1%	128,679	185,579	44.2%	-24%
New-vehicle dep. sales	18,795,482	19,545,287	+4%	16,302,280	13,798,152	- 15.4%	-27%
As % of total sales	59.0%	58.6%		57.20%	52.30%		
Used-vehicle dep. sales	9,265,366	9,821,093	+6%	8,164,415	8,454,020	3.5%	-9%
As % of total sales	29.1%	29.4%		28.6%	32.%		
Service & Parts dep. sales	3,794,920	4,013,121	+6%	4,051,172	4,128,580	1.9%	9%
As % of total sales	11.9%	12%		14.2%	15.7%		

Figure 8.1 **Aftermarket income, 2009**

Source: NADA DATA (2009)

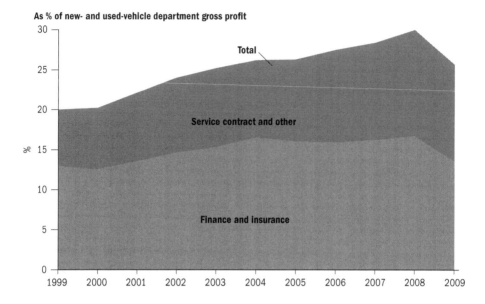

Table 8.5 **Profile of dealerships' service and parts operations, 2009**

	Average dealership	All dealers
Total service and parts sales	$4,128,580	$76.21 billion
Total revenues gross margin as percentage of P&S sales	25%	
Total net profit as percentage of P&S sales	4%	
Total P&S sales per customer repair order	$217	
Number of technicians (including body)	14	249,926
Number of service bays (excluding body)	17	

Paul Taylor, chief economist for NADA's Industry Analysis Division, identifies some interesting trends regarding the aftermarket business. Supply-chain management, logistics, service and customer satisfaction seem to be the main value drivers for this industry.

- Nowadays, the idea is to "put consumers in the driving seat" – by giving dealers *greater independence from car-makers*, promoting *inter-brand competition*, and *introducing competition into the aftermarket*. The customer usually has time constraints and asks for the car to be serviced by the next day: if the dealer cannot meet the deadline, for example, due to a delay in obtaining a certain part, the customer simply decides to go elsewhere. In order to better manage the time dimension, similarly, dealers apply pressure on the manufacturer in order to have the correct parts at the correct place within the correct timeframe.

- There is a broad range of parts that must be stocked in order to service cars within the required timeframes. PDCs (parts distribution centres) and their dealer networks have to stock hundreds of thousands of parts in multiple locations in order to achieve the required service levels.

- Parts managers at the PDCs have to deal with long lead times from manufacturers, large minimum order quantities and frequently "last time buy" decisions. Some information on timescales: order lead times normally range from 1 to 3 days and because of storage capacity constraints, parts need to be replenished frequently, sometimes up to twice a day. Those kinds of supply conditions can easily explain the creation of geographically positioned super dealers acting as stocking hubs.

- To manage such a complex and multilevel supply chain, the construction of a central control system is imperative.

8.5 Magneti Marelli: history, business and market

Magneti Marelli, founded in 1919, is an international group leader in developing and manufacturing high-tech automotive systems and components. The company is based in Italy (Corbetta, Milan) with 77 production units, 11 R&D centres and 26 application centres in 18 countries and a workforce of around 32,000 people.

Magneti Marelli is renowned as a world class global automotive supplier The group supplies all the leading car-makers in Europe, North and South America and Asia, generating a turnover of around €5 billion in 2009 (at around 5.4% for Research & Development and 5% for general investments).

Magneti Marelli is part of the Fiat Group. The company showed an interesting sales breakdown for 2009:

- **Channel.** 89% of sales come from OE, 6% from IAM and 5% from OES

- **Region/Country.** Italy is the main market with 27% of sales, followed by other Europe (23%), South America (17%), Germany (13%), France (6%), North America (4%), China (3%), Spain (3%), UK (1%) and others (3%).

- **Customer.** Fiat Group is the main client (49% of the total sales), followed by other OEM such as VW (12%), GM (4%), Daimler (4%), PSA (4%), Sevel (4%), BMW (3%), RSA Nissan (2%), Ford (2%) and also some Chinese customers (1%), Japanese customers (2%), motorcycles (1%) and others (12%).

Within the scope of its mission as a worldwide automotive systems and components supplier, Magneti Marelli aims at combining quality and competitive offering, technology and versatility, with the goal of making key technologies available to the final user at a very competitive price. Through constant innovation, Magneti Marelli provides its know-how and significant expertise in electronics, through a process of ongoing innovation, in order to develop intelligent systems for active and passive vehicle safety, on board comfort and powertrain technologies. Annex 2 shows the company's organization chart.

The main Magneti Marelli business areas (Annex 3) are automotive lighting, electronic systems, powertrain, suspension systems, exhaust systems, motorsport, plastic components and modules and Magneti Marelli aftermarket parts and services; each of those business lines has a different turnover and contribution to the total revenue.

8.5.1 Magneti Marelli aftermarket parts and services

Magneti Marelli competes in the global aftermarket as a provider of parts and services for the OES and IAM segments of the automotive market (automobiles and commercial vehicles). In 2009, the business unit turned over €237 million, accounting for 11% of the Magneti Marelli total revenues.

The OES segment guarantees 42% of sales, while IAM generates around 58% of sales. A breakdown of the IAM segment shows the weighting of each customer: spare parts dealers with 68% of sales in the segment, spare parts wholesalers (22%), manufacturers (6%) and end users (4%).

The story of Magneti Marelli Aftermarket started in 1929 (see Table 8.6 for the key steps of Magneti Marelli aftermarket's history) – even though the "Aftermarket division" was established in 1985. In the 1960s Magneti Marelli was acquired by Fiat Group and it started growing in the OE and aftermarket for all brands and OEM in Europe, Asia and America.

In recent years, the aftermarket business of Magneti Marelli has passed through the different stages of Fiat Group. In early 2000, the company was sold to an external Italian group of entrepreneurs (RGZ) that acquired a majority of the Magneti Marelli aftermarket business. But, when Sergio Marchionne took over Fiat Group and automotives were reaffirmed as the core business of the group, Magneti Marelli Aftermarket Parts and Service was re-acquired (in 2007). Since then, Magneti Marelli serves both IAM and OES, including all the car-makers, delivering to their dealers and also to the independent retailers.

In the aftermarket segment, the Magneti Marelli programme has to have a full range and full coverage of the vehicle fleet, working hand-in-hand with high-level partners: the major component makers.

Magneti Marelli delivers products to the market via its own package, with the Magneti Marelli brand. Not all the parts are manufactured by Magneti Marelli: the company also purchases some products from partners and markets them under the Magneti Marelli brand.

Magneti Marelli is a service network too, marketed with the "Checkstar" name; Checkstar is a network of approximately 5,000 repair shops, mainly in Italy, Poland, Spain and Latin America.

Table 8.6 **Key historical highlights**

1919	The Fabbrica Italiana Magneti Marelli (FIMM) was founded
1929	The company starts to establish networks in many European countries
1931	The first accumulator is produced
1935	Start of spark plug production
1947	The Electronics Division is born
1967	Magneti Marelli becomes part of the Fiat Group
1971	The first research centre for the development of automotive electronics is born
1972	Presentation of the first diagnosing system for automobiles at the Turin Motor Show
1985	Creation of the Aftermarket Division with a network of 300 workshops
2002	The Aftermarket division is sold to RGZ; the company RGZ Magneti Marelli Aftermarket S.p.A. is established
2005	The Checkstar Service Network is born
2007	Fiat Group buys back the Aftermarket division from the RGZ Group

The main markets for Magneti Marelli Aftermarket are Germany, France, Poland, Greece and Italy; Italy has control in Brazil (through Cofap) and Argentina (through Repestos). Italy and Brazil respectively account for 28% and 43% of the IAM total revenue, followed by Spain and France with 7% each, Germany and Poland with 5% each, Argentina with 3% and Greece with 2%.

Magneti Marelli Aftermarket Parts and Service (AMP&S) researches, selects and distributes original or equivalent to original quality spare parts and guarantees quality and reliability of the commercialized product. Its mission is focused on offering a multi-brand open platform of products by bundling the Magneti Marelli manufactured parts and growing a network of alliances with excellent partners such as car-makers, car systems and parts manufacturers.

The main goals of AMP&S are: developing and providing support, technical assistance and diagnostic, continuous training to the network of repair shops (when possible, under the brand of Magneti Marelli Checkstar Service), and distributing spare parts to the independent aftermarket to capitalize on the long-term partnerships with the main players in the distribution and logistics field.

In the automotive aftermarket, Magneti Marelli distributes its proprietary brands (Magneti Marelli, Seima, Cromodora, Vitaloni, etc.) and other brands such as Phillips, Continental, Brembo, Mahle, Pagid, Behr and Federal Mogul, all synonymous with high quality.

AMP&S offers a wide range (about 34,000 part numbers subdivided into 30 product lines) of original equipment or original quality equivalent spare parts (Table 8.7), backed by a service network of about 4,800 authorized workshops throughout the world (1,800 in Italy, 1,200 in Spain and Portugal, 160 in Greece, 80 in Turkey, 130 in Poland, 32 in Croatia, 1,350 in Brazil, and 40 in Argentina, Paraguay and Uruguay). In operation since 1965, the Magneti Marelli workshops network currently includes specialized workshops in nine countries and two continents (Annex 4).

Table 8.7 **AMP&S product range: spare parts**

Mechanical components	Electrical/electronic components
Oil pumps	Ignition
Fuel pumps	Switches
Water pumps	Small motors
Shock absorbers	Rotary motors
Brake hydraulics	Lambda sensors
Brake pads/shoes	Electronic system
Brake discs/rotors	Engine spare parts
Wheel bearing kits	Alternators spare parts
Pre-assembled brake kits	On-board instrumentation
Consumable/maintenance parts	**Body parts components**
Batteries	Lamps
Lubricants	Lighting
Glow-plugs	Radiators
Spark-plugs	Cabin air filters
Air, oil, fuel filters	Heating systems
Spark plug cable kits	Rear-view mirrors
Windshield wiper blades	Electric window winders

8.6 Mopar

Mopar, a contraction of "motor parts", is a Chrysler Group LLC brand (Box 8.2). Mopar parts are original equipment manufactured parts for Chrysler vehicles. Mopar is Chrysler Group LLC's service, parts and customer-care brand, which means it supplies automotive parts and services for the Chrysler Group. Mopar provides quality replacement parts for Chrysler automobiles, as well as producing aftermarket parts designed for performance on both the street and the racing circuit.

Mopar (see Box 8.3 for its history) distributes approximately 280,000 different parts and accessories, in more than 90 countries, and it represents the single source for all original equipment parts for Chrysler, Dodge, Jeep and Ram Truck vehicles.

Mopar parts are engineered and tested by the same teams that create factory-authorized vehicle specifications for Chrysler, Dodge, Jeep, Ram, SRT and Fiat vehicles. This implies a uniqueness for the brand towards the aftermarket.

In 2009, Mopar market share in the aftermarket was 30%, with an industry average of 25–35% (R.L. Polk and Chrysler Data, 2008).[5] The forecast showed a certain

5 R.L. Polk is a consulting agency providing insights, market data and marketing solutions for the automotive sector.

stabilization of parts demand in 2010, and a rebounding for 2012, by the improvement of vehicle volume and age.

Box 8.2 **Story of the Chrysler Group**

Chrysler Group LLC is an American-based multinational auto-maker headquartered in the Auburn Hills, a suburb of Detroit in Michigan.

The company was founded by Walter Chrysler (1875–1940) on 6 June 1925, when the Maxwell Motor Company (est. 1904) was reorganized into the Chrysler Corporation; over the years, it has become the major global automotive group. In 1998, it was acquired by Daimler-Benz to form DaimlerChrysler and after 9 years, in 2007, Chrysler Group fell under the control of the financial group Cerberus Capital Management, while DaimlerChrysler became Daimler AG.

On 10 June 2009, Chrysler LLC emerged from a Chapter 11 bankruptcy reorganization and substantially all of its operations were sold to a new company: Chrysler Group LLC merged with the Italian auto-maker Fiat. Initially holding a 20% stake in Chrysler Group, Fiat's stake was raised to 53.5% thanks to the acquisition of the equity interests held by the US Treasury (6% in June 2011) and Canada (1.5% in July 2011). Indeed, in 2010, the new Fiat Automobile SpA acquired majority control of Chrysler Group. It is reported that Chrysler was heavy on fleet sales in 2010, hitting as high as 56% of total sales in February of that year. For the whole year, 38% of sales of Chrysler were to fleet customers. The industry average was 19%. However, the company hopes to reduce its fleet sales to the industry average in 2011 with a renewed product line-up.

Chrysler is the world's 16th largest vehicle manufacturer as ranked by OICA in 2009. Total Chrysler vehicle production was about 1 million vehicles that year.

Mopar' birth and growth is an interesting story (Annex 5 outlines the 72-year history of the brand, starting from the development of its logo).

Box 8.3 **History of Chrysler**

In the 1930s, Chrysler created a formal vehicle parts division under the MoPar brand, with the result that "Mopar" remains a colloquial term for vehicles produced by Chrysler Corporation.

1959–1963. Prior to 1960, Chrysler had very little involvement in the "aftermarket" sector. Toward the end of the 1950s, Chrysler began to look at possible advantages that market entrance could generate. The aftermarket had great profit potential, as well as market stability. Chrysler caught on at a bad time: auto owners tended to spend more money to keep their older cars running, as opposed to buying new vehicles. Along with penetrating the automotive aftermarket, in November of 1963, Chrysler announced plans for the elimination of all of its wholesalers.

1964–1971. Chrysler's biggest problem at this time was that Chrysler dealers could not compete with the wholesalers on price. The solution for Chrysler was to go back to the depot system used in earlier years. In July 1964, a depot network consisting of 18 units was set up, divided into area depots, regional depots and national depots. By 1965, Chrysler parts were being distributed by two separate systems: the Dealer Parts Sales Group supplied Chrysler parts through Chrysler dealers and wholesalers; and the Independent Aftermarket Parts Sales Group distributed Mopar parts through franchised warehouse distributors.

1972–1984. Chrysler developed newer methods of distribution, inventory control and tracking systems. With widespread advances in technology, Chrysler was able to meet supply and demand at a greater rate than in earlier years; wholesalers were out of the picture and Chrysler only dealt with aftermarket parts through the dealer network. Starting from 1973, Mopar established a dedicated parts delivery service, becoming the industry standard.

1985–1990. Chrysler continued to grow. An ideal form of recognition "Chrysler Corporation Genuine Parts" was incorporated into the Mopar logo, in order to differentiate genuine Chrysler parts from aftermarket and counterfeit parts.

2002–2007. In 2002 the Mopar brand was re-launched, integrating Mopar and dealer inventory and top level motorsport participation; in 2007 a new, state-of-the-art Dealer Daily Parts Stock Replenishment service was initiated.

2009 – Today, in collaboration with Fiat, the main goal is to strengthen Mopar and to present it as a brand able to provide excellence and to add value to Chrysler brands.

Recent internal research identified some key associations with the Mopar brand, which stands for quality, speed, power and passion. Moreover, after-sales specialists recognize outstanding brand equity in Mopar. The increasing need to be more focused on customers, service and brand equity is forcing Mopar more and more towards new initiatives that can drive up revenue and market share.

The Chrysler distribution structure, by 2009, was composed of 2,600 dealers: each dealer is an OES for the aftermarket and some of them are parts wholesalers too (around 500). Mopar, by 2010, had 20 facilities: among those, five were national-level parts distribution centres (PDCs) and 15 were field PDCs, located in different states. Mopar can boast, globally, a space of 9 million square feet. Mopar is able to handle more than 175,000 order lines daily, for more than 3,000 shipping addresses. The dealer deliveries complete around 70% before 7:00 am and 90% before 10:00 am.

The following are Mopar's main strategic goals:

- **Customer satisfaction and retention**. Strengthening every element of the aftersales customer experience and developing new customer touch-points able to let customers experience a superior service.

- **Product portfolio**. Expanding product offerings to maximize the growth potential and add value to the final customer by offering a shorter time to market for accessories and remanufactured parts and using a smart pricing programme to drive the market.

- **Channel innovation**. Enhancing and redefining the distribution structure, also looking at transformation of wholesale retailers and independent repairers (continually growing in terms of numbers, business weight and sales) and at new forms of sales channel (e.g. the internet). Recent research shows that around 70% of Americans use the internet in order to find and eventually chose a dealer).

- **Network capacity**. Enhancing existing and developing more competences in terms of people, tools and assets: for example the number of technicians and service advisers, weekend and extended hours, and Express Lane development. Specifically, the so-called "Express Lane" is more than just an oil change service. The highly trained, professional technicians perform a complete preventative maintenance check of a vehicle's major components to keep the vehicle safe, reliable and in good operating condition. It's fast, convenient and helps prevent costly breakdowns. It's a quick service strategy, able to offer: oil change, quick tyre changes, windshield wipers and blades, fluid level top-ups, brakes adjustment, battery checks and so on.

References

Krebs, M. (2008, November 11). Auto affordability worsens, Comerica reports. *Auto Observer.* Retrieved from http://www.edmunds.com/autoobserver-archive/2008/11/auto-affordability-worsens-comerica-reports.html

McCall, B. (1999, July 18). King of the road. [Review of the book *The Distance to the Moon: A Road Trip into the American Dream,* by J. Morgan]. *The New York Times.* Retrieved from http://www.nytimes.com/1999/07/18/books/king-of-the-road.html

NADA DATA (2009). *Economic Impact of America's New-car and New-truck Dealers: A Dealership and Industry Review.* Retrieved from http://leblog.gerpisa.org/system/files/NADA_Data_2009_final_091109.pdf

R.L. Polk & Co. (2009). Automotive Buy Flow Study: The Automotive Shopping Process. Retrieved from http://www.gstatic.com/ads/research/en/2009_AutoBuyFlowStudy.pdf.

Shi, D.E. (2001, March 25). Americans and cars: our love is here to stay. *Chicago Tribune.*

Streitfeld, R. (2009, March 14). U.S. car repair shops getting mileage out of thriftier times. *CNN.* Retrieved from http://edition.cnn.com/2009/US/03/14/car.repairs/index.html.

Annex 1. Aftermarket size and potential

The size and growth rate of the automotive aftermarket depends primarily on a number of factors:

1. **Number of vehicles on the road.** The number of vehicles on US roads grew significantly in recent years, fuelling ongoing demand for products and services offered by automotive dealers.

2. **Average age of the cars.** The average age of vehicles on the road has increased in recent years and it is now estimated at 10 years for cars and almost 9 years for light trucks. This phenomenon directly affects the demand for maintenance and repair services, especially for exhaust systems, brakes, shocks, suspension, engine repairs, oil changes, and other related services. The common prediction of specialists such as Standard & Poor's and the Capstone Financial Group shows that the positive trend is going to continue for several years.

3. **Quality advances in cars.** Manufacturers are able to guarantee high-quality vehicles, with better performance, made of high-quality components (especially the consumable components such as oil, filters, etc.), that are more and more durable. This phenomenon directly affects the demand for maintenance and repair services, causing a negative trend (the more durable the components, the greater the length in maintenance intervals).

4. **Number of annual miles per vehicle.** A steady increase in total miles driven reached a peak of 3 trillion miles in 2006; the miles driven are estimated, on average, for 2009, at 12,000. The more miles driven, the more the wear and tear, the greater the need for maintenance and repair. However, due to increasing fuel prices and the economic downturn, an adverse downward trend in service and repair is recognizable.

5. **Technology advances in cars.** Cars have become more and more computerized and also complicated. Due to their increased complexity, today's cars require specialized tools, skills and computer software for service and repair. This trend can potentially favour the aftermarket. Fewer car owners are capable of repairing their own vehicles, opting for service providers who have the specialist equipment and possess all the skills required. Especially owners of new late model cars are often forced to return to the dealership for service and repair.

6. **Large untapped market of unperformed maintenance.** According to the Automotive Aftermarket Industry Association (AAIA),[6] there is over $55 billion, per annum, of unperformed and underperformed maintenance

6 http://www.trade.gov/static/Automotive%20Parts%20Industry%20Assessment%202010%20rev3.pdf

by vehicle owners. A 2008 study conducted by the Car Care Council esti-mates that 80% of vehicles need service and parts.[7] The study shows that one in ten drivers continue to drive, ignoring the "check engine" signal. This unperformed maintenance represents a significant untapped market for auto franchises. While in the current economic climate customers are more likely to defer expensive repairs on their cars, they are more likely to repair them eventually than to replace them.

7. **Growing used car sales.** While new car sales are declining, there is increasing demand for used cars. The fact is that the price for an average good quality car is increasing substantially. Strong used car sales increase demand for the services of auto repair and auto reconditioning, a signifi-cant business opportunity for dealers with used-car reselling businesses.

8. **Increased demand for fuel efficiency.** Before the economic downturn, US auto manufacturers were already losing sales to Japanese car-makers. Fluctuating fuel prices have resulted in a shift in consumer demand from big, gas guzzling cars, pick-up trucks and SUVs to smaller, fuel-efficient Japanese cars. Federal Regulations stipulate that improving fuel efficiency must be a cornerstone of future strategy for auto manufacturers. The gov-ernment bailout of the industry is contingent on manufacturers produc-ing fuel efficient vehicles, reducing emissions and developing alternative fuel vehicles such as hybrid and electric cars.

9. **Lower affordability of cars.** According to Comerica Bank's Auto Afford-ability Index, new cars are becoming much more expensive relative to average family income levels (Krebs, 2008). In 2008, the average price of a new car sold in the United States was about $28,400. A car is becom-ing an increasingly expensive purchase; therefore consumers are preserv-ing their investment through maintenance and repair. This benefits the aftermarket. In addition, the increased cost of cars relative to income has stimulated demand for good quality used cars with consequent increased demand for aftermarket products and services.

7 http://www.carcare.org

Annex 2. Magneti Marelli organization chart

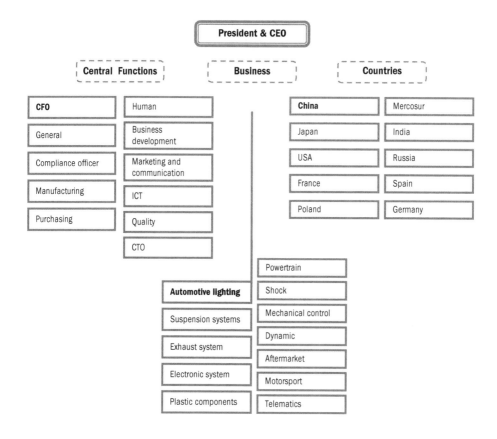

Annex 3. Magneti Marelli business areas

Electronic systems (instrument clusters; infotainment & telematics, lighting & body electronics) is the Magneti Marelli division with headquarters in Corbetta (Milan) that deals with automotive electronics. The significant numbers for 2009 for this business line were as follows: total turnover of €501 million (11% of the total revenues), an R&D expenditure equal to 15% of the turnover on investments equal to 6.8%; it is present in eight countries spanning four continents.

Powertrain (gasoline, diesel and multi-fuel engine control systems; automated manual transmission "Freechoice" gearboxes) is a business line dedicated to engines and transmission components production for cars, motorbikes and light vehicles. It had €850 million of revenues (18% of the total revenues), with two R&D centres, four application centres and 11 manufacturing sites, located in four continents and seven countries.

Suspension systems, Cofap – shock absorbers, dynamic systems (suspension; shock absorber; electronically controlled shock absorbers), is the business unit that designs and manufactures suspension modules and components for motor vehicles. The significant numbers for 2009 pertaining to this business line were as follows: total turnover of €808.1 million (14% of the total revenues), an R&D expenditure equal to 1% of the turnover and investments equal to 2.9%. It has 13 production facilities and two research centres and a presence in four continents and five nations.

Exhaust systems (exhaust systems, catalytic converter and silencing systems) is the business line that develops and produces exhaust systems for cars and engine-powered vehicles, using advanced technologies in terms of performance and quality. The business unit significant numbers for 2009 were as follows: €543 million of actual turnover (10% of the total revenues), an R&D expense equal to 1% of turnover and an investment equal to 3%. It consists of seven production plants and four research and development centres.

Motorsport (specific electronic and electro-mechanical systems for championships at the cutting edge of technology, in F1, in MotoGP, SBK and the WRC). Magneti Marelli's Motorsport Department, with 1% of total revenues, is involved with the design, manufacture and technical sales support for a complete range of parts, hardware and software products for racing applications and motor racing championships. The business line is based in Corbetta (MI), with plants in Venaria (TO) and Bologna, and application centres in France, the UK, USA, Brazil and Japan. This highly qualified department that comprises a team of over 100 specialized engineers and technicians, enables Magneti Marelli to partner the top teams in Formula 1, WRC, MotoGP, Superbike, GP2, FIA GT and other championships. For these competitions, Magneti Marelli develops and produces specific electronic and electro-mechanical components, in particular for engine control and data acquisition. It also provides displays, telemetry systems, alternators, voltage regulators, ignition coils, sensors, injectors, pressure regulators, fuel pumps and software applications. Magneti Marelli's involvement with motor racing is connected to the great impulse that Magneti Marelli has always devoted to innovation.

Plastic components and modules, the division that takes care of products and projects such as dashboards, fuel systems centre consoles, bumpers and fuel systems, has to date been an activity undergoing an integration process in Magneti Marelli. It makes 8% of the total revenues.

Aftermarket Parts and Services, Magneti Marelli Aftermarket Parts and Services is positioned in the global aftermarket as a provider of spare parts and services for OEM and IAM segments of the automotive market (automobiles and commercial vehicles). The business unit achieved in 2009 a turnover of €237 million with 446 people employed in seven countries spanning two continents: Europe and South America. It is present in 82 markets with Argentina, Brazil, France, Germany, Italy, Poland and Spain as the base for seven sales organizations.

Table 8.8 **Magneti Marelli product range**

Automotive lighting	headlamp; rear lamp technologies
Powertrain parts	gasoline engine control; diesel engine control; transmission
Suspension systems	suspension modules; shock absorbers
Exhaust systems	emission abatement system; silencing system
Electronic systems	instrument clusters; telematics; displays; infotainment & navigation

Annex 4. Corporate structure of Magneti Marelli aftermarket

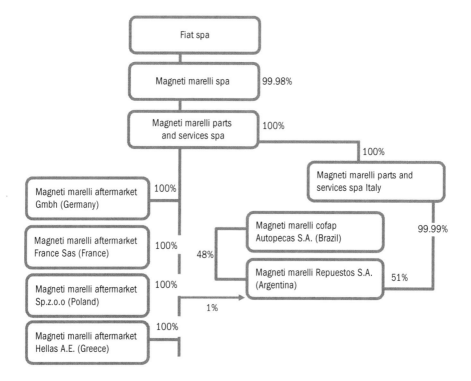

Annex 5. Mopar: 72 years of history

In 1928, when Chrysler acquired Dodge, the need for a dedicated parts manufac-turer, supplier and distribution system to support the growing enterprise led to the formation of the Chrysler Motor Parts Corporation (CMPC) in 1929.

From 1933 to 1937 Chrysler Motor Parts featured a logo with the letters **D, C, P** and **D**, for Dodge Chrysler, Plymouth, and Desoto. This led to the Mopar trademark becoming one of the most familiar trademarks in automotive history. But Mopar became a trademark for a line of antifreeze products in 1937. The genius was Nel-son L. Farley, Chrysler Division's sales promotional manager in the 1930s. Farley had established a think-tank called the Activities Council, whose purpose was to brainstorm new merchandising ideas and report back to him. In the spring of 1937, this activities council was working on the creation of a product name to put on cans of Chrysler Motor Parts antifreeze that was being used in their cars. The group, after many suggestions, came up with a simple name that would be easy to remem-ber: a combination of the words motors and parts; hence the word "Mopar". Now Chrysler needed a logotype for the trade name. The first attempt, created by a man named Burke Bartlett, was a bright purple logo arranged in a vertical arrow. The next design became one of the most famous and distinctive trademarks of the cen-tury, the unique signpost of the Chrysler Parts Division. The Activities Council then came up with a way to introduce the new acronym to the public. And in 1937 they created a character named "Mr Mopar" who made his debut in the form of a camel. A year or two earlier, a man named Vern Dupuis had made a small "mechanical man" fashioned out of parts. The group found this mechanical man, named him "ACCY", an abbreviation for accessory, and put him in front of the camel. Eleven years later when Dupuis was in the Merchandising and Development Depart-ment he modified "ACCY" into a moving and speaking robot and renamed him "Mr Mopar". A later version of this robot made television appearances from coast to coast. Later, the familiar Pentastar of Chrysler and the Mopar signature in process blue was seen on the package designs and labelling of more than 40,000 quality-engineered original equipment replacement parts. The name "Mopar" stands for quality engineering. The colour of the logo, like Chrysler, is always blue.

Today the logo is a blue M, subscripted by "MOPAR" in black letters.

9

iGuzzini Illuminazione and the challenge of LEDs on the global market

Sara Paoletti
Istituto Adriano Olivetti (ISTAO), Italy

Stefano Grugnetti
Istituto Adriano Olivetti (ISTAO), Italy

Lorenzo Palego
Istituto Adriano Olivetti (ISTAO), Italy

This is the story of a family that, by progressively taking on the challenges of the market, has traced a path of growth leading it to become one of Europe's leaders in the lighting industry. Its innumerable achievements worldwide over its 50 years of activity are the result of a business and management style that has supported an innate passion for architecture and design, with a strong organizational competence and an ongoing commitment to optimization of the "team". Current challenges, on the other hand, are no less arduous, although different from those of the past: technological innovation changes the paradigms of the market; the lengthening of the subcontracting chain due to varying supply imperatives generates changes on the supply chain side; and the need to protect and grow markets offers new challenges from the cultural and organizational point of view. What strategic choices will guide the company into the future?

9.1 Light, essence of life

> Our mission is to improve the quality of light and, therefore, the quality of
> life of people (iGuzzini mission statement).

In 1860 Joseph Swan was the first person to pass an electric current through thin carbon filaments, producing a bright light – however briefly. Nearly 20 years later, Thomas Edison extended the duration of light to several hundred hours and patented electric power distribution, leading to the era of artificial lighting. There have been great technological advances since then, from the point of view of efficiency and design, but it is only recently that the effects of artificial light on the human body have been considered.

Light plays a fundamental role, not only in enabling us to see but also in helping to adjust the delicate physiological mechanisms underlying the health, emotional stability and vitality[1] of human beings. And iGuzzini was among the first companies in Europe to place increasing emphasis on these issues and on aspects more recently associated with eco-sustainability and energy saving.

Founded in 1959 by the sons of Mariano Guzzini,[2] iGuzzini is one of the European leaders in the lighting industry. The company's commitment places at the heart of its projects "Education in the conscientious use of light, for the welfare of people and for the affirmation of architecture, cultural heritage and the natural environment." These values, which have been part of the history of the Recanati enterprise, have been the focus of numerous media campaigns developed over the past decades in support of the brand[3] and are the cornerstones of the company's culture and of its commitment to disseminating that culture.

Thanks to its ability to develop relationships of synergy with the world of architecture and industrial design, iGuzzini has over the years assumed a pioneering role in effectively combining technology, performance and design. These elements, united with a modern organization, have enabled iGuzzini to become a major player in the European lighting sector and continue to contribute to the development and success of the company.

Since the start of the new millennium, however, the lighting industry has been undergoing a transformation, triggered in particular by the process of technological innovation under way with the advent of LED technology, which brings to the company new strategic and organizational challenges.

In November 2012, the Chairman, Adolfo Guzzini, representing the third generation of the industrial family, stated in a press release:

1 From *La Luce che Cura* (*The Light That Heals*) by Fabio Marchesi (2002), engineer, scientist, researcher and member of the New York Academy of Sciences, who is considered one of the top national experts on the therapeutic applications of light.
2 Father of Raimondo, Giovanni, Virgilio, Giuseppe, Giannunzio and Adolfo.
3 The first advertising campaign of the iGuzzini brand, aimed at raising awareness of intelligent consumption, dates back to 1982.

> Since 2009 our company has supplied tens of thousands of new gen-
> eration LED devices worldwide, renewing and adapting public lighting
> systems which often date back to the '70s, thus bringing about a substan-
> tial reduction in energy consumption and light pollution... Thanks to
> these systems, not only has energy consumption been reduced but lamp
> replacement costs will be reduced to zero, given that the life of LEDs in
> quality appliances can exceed 10 years.

With the increasing dissemination of LEDs, iGuzzini owners and management
are now faced with a complex challenge: how to rethink their product-market mix
in order to embrace the opportunities offered by new technology, while at the same
time maintaining and developing traditional production, which has achieved a certain level of excellence. How to continue the process of internationalization outside
Europe, which began in particular with the opening of the commercial branches
and the plant in China? How to optimize the organizational process on a multinational and multicultural scale?

9.2 The European lighting market

To better understand the place of iGuzzini Illuminazione in today's competitive
scenario, it is important to examine, however briefly, the market in which it operates and the dynamics involved.

9.2.1 Production and consumption of lighting products in Europe

The lighting industry in Europe recorded a production value of €10 billion in 2010,
employing around 72,000 people. The sector shows a very high degree of openness,
with an export rate of 70% of production value and with imports accounting for
74% of domestic consumption (see Table 9.1).

Thanks to a positive performance in international markets, European production increased by 4% in 2011. Exports, after the financial collapse of 2009, grew
steadily over the following two years, reaching €7.946 million in 2011, a year in
which more than 50% of the production of lighting fixtures was attributable to the
top 20 companies in Western Europe.

Table 9.1 **Lighting industry in Europe (2010)**

Source: CSIL (Centro Studi Industria Leggera – Light Industry Research Centre)

Base data	Values
Production (€ millions)	10.193
Exports (€ millions)	7.176
Imports (€ millions)	8.604
Consumption (€ millions)	11.621
Export/Production	70.4%
Import/Consumption	74.0%
Employees	72,000

The lighting sector may be divided into four major product areas (residential, commercial, industrial and outdoor products) with significant specialization within enterprises.

The residential and the commercial sector together account for over 60% of the sector's supply in Europe; the production of outdoor lighting products has witnessed a growth trend in recent years, while there has been a slight fall in relation to industrial lighting appliances (see Fig. 9.1).

Figure 9.1 **Distribution in the supply of lighting by product segment in Europe (%, 2006, 2008, 2010)**

Source: CSIL (Centro Studi Industria Leggera – Light Industry Research Centre)

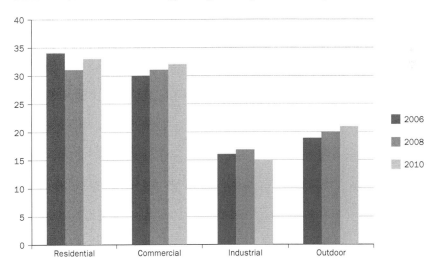

Many European companies specialize in the residential sector (Briloner, Globo Handels, National Lighting, Paulmann, WOFI Leuchtne); others have a portfolio of products focused on the commercial segment (Anosrg, Cooper Safety, Erco, Lis, LTS Licht, Lival, Waldman), the industrial segment (Beghelli) or the product segment for foreign markets (Bega Group, Blachere Illumination, Hess, Konstsmide, MK Illumination, Schréder, Waldmann).

iGuzzini Illuminazione operates on the European market with a diversified product portfolio in the four sectors, although with a clear emphasis on the lighting design field;[4] i.e. in the commercial and industrial fields both indoor and outdoor.

The Austrian company Zumtobel is still the European leader (taking into account only Western Europe), based on the total production of lighting devices. The main European manufacturers next in line are: Philips Lighting (the Netherlands), Eglo (Austria), Philips Consumer Luminaires (Belgium) and Trilux (Germany).

In 2010, iGuzzini Illuminazione was one of the top 15 producers in Europe and the third largest in Italy, after Targetti Poulsen and Disano. Given the strong specialization of the company in the lighting design sector, it is interesting to note that the Recanati company is the seventh in Europe in the outdoor lighting sector[5] (the first in Italy) and lies in fourth place in the specific area of outdoor residential lighting.

9.2.2 The lighting sector in Italy

The lighting appliance sector in Italy recorded a growth trend in the 15 years prior to the crisis that began in 2008–2009 (see Fig. 9.2 for turnover and Fig. 9.3 for import/export). Italy, after Germany, is the second largest producer in the Western European markets, with a market share of approximately 20% and export levels of slightly over 50%.

---

4 The fields of application for iGuzzini products are the following: architectural, art and culture, large spaces and sports/transport areas, street lighting, urban lighting, entertainment and accommodation facilities, places of worship, residential, commercial spaces, offices and education.

5 Classifications taken from *The European Market for Lighting Systems* (CSIL, 2011).

Figure 9.2 **Lighting appliances, production turnover, Italy (1995–2008) (€ millions)**
Source: Research Centre Cosmit/Federlegno

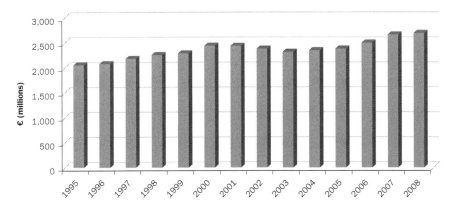

Figure 9.3 **Lighting appliances, exports and imports, Italy (2005–2010) (€ millions)**
Source: ISTAO based on Coeweb data

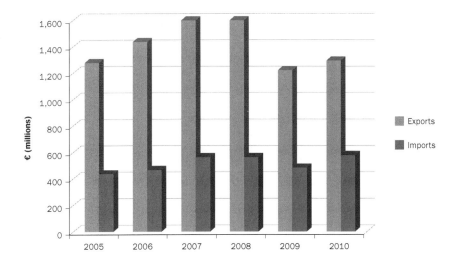

Shifting the structural analysis to the regional level, it emerges that the top three regions with the highest number of enterprises in the sector of "Manufacture of lighting appliances and electric lamps" are Lombardy, Veneto and Tuscany, where a total of 56% of acting enterprises have their operations.

The regions that are home to enterprises with an average size greater than the sector average are: The Marches (20.3 employees per company), Emilia-Romagna (15.1 employees per company), Trentino-Alto Adige and Lombardy (14.6 employees per company). Tuscany and Veneto, although with smaller average company sizes (9.5), are characterized by dedicated production zones specialized in lighting: for example the production network that has grown around the activities of Targetti in Tuscany or the Veneto Lighting Systems District.

9.2.3 LED technology and new development scenarios in the lighting sector

Among the factors with the greatest influence on the competitive backdrop to the industry, the growing popularity of LED technology (light emitting diode) is of particular importance.

An LED is a diode, or a small semiconductor that emits light when an electrical pulse passes through it. LEDs can achieve significant energy savings and have a much longer life than traditional light sources.[6] This is a radical technological innovation in the lighting industry, capable of satisfying increasing combined demands for energy savings, eco-sustainability and efficiency: it is now possible to produce more and better quality light, reducing energy requirements and hence CO_2 emissions, thanks to LED technology.

The market has grown exponentially in recent years, increasing by 400% between 2005 and 2010 (see Fig. 9.4). Although some major LED manufacturers, such as Philips and OSRAM, still produce traditional light sources, it is not unlikely that current technology will be replaced by LED technology during the decade (therefore by 2020), given the growth rate of this market. In Europe, the installation of devices that use LEDs as a light source increased in 2011 by almost 60%.

---

6 Previously, a light source existed to which a reflector was applied, which emitted a beam of light that was narrow or wide depending on its form and specificity (matt, gloss), and connected to a dissipater and a power supply. LED technology ushered in a very different world in which the basic technological components of lamps actually changed. The reflector was connected to a diode and a heat dissipater that had the effect of lengthening the life of the appliance.

Figure 9.4 **LED consumption trend in Western Europe and on the world market (2005–2010) (US$ millions)**

Source: CSIL (Centro Studi Industria Leggera – Light Industry Research Centre)

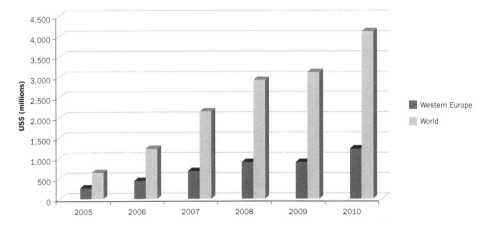

LED technology, in fact, will substantially change business processes and competitive structure. It is reasonable to assume that the following may occur:

- **Greater vertical concentration of industry**. A number of large groups that, until a few years ago, produced light sources and currently produce LEDs, are integrating downstream by acquiring enterprises that specialize in the production of lamps and electronics.

- **Diffusion of small assembly enterprises**. Small businesses are developing in several European countries that are able to assemble LEDs on an artisan basis – mainly Asian imports – in low cost lighting devices.

The nature of the competition that will inevitably be encountered by companies in the lighting sector will therefore depend on the growing importance assumed by the use of the LED light source.

The use of LEDs has gradually led, on the other hand, to greater organizational complexity and represents both a threat and an opportunity for European lighting enterprises that hope to achieve competitive advantage. In this transition between traditional and LED lighting, indeed, the expansion of the production platform and of buying and selling codes becomes indispensable, and the impact will be significant from the economic and financial as well as logistical point of view. Moreover, LED technology itself has not yet reached the stage of standardization and maturity, and constant technological change is the order of the day.[7]

7 Precisely in order to define standards and specifications for the interfaces of LED systems to make them interchangeable and to "systematize" and harmonize the results and applications of the ongoing technological innovations under way, the Zhaga consortium was set up, of which iGuzzini Illuminazione is a "regular member".

9.3 Origin and development of iGuzzini Illuminazione

9.3.1 A story that began a long time ago

iGuzzini Illuminazione, founded in 1959, together with F.lli Guzzini (founded in 1912), Teuco Guzzini (founded in 1972) and Gitronica (founded in 1990), belongs to the Guzzini Group (the family finance company, FIMAG/Finanziaria Mariano Guzzini, dates back to 1982).

iGuzzini Illuminazione was founded as a "rib" of the business concern that started out a hundred years ago. In 1912 Enrico Guzzini, the head of the family business, founded F.lli Guzzini with his three children on his return from Argentina, to which he had emigrated several years previously: it was a small craft business specializing in the processing of animal horn. In 1938, it was the first in the world to introduce acrylic into the tableware sector, a cutting-edge material at the time which was applied exclusively in the aviation industry.

After World War II, the third generation entered the company and it became necessary to develop the business by identifying new market opportunities to enable the different family members to express their potential and realize their individual aspirations.

In 1959 the older children of Mariano founded Harvey Creazioni (subsequently iGuzzini Illuminazione) independently from F.lli Guzzini. Thus began the production of decorative lamps using acrylic, and they were able to exploit the commercial channels (primarily homeware and giftware shops) that had been previously developed by F.lli Guzzini.

The new approach to products based on the principles of contemporary design[8] introduced by the third generation contributed at once to the success of iGuzzini Illuminazione. In the early 1960s Luigi Massoni was hired as Art Director of Harvey Creations (a new role in the contemporary industrial field, and all the more so in small businesses) and his younger brother Adolfo entered the company; each of these events represented a new phase in the company's development. With the development of coordinated lines, an innovative product logic was immediately set in motion. A catalogue was created by careful selection of the collections, and the range was gradually expanded. The link was also reinforced with the world of designers and specialized magazines, the company logo was redesigned (introducing the name *Guzzini*) and new emphasis began to be placed on the brand and on other intangible values. The way in which products were presented on the market, finally, was revolutionized (from packaging to display at sales outlets) and, for the

---

8 In the 1950s, industrial design came to prominence, in the wake of the American cultural model, in Italy and especially in Milan. In 1954, in particular, La Rinascente department store for the first time promoted the Compasso d'Oro award for objects with the best industrial design, and in 1956 the ADI (Association for Industrial Design) was founded.

first time, the company focused strongly on direct communication through participation in economic and cultural events.

The business evolution of iGuzzini Illuminazione was supported by a strong thrust towards internationalization as an important driver of development, at a time when Italian companies operating in the furniture and design field were focused mainly on the domestic market.

In addition to identifying major national distributors of furniture and accessories in Germany, Holland and the UK, charged with selling the products in their respective markets, iGuzzini Illuminazione, through joint venture agreements, created new business opportunities in two strategic geographic areas: Yugoslavia, with the aim of opening up a commercial "passage" in Eastern Europe, and Canada, the gateway to the United States.

The energy crisis of the early 1970s brought about a number of economic and cultural changes which were to strongly impact on corporate strategies. The dramatic increase in the price of oil and consequently of plastic, and the growing perception that oil was an anti-ecological product, drove the company to assess other market opportunities. The knowledge of the American environment and the openness to new concepts of lighting technology that were not yet explored in Italy were to represent the key factors for business success. The importance of lighting was expressed in the concept of "dedicated" light, and innovative products were developed that required new technologies as well as an efficient and flexible industrial production organization.

The combination of technology, performance and Italian design, combined with the right price, became the winning strategy for old and new markets alike.

Forty years later, iGuzzini Illuminazione still reveals its strong international vocation, evidenced in recent years by the opening of a production facility in China, a reference point for the Far Eastern markets (see Section 9.3.6).

9.3.2 iGuzzini in Italy and in the world

In 2010 iGuzzini achieved sales of €175.4 million (69% abroad and 31% in Italy) and had 1,268 employees. In 2011 the consolidated turnover amounted to €186 million, showing a slight increase of about 6% during a time of economic crisis.

The company, which has its headquarters in Recanati, had the following structure in 2011 on the Italian market: 17 agencies, one commercial office and one branch. In Europe there were 11 branches, one representation office and 17 distributors, while in the rest of the world iGuzzini had five branches, three representation offices and 22 distributors (see Fig. 9.5).

iGuzzini achieved ISO 9001 (Quality) certification in 1994, ISO 14001 (Environment) in 2006 and in 2008 it adopted an organizational model of management in accordance with Legislative Decree 231/2001 on the administrative liability of companies.

Figure 9.5 **iGuzzini in Italy and in the world**

Source: iGuzzini Illuminazione

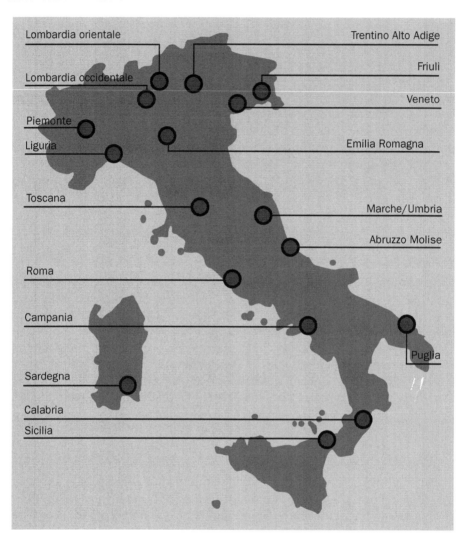

9.3.3 Technology, design and organizational creativity: the drivers of competitive advantage

The company's competitive advantage is based on a number of drivers of development: innovation, design, technology, organizational creativity and design service.

The management of these elements in a context of quality of processes (and of products) has ensured the success of the company over the years.

For iGuzzini Illuminazione, creating innovation means continuously reinterpreting the products over time, based on changing with the times and following consumer needs. Local cultural considerations, spaces and lifestyles impose different performance demands in both technical and design terms. Knowledge becomes fundamental, as does the awareness and sensitivity of customers and their expectations in relation to the design of the products.

The organizational practices of iGuzzini are based on logics of indirect cooperation rather than considerations of function or area. This process enables skills to become established which generate efficiency and innovation over the long term. To capitalize on the experience gained, it is important to verify and record the product results on the market. Rapid innovation can only be achieved in this way, leaving room for creativity. This is a clear example of the open innovation model.[9]

The first phase of the process of developing a new product is the analysis of customer needs (see Fig. 9.6). In this context, knowledge is required of market trends and emerging technologies. **Concept cards** are then developed which are analysed by general management in order to make an initial macroselection of the most promising ideas.

The second phase of the process of developing a new product – the pre-project phase – involves collaboration: the designer works with design groups, criteria are set for the assessment of product-target-channel consistency, the product design is defined and this passes to a **management design review**.

The third stage involves the final selection of projects (both internal and external) and the simultaneous enrichment and completion of the concept cards. The products to be developed are then decided, based on the competitive environment, and the necessary executive investments are then determined and approved.

This is followed by the stages of **final working design** and **prototyped design**, which also leads to the establishment of the final industrial cost.

Figure 9.6 **Process of developing a new product**

Source: ISTAO

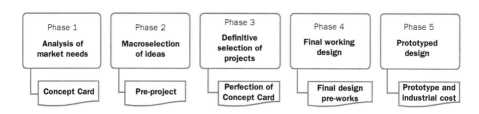

9 The reference is to the model developed by Henry Chesbrough whose concept of "open innovation" refers to the company's use of external sources of technology and innovation to stimulate domestic growth. The application of the model of open innovation should induce companies to better exploit external ideas and technologies in their business, enabling the simultaneous application of their own ideas not used by other companies.

The principal stages of the design process for a new product are followed by the start of production, the definition of commercial communications strategies and the market launch. The monitoring of the sales performance occurs after 6–12 months.

Design is divided into three main areas, one for outdoor products, the second for indoor products and the third for office products.

The accumulation of experiences at the design phase occurs by means of **control cards** which may be product-based (the homogeneous families must follow particular standards) or related to the technology used. These data sheets represent corporate know-how which is shared and transferred from one design group to another.

All iGuzzini processes are managed and controlled following high standards of quality and continuous improvement, and in 1992 the company used the services of two laboratories (one regulatory and one photometric) certified by the Italian Quality Mark (IMQ), aimed at ensuring the safety of its products.

Innovation for iGuzzini Illuminazione is represented primarily in lighting design and application, but the company has always striven for "product-service" excellence. As well as having been the first to develop an outdoor line in addition to their indoor lines, with the same performance and quality standards, the company has placed service at the core of its offering (see Fig. 9.7).

Figure 9.7 **Extent of the iGuzzini service**

Source: ISTAO

In the future, too, service will be a strategic driver while growing importance will be attached to research and development aimed at studying the impact of the technological innovations proposed by large producers of lighting components and sources, aimed at optimizing their application.

9.3.4 A flexible industry with an artisan soul

Although the shift from artisan to industrial enterprise was necessary when the company entered the lighting engineering segment, it nevertheless managed to maintain strong flexibility from the point of view of organization, production and logistics, thus enabling it to enjoy a significant competitive advantage in the end market. Flexibility that, on the other hand, translates into a high number of codes for finished products,[10] whose portfolio is continually updated (about 800 new ones are managed each year).

After a recent reorganization, there is currently a single area within iGuzzini Illuminazione which incorporates the logistics, the production and the purchasing departments.

Another important change in recent years has been the online integration of suppliers and sub-controllers that has enabled the gradual transition from a classical planning model of ERP (enterprise resource planning) and MRP (material requirements planning) to a management lead-time with the ability to activate a process of rapid budgeting that has led to significantly improved efficiencies.

There has also been a transition from a **make-to-stock** production model, which covered 55% of the codes, to a management model with a higher percentage of **assembly to order** and **make to order**.[11] The production process evolves with the contribution of various processes carried out in the following departments:

- Technological, where the main components are produced

- Mechanical, in turn organized into small islands (cold-rolled sheet processing, plate turning, die-casting, jet machining, laser cutting)

- Injection (monotechnology)

- Painting

- Finished products (assembly and control)

---

10 Almost 11,000 in 2011, of which 3,500 related to special products, in addition to the 50,000 semi-finished codes.
11 Make to stock refers to products with higher rotation that are produced for the warehouse through a system of forecasting and planning of stocks. Assembly to order is characterized by a lower rotation than make to stock and involves programming the inventory management of components. Make to order refers to those products such as the special codes which are created ad hoc or which involve even minimal changes (such as a colour change) over the product in the catalogue, which are produced only to order and which are not kept in stock, including components.

The company also utilizes an efficient and loyal network of subcontractors, assemblers (mostly local) and a number of foreign sub-suppliers of finished products (Serbia, France, Romania). The product is developed in Italy, where the prototyping occurs and where the control technical specifications are defined for the final inspection required for the sub-suppliers.

The purchase of raw materials is centralized, then they are passed to the network of suppliers and subcontractors on account for manufacture. The electronics suppliers are very often also suppliers of traditional sources (e.g. Osram and Philips), while suppliers of LEDs are mainly of Asian origin. Given the exponential growth in demand for LEDs worldwide, the delivery times are gradually lengthening, with clear impacts on the lead-time of enterprises downstream.

A logistics hub of 14,000 m^2, equipped with various types of warehouses (vertical, automatic TRASLO [stacker crane], COMBI [truck] with pallet system), was created in 2001 at the Recanati headquarters, aimed at optimizing the movement of materials and goods,

9.3.5 From "product" to "design": a challenging selling-point

iGuzzini Illuminazione's transition from decorative lighting to technical lighting design occurred in the mid-1970s, when the oil crisis – with its inevitable impact on the raw materials market – forced the company to explore new production avenues.

It was during this period that the company transformed from an artisan into an industrial enterprise, accompanied by radical change in its business culture and technical-production organization. Plastics processing was supplemented by metal processing with die-casting, and the need therefore arose to take on new highly specialized technical personnel within the company, just as it would become gradually necessary to alter its presence on the market.

Familiarity with the American scene favoured this process of "productive conversion", offering new ideas and starting-points for products and lighting management that were not yet widely known in Europe. It therefore became necessary to stimulate the market by developing a new avenue of demand.

Whereas in the decorative lighting segment, the most important element of the product lay in the shape of the lamp, light itself became the key aspect in the architectural segment. There was thus a transition from the concept of "object" to that of "design", with the need to gradually generate demand for "light direction" of various living and working areas.

In the transition from decorative lighting to architectural lighting, therefore, a radical change occurred in the relevant product concepts and associated targets, and it became necessary to rethink the sales chain (design, for example, is for the most part a collective expression). iGuzzini Illuminazione's first point of reference was initially the dealer, who in turn dealt with private customers; however, in the technical lighting industry the company was required to deal with new professional figures (designer, interior decorator, architect), who played key roles in coordinating the various activities necessary to satisfy customers' needs.

The first iGuzzini distributors were lighting boutiques. In this new phase of the company's development, the intermediary role of "specifiers"[12] became a crucial part of the sales chain, as did the involvement of electrical wholesalers.

Collaboration with leading lighting designers was of crucial importance for the fine-tuning and implementation of this change in culture, organization and market approach, as was the definition of two strategies successfully pursued by the company:

- Extensive ongoing training

- Communication of the brand

The company began a training school as far back as the early 1980s. Today, there are over 5,000 architects and intermediaries involved each year in training activities, conducted at the Recanati headquarters as well as internationally.

iGuzzini was innovative in the way it extended its training and cultural processes to the market, nurturing the growth of its own organizational and relational capital. For example, alongside the traditional sellers, new figures arose such as that of technical sales engineer, to provide assistance in developing the lighting design project and to be a source of information for architects and specifiers.

These relationships are of a complexity in keeping with the nature of the projects (with particular reference to those contacts) and with their level of internationalization.

Corporate communications stemmed from the basic need to generate new demand and it turned into a genuine cultural project which differentiated the company from its competitors. In 1982, the company for the first time developed an advertising campaign by using well-known weekly magazines to achieve great visual impact. The content of the first advertising launches focused on the value of light rather than on product design and was aimed at promoting brand awareness and conveying the image of "industrial lighting design". Subsequently, even where extended to newspapers and international markets, the campaigns retained the connotation of institutional messages in support of the company's brand and values. One of the most successful examples was the campaign "*Con iGuzzini contro l'inquinamento luminoso*" ("With iGuzzini against light pollution") which was launched in 1994 and played a significant role in securing the first public procurement orders.

12 These are figures (designers, technical studios, architects, engineers) operating in business-to-business markets who are in a position to influence purchasing processes and to play a key role with regard to selection by advising, recommending or prescribing brands of companies, products or services to customers and/or distributors.

9.3.6 The process of internationalization and entry into China

Internationalization was certainly a major challenge for iGuzzini. It started 30 years ago and is still one of the main drivers of development.[13] The project to integrate branches was pursued with rigour and determination. It was made possible through targeted investments in information systems and thanks to an organizational effort dedicated to creating a global culture based on shared values.

Today the company has 17 operational European and non-European branches. Between 2002 and 2010, commercial facilities were created in China, Singapore, Hong Kong-Macao-Taiwan, Russia, Dubai, North America, Sweden, Finland and Turkey.

The first foreign branches (companies) were created as subsidiaries, but had local distributors as shareholders. Although in the past these structures were completely independent, in more recent years they were gradually integrated into the corporate system.

The organization of branches is based on the nature of the markets served, within which there can be considerable variation in the distribution structure, the working mechanisms and in those involved in the sales process. The general specifiers (architects) and particular specifiers (light designers) are in general privileged partners at the start of the process of selling a lighting product. Markets exist in which the light designer is a figure of gradually increasing importance, whereas in other markets the architect plays the dominant role. The commercial structure of the enterprise thus presents different solutions depending on the specific conditions that characterize the particular markets served.

The "China Project" is prominent among the most important internationalization projects: through it, the company has gained a competitive advantage in the markets of the Far East, thanks primarily to product availability, prompt deliveries and design.

Certainly the development of the entry strategy into China has required commitment and planning acumen. The first distribution agreement for Hong Kong and the opening of a branch office there dates back to 2002. The opening of the representation office in Beijing followed in 2003, and the opening of a production plant there was considered: this finally occurred in 2007. In 2005 a sales office was opened in Shanghai and, two years later, in Singapore. In 2010 the sales office in Chengdu was opened.

---

13 The internationalization process began to take shape in the mid-1980s. In just ten years a European network developed which consisted of commercial companies operating in their own territories as nodes of a single network of services, initially Germany, France, Spain, the United Kingdom, and subsequently – after the 1990s – Norway, Denmark, Sweden, Benelux and Switzerland.

The decision to open a production plant in China was based on a careful assessment of the level of technological expertise which the network of local suppliers would be able to make use of. The plant, as a "greenfield" operation, was located in the Shanghai area for three fundamental reasons.

The first relates to the exploitation of localization economies: greater market potential of this geographical area, more modern physical infrastructure, availability of technical expertise for the development of an efficient supply chain and, not least, a more beneficial level of taxation.[14] The second reason relates to the fact that Shanghai is a city with a strong international presence which facilitates the adjustment of personnel to a new working environment and to their stay in China for medium to long periods. The third reason is related to the reference target of the plant, which acts as a production-logistics-services platform for the development of commercial relations with the rest of Asia.

Business activity in China is based essentially on the specification of international architects and local light designers whose contribution led to the company being awarded major projects in the Olympic Games in Beijing (2008) and at the Shanghai Expo (2010).

Today, iGuzzini boasts elevated brand awareness thanks to communications investments in specialized magazines and the translation into Chinese of the pay-off "better light for better life". Clients over time have developed a positive perception of the company and its professionalism through both its products and its intensive direct marketing activities.

The most critical issue on the market is competition from local producers, in terms of price, and the insufficient consideration given to high-end products.

Despite the fact that delocalization in China was based mainly on the desire to implement a "local for local" strategy – also in light of the low impact of labour costs on the lighting design product[15] – currently about 80% of Chinese production is destined for the European market and only 20% is sold locally.

The second phase of the internationalization project in China that began recently is aimed at integrating the areas of South-East Asia, ensuring that Shanghai is the reference point as a "training" centre. The specificity of local cultural factors, as has

---

14 China is a difficult country to penetrate not only because of the complexity of the market but also because of the regulatory barriers to market access and, in particular, to the need to obtain specific product certifications for marketing and sale.

15 70–80% of the cost of production is in fact attributable to electronic components and the light source.

been learnt from this experience, has led to the need for differentiation in terms of product characteristics as well as price, in order to be able to effectively manage the process of internationalization. The creation of optimal market conditions is one of the objectives of iGuzzini's medium-term strategy and they are, in a sense, based on the dissemination of the "culture of light" at the global level, but this could still require ad hoc product lines to be designed specifically for non-European markets, which accounted for 25% of total revenues in 2011 (see Table 9.2).

Table 9.2 **Geographical areas of iGuzzini Illuminazione revenues (2010–2011) (€)**
Source: ISTAO

Revenues by area	31 December 2011	31 December 2010	Variation %
Italy	58,316,806	53,580,582	8.8%
EU	82,173,663	79,972,838	2.8%
Non EU	46,108,660	41,805,723	10.3%
Total revenues	186,599,129	175,359,143	6.4%

In large markets and those with strong growth (e.g. Brazil, China or India), quality standards do not yet match those in Europe, even in the high quality sector in which the company operates, and the demand there is not yet ready or evolved, despite the fact that avant-garde architecture is to be found there. It therefore becomes important to obtain up-to-date information and to make contacts and relationships with key specifiers, architects and opinion leaders with a view to designing products and services that are consistent with the maturity of the market, fully satisfying its demands as well as meeting hidden needs.

9.3.7 A family business and managerial enterprise: a successful team

We have spoken in broad terms about continuous innovation, the importance of design, and of internationalization as being among the strategic factors that have led to the success of iGuzzini, but one cannot omit one key organizational factor, namely the strong sense of belonging to the company. The creation of a successful organizational model has managed over the years to transform an entrepreneurial intuition into a successful experiment, ensuring its prosperity over the long term.

A first important step in this direction came in the early 1990s, with the transition from a family business to a managerial enterprise. The entrepreneurs delegated their management role to a pool of trusted managers, in order to devote more time to their role as "creators" and "trainers".

The organizational system that is based on an interfunctional type of model is supported by a significant human resources structure that handles growth, training and development of resources, both internally and in the branches. The IT function is also crucial for the coordination and interconnection of the different areas of the company. The various software systems adopted by iGuzzini were mostly developed internally, to ensure the maximum level of customization and flexibility, and were subsequently linked with the foreign branches in order to ensure effective internal communication.

Despite the fact that the location of the company and the infrastructure of the territory are not particularly favourable, iGuzzini manages to have broad appeal at the national and international level. Numerous collaborations have begun with Italian and foreign training institutes, enabling the enterprise to obtain high-level technical and managerial resources. There is a preference for recruiting young people who still have links with the territory, to ensure that loyalty is created over the long term. Job postings, job rotation and continuous training are among the key means used to ensure that more opportunities for employees are created.

The system of training and development of human resources developed by iGuzzini not only offers the opportunity to enhance specialist skills, but also aims to develop soft skills and management expertise at different levels of management. In 2010, the company delivered a total of 29,000 hours of training, funded for the most part. The training course for new recruits is standard. It is held in Recanati and is also available for personnel employed in the branches. Training activities are regularly outsourced.

9.3.8 New challenges on the global market

The matters discussed above highlight a number of key factors of change in the market which represent clear opportunities, but they may also represent threats – especially with regard to global competition – and they require the continuous rethinking of the company's strategic behaviour.

In particular the advent of LEDs from the technology point of view will change the balance on several fronts:

- **Supply chain**. A significant amount of LED production occurs in Asian countries, therefore the optimization of the logistics function and the strategic decisions made in terms of technology suppliers are increasingly becoming a key factor.

- **System of competition**. There is a significant threat that LED manufacturers and new "assemblers" will enter the lamp market, and this is gradually intensifying competition on the price front.

- **Organizational challenge**. The need to bring to market new LED technology products as well as to maintain existing products will generate management complexity in terms of production platforms and product warehousing.

At the same time, the growth in demand from Asian countries is forcing European companies to reposition themselves strategically; the decision to focus on the Chinese market for the last decade, with its dual status as target market and supply market, is currently of benefit to iGuzzini, but it is not sufficient for it to become leader in the new markets.

Currently the company's strategy is to differentiate itself by seeking to optimize its presence in more segments of the selected markets, including niche markets. The emergence of LED technology requires iGuzzini to review competitive levers and to reposition itself in an ideal equilibrium between quality and price. One of the challenges that the company is already facing is how to meet the demands for product customization required by customers while maintaining control over the growing complexity of the company's management structure.

The market spaces which the company has managed to conquer by focusing on the quality of the design/product and on the service (planning) must today be maintained and expanded. Communications policy must also be reviewed to make sure that it is consistent with the new strategies and the new image and perception of iGuzzini Illuminazione on the market.

Innovation, too, must also be focused in order to avoid dispersion of efforts especially in a declining market characterized by more intense competitiveness.

9.4 Conclusions

iGuzzini Illuminazione is now operating in a global environment subject to profound change. In particular, the theme of product innovation and the new market prospects offered by the altered global geographic-economic landscape are gradually changing the competitive environment, forcing industry players to redesign their medium- and long-term strategies.

There are numerous issues that face management and owners alike.

- How should iGuzzini tackle the challenges of the market, given that the technology landscape is constantly evolving?

- What will be the growth drivers for iGuzzini Illuminazione?

- How can one continue to follow a strategy of extreme differentiation in terms of products-markets while maintaining organizational and economic efficiencies? What can we learn, here, from the experience in China?

The development, success, identity and the organizational structure of iGuzzini Illuminazione in the near future will depend on the answers to these questions, and on the manner in which the company will decide to tackle the global market challenges identified in this case study.

References

CSIL (Centre for Industrial Studies) (2011). *The European Market for Lighting Systems*. Milan: CSIL.

Marchesi, F. (2002). *La Luce che Cura*. Milan: Tecniche Nuove.

10

After all the music. . .

. . .the repositioning of MTV Italia

Giulia Ferrari
SDA Bocconi School of Management, Italy

Dino Ruta
SDA Bocconi School of Management, Italy

Severino Salvemini
SDA Bocconi School of Management, Italy

In September 2008, Gian Paolo Tagliavia, Managing Director of MTV Italia, received the news that he would be named its future CEO. The top management changes began in July and portended the immediacy of the new strategic directions. MTV Italia had, in fact, been facing a scenario that undermined the business model on which the broadcaster had based its fortune since 1997: revenues from advertising that year recorded a first decline, and the internet and new technologies brought with them new distribution channels. MTV Italia therefore had to rethink its offer in order to remain fresh and contemporary, yet earn the trust and loyalty of its target audience and reaffirm its catalytic role in attracting their attention. The case describes the birth, success and evolution of the MTV phenomenon, both nationally and internationally, and offers several points for reflection on its strategic and organizational capabilities, and how to sustain competitive advantage through strategies and techniques that can evolve over time.

30 September 2008

Gian Paolo Tagliavia had been working until late August at his office in Corso Europa in Milan. Appointed Managing Director of MTV Italia[1] in July (after serving as Head of Online since 2005), he had to handle a full schedule for 2008/9, but he had wasted no time in drawing up strategic guidelines for the upcoming season. Now he could finally enjoy the summer holidays. He was about to leave for Sicily to go to the annual grape harvest at his father-in-law's winery, when a phone call disrupted both his vacation and work plans: Telecom Italia Media (which held a controlling interest of 51% in MTV Italia) had nominated him future CEO of MTV Italia. Looking for confirmation, Tagliavia called Antonio Campo Dall'Orto (CEO of MTV Italia from 1997 to 2008) who told him to open a bottle to celebrate. "Here's to you Gian Paolo! You are the right man in every way to be at the helm of the company!". . .

MTV is the number one brand in the world for youth entertainment, reaching more than half a billion households. The channel is the cultural home of the Millennial Generation, music fans and artists, and is a pioneer in creating innovative programming for young people. MTV reflects and creates pop culture with its Emmy,[2] Grammy,[3] and Peabody[4] award-winning content built around compelling storytelling, music discovery and activism that spans television, online and mobile platforms. MTV is a subsidiary of Viacom Media Networks,[5] along with Bet Networks, Bet, Addicting Games, CMT, Comedy Central, Game Trailers, Logo, MTV, MTV2, MTVU, Tr3s: MTV, Música y Más, Neopets, Nickelodeon, Nick Jr, Nick at Nite, Nick Toons, Parents Connect, Scratch, Shockwave, Spike, TeenNick, TV Land, VH1 and

---

1 In July 2008, Gian Paolo Tagliavia, Head of Multimedia and DTT at Telecom Italia Media, was nominated Managing Director of MTV Italia, under the CEO and Managing Director of MTV Europe, Antonio Campo Dall'Orto. Along with Tagliavia, two other managers were also promoted: Alberto Rossini moved from Head of Content for Telecom Italia Media to cover the same position for MTV Southern Europe; and Head of Talent and Music Luca De Gennaro expanded his territory from Italy to Southern Europe.

2 The Emmy is the most important international television award, dedicated to various sectors of the television industry including entertainment, news, documentaries and sport. Emmys are awarded annually during three separate ceremonies organized by three different organizations.

3 Grammy Awards are one of the most prestigious awards in the United States for achievements in the music industry, covering 105 different categories, subdivided over 30 musical genres from pop to gospel to hip-hop.

4 The George Foster Peabody Award (known simply as the Peabody Award) is an annual international award for excellence in radio and television broadcasting. The Peabody Award honours distinction and success in the United States in the fields of broadcast journalism, documentary filmmaking, educational programming and entertainment for teenagers.

5 Viacom Media Networks (formerly MTV Networks International – MTVNI) is owned by Viacom Inc.

VH1 Classic. After years of success and unstoppable geographic expansion, from 2007 to 2008 Viacom Media Networks experienced some changes: a drop in audience and consequently in revenues for MTV USA. Some national MTVs, including MTV Italia, also recorded their first negative figures. For some years, the content industries had been undergoing structural changes due to technological innovation, the evolution in consumer habits, the redefinition of competitive spaces and the explosion of distribution channels. The entrepreneurial momentum of market newcomers and incumbents led successful companies to reassess the sustainability of their offering and to rethink it from a strategic standpoint.

10.1 Background (1997–2002)

10.1.1 MTV in the US and geographic expansion

In 1981, Reagan succeeded Carter to become the 40th President of the United States of America, Metallica were born and Bob Marley and Rino Gaetano passed away, Pope John Paul II was seriously wounded in St Peter's Square, Coca-Cola opened its first factory in China and IBM launched its first personal computer. In August of the same year, the debut of MTV was announced by John Lack with the words "Ladies and gentlemen, rock and roll" played over footage of the first Space Shuttle mission, along with *Video Killed the Radio Star*, the music video by the Buggles. MTV, short for Music Television, was the first ever television channel dedicated to music. It was launched by Warner Amex Satellite Entertainment Company (WASEC), a joint venture between Warner Communications and American Express. The brains behind the new venture were John Lack, 35, Vice President and COO of WASEC; Bob Pittman, 27, Head of Programming and future CEO of MTV from 1983 to 1986; and Tom Freston, 36, the broadcaster's Head of Marketing, creator of the "I Want My MTV" campaign and CEO of MTV Networks from 1987 to 2004. Frank Olinsky designed the logo, an "M" in bold sans serif script and "TV" spray-painted on the right. When deciding which corporate colours to use, drawing inspiration from the world of graffiti and the idea that rock and roll is constantly changing, the network opted to allow the logo to be any colour or material. Since then generations of graphic designers have played with it. In 1984, the company was renamed MTV Networks (MTVN); in 1986, MTVN was acquired by Viacom Inc. (Viacom).

The channel's original format consisted of a combination of videos and VJs; that is, music videos produced by record companies for promotional aims presented by young video jockeys. Music genres ranged from new wave to hard rock and heavy metal (Adam Ant, Blondie, Eurythmics, Culture Club, Prince, Ultravox, Duran Duran, The Police, etc.), in addition to classic rock (David Bowie, Billy Joel, Rolling Stones, Rod Stewart, The Who and Dire Straits. (The single *Money for Nothing* by this last band referred to MTV in the lyrics, including the slogan "I Want My

MTV".[6]) Subsequently, MTV offered a combination of pop and hard rock, bringing together Metallica, Nirvana and Guns N' Roses with Michael Jackson and Madonna[7] and introduced genres such as hip-hop and rap. In 1985, the Video Hits One (VH1) channel was founded, broadcasting light popular music, rhythm and blues, jazz, country and classical music. At the same time, a new form of music video was emerging, one that was more creative, entertaining, artistic, experimental and technically complex than in the 1980s. Music video directors included the likes of Spike Jonze, Michel Gondry, David Fincher, Jonathan Glazer and others. MTV became a true "image factory".[8] In 1990, MTVN launched new channels (VH1 Classic, MTV2, UMTV, MTV Hits) featuring specific musical offerings, while the main channel, MTV, became less musical and started experimenting with unusual and innovative programmes: *Remote Control*, the reality show *Real World*, and the cartoons *Beavis and Butt-Head* and *Daria*.

In 1987 international expansion[9] began when MTVN launched MTV Europe, the first overseas channel, and created MTV Networks International (MTVNI) to run all overseas channels. Initially, MTV Europe replicated US programming, but soon (around the mid-1990s), MTVNI began to create separate channels in various European countries following a "think globally, act locally" policy; the basic formula was 30% joint programming and 70% diversified by country. While the company entered some countries independently, in others, such as Brazil and Italy, MTVNI relied on local partners. Although this decision carried strategic and operational risks, it also allowed better management of the production and programming of local content and penetration of markets that were less than enthusiastic about "made in the USA" globalization.[10] "MTV had to be indigenous to each marketplace. It would have the MTV look and feel, but with VJs from those countries and a playlist that appealed to the local audience" (Sara Levinson, Executive Vice President MTVN, 1990).

6 "I Want My MTV" was the first massive advertising campaign for MTV, launched in 1982. The strategy was to feature internationally renowned artists (David Bowie, The Police, Kiss, Culture Club, Billy Idol, Hall & Oates, Cyndi Lauper, Madonna, Lionel Richie, Ric Ocasek, John Mellencamp, Peter Wolf, Joe Elliott, Stevie Nicks, Rick Springfield and Mick Jagger). These artists would interact with the MTV on-air logo and encourage viewers to add MTV to the channels they watched.

7 On 2 December 1983 Michael Jackson's 14-minute-long *Thriller* video debuted on MTV. The following year, the channel produced the first MTV Video Music Awards (VMAs), showcasing Madonna's memorable performance of *Like a Virgin*.

8 http://www.youtube.com/watch?v=LATTM7DkvWo&feature=related

9 Beyond motivations deriving from its business strategies, a big push towards internationalization came from record companies. In fact, the recording world consisted of a few multinationals that produced almost all albums. So in the broadcaster's internationalization, record companies saw a chance to expand and coordinate the launch of music products on a global scale.

10 Twenty years after the debut of MTV Europe, MTVNI continued to develop its localization strategy. Bill Roedy, Vice President of MTVN, commented during the latest offering of MTV Arabia: "This will not be MTV USA. It is MTV Arabia produced by Arabs for Arabs."

10.1.2 The early years of MTV Italia

On 1 September 1997, the strategic turnaround of MTV Italia was put into effect with the decision to broadcast on the free television market. MTV Italia's music programming moved from Tele +3 (where it had been aired for 13 hours a day since October 1995) to the Rete A frequencies (covering 21 hours of daily air time). This completed the creation of MTV Italia, the only national MTV channel broadcast terrestrially. However, it was only on 1 May 2001 when MTV Italia, the result of a joint venture between Beta Television (51%) and Viacom (49%), found its true television home. After overcoming the risk of blackout due to the Maccanico Law,[11] which sparked a widespread protest,[12] MTV Italia moved from Rete A frequencies to Tmc2 (owned by Telecom Italia Spa). The CEO was Antonio Campo Dall'Orto (born in Conegliano, Italy in 1964). With a BA in Economics and a Master's in Business Communications, Dall'Orto was a former marketing consultant, assistant to Mediaset's Head of Sector Leonardo Pasquinelli, and later Assistant Director of Canale 5 under Giorgio Gori.[13]

In 1997, MTV Italia started broadcasting from London using Italian VJs.[14] In early 1999, 50% of the programming continued to come from London and the remainder consisted of Italian productions transmitted via satellite to London and then back to Rete A. By the end of the year, the entire production of MTV Italia moved to Cinevideo Studios in the suburbs of Milan.

10.1.2.1 The initial response

The first surveys that MTV Italia commissioned immediately revealed interesting data on usage and appeal. For example, 50% of viewers watched MTV at home, 29% at a friend's house and 21% in bars, clubs or gyms (CRA Nielsen, October 1998).[15] In addition, 93% of viewers liked the MTV Italia graphics, 88% said they loved the programmes, 86% the VJs, and 69% the programme promos (Eurisko, April 1999).

---

11 Law Number 249 of 31 July 1997: "Establishment of the communications and regulations governing telecommunications and broadcasting". The eponymous Maccanico Law aimed to provide more complete television communication legislation. It also addressed the antitrust issue, in accordance with the principles of pluralism previously established by the 1990 Mammì Law. In 1999, commercial television companies were invited to bid on concessions for broadcasting frequencies, but Rete A did not meet the two criteria of nationality and dominant influence.

12 Among the signatories of an open letter to save MTV Italia were Walter Veltroni, Giovanna Melandri, Jovanotti, Pino Daniele, Renzo Arbore, Fernanda Pivano, Ettore Scola, Romeo Gigli, Fulco Pratesi, Lucio Dalla, Sting and Madonna.

13 In 1989, Giorgio Gori was Head of Programming for the three Fininvest networks (Berlusconi Group). In 1991, when Fininvest established network departments, he became Director of Canale 5. In 2001, he founded Casa di Produzione Televisiva Magnolia (Magnolia Television Production House).

14 Administrative headquarters are in Milan.

15 http://www.nielsen.com/uk/en.html

Viewers were also asked how they accessed and exited MTV Italia. In terms of accessing the channel, 22% said they tuned in directly when they switched on their televisions and 17% watched MTV Italia when they had friends to dinner. As for the question "When you stop watching MTV what do you do?" 58% of respondents claimed they started zapping, 39% turned the TV off, and only 28% tuned in to other channels (Eurisko, 1999).

10.1.2.2 Organization and programming

Figure 10.1 illustrates the original structure of MTV Italia:

Figure 10.1 **MTV Italia organizational structure**

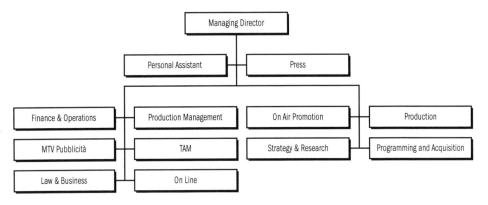

Programming and Acquisitions, headed by Alberto Rossini, was the department that planned the schedule, and purchased television shows and music programming. Rossini defined MTV Italia as a "program-centric" organization; the work of the other corporate departments depended on scheduling demands. MTV Italia's small physical structure fostered constant communication between managers. Even though the organization was built on a hierarchical structure, the different levels worked closely together. There was continuous interaction and collaboration between the highest level executives and people in lower positions. The company followed three criteria when setting up the programme schedule: first network identity, followed by cost control and finally audience maximization.

> The financial limitations, without a doubt, have an impact. I come from
> Mediaset[16] and I know the costs there and here. People at Mediaset don't

16 Mediaset, the first network of private broadcasters in Italy, consisted of Canale 5, Italy 1 and Rete 4, three analogue free-to-air national networks, funded entirely by advertising and managed exclusively by the distribution company Publitalia '80. By the 1990s, the three networks reached a total audience index equal to the three state networks, thanks to a wide variety of programmes, TG5 news directed by Enrico Mentana, and a new generation of successful presenters such as Gerry Scotti, Fiorello, Ezio Greggio, Marco Columbro, Lorella Cuccarini, Alberto Castagna, Amadeus, Simona Ventura and Maria De

believe that we produce our programming with such a small budget, and people working at MTV can't believe the programme costs of other [shows] ... there's no comparison. TRL, for example, is a programme where the writer, director and producer are the same person (Massimo Lopresti) and then there are four people who work with him, two are interns and two other junior staff members who came on board a year ago. This is a flagship afternoon program. . . made up of 5–6 people, of whom only one is an MTV veteran (Alberto Rossini, 2002).

Even the nature of MTV Italia's distribution (over the air) had an impact on the programming.

MTV UK, unlike MTV Italia, is nearly an all-music channel. This is because MTV UK is an encrypted satellite channel, so there isn't any issue about what other programmes potentially compete with it at any given hour. Having a larger spread, we absolutely have to take into account what other channels are doing at the same time: music alone is not enough. Our viewers zap through various channels, because they also want some entertainment. We face different scenarios because we are unencrypted. This is the fundamental difference (Stefano Orsucci, Head of Production, 2001).

Each local MTV channel was independent from the others in terms of programming: they could choose whether to import programmes designed by their sister companies, or adapt them, coproduce them or propose their own concepts to the network.[17] MTV Italia programmes could be produced in house or outsourced. The MTV Italia format was the outcome of ideas of various production teams. Once they proposed an idea, it was analysed by different producers in special meetings or creative conferences that took place at regular intervals (five times a year, one every two or three months). On average, out of ten proposed projects, only two or three were deemed feasible and a pilot episode was produced. If it was popular with viewers, then the show was continued.

In terms of the production and/or acquisition dichotomy, the programmes broadcast by MTV Italia between 2001 and 2002 can be classified as shown in Table 10.1.

Filippi. After 2000, with the debut in Italy of *Big Brother*, broadcast on Canale 5, and other innovative television formats, new and mostly female faces joined the network such as Daria Bignardi, Barbara D'Urso, Alessia Marcuzzi, Federica Panicucci and Michelle Hunziker. Since 1999, Mediaset has been present in the multimedia sector through the internet with a range of services available on the www.mediaset.it portal (formerly called MOL – Mediaset On Line): free and exclusive high quality videos (Video Mediaset), news (TGcom) and sports (Sport Mediaset), e-commerce (Mediashopping), a network community, mobile phone services and corporate information (Qui Mediaset).

17   MTV Italia designed shows such as *Web Chart* and *Stylissimo* that were exported elsewhere; the Italian broadcaster also acquired some TV series and Japanese cartoons that had never been aired before by other MTVs.

Table 10.1 **MTV Italia programme classification**

Acquired programmes	Imported and modified formats	MTV Italia format
Hit List Espana	Total Request Live - TRL	Ca' Volo
Hit List UK	Mad 4 Hits	Sexy Dolls
US Top 20	Select	Sonic
Superock	Brand: new	Stylissimo
Yo!	Dance Floor Chart	Singles
Cartoons	Hit List Italia	Loveline
Undressed	Week In Rock	Kitchen
Jackass	Say What?	Romalive
Becoming	Videoclash	MTV Trip

The distinctive features of MTV Italia emerged from the vertical and horizontal programming flow: original, innovative products with fragmented formats (most shows were made up of different theme-based "units" tied together by VJs); interactivity and an international focus;[18] and aestheticism (MTV was the epicentre of the company image and again this depended on its importance in youth culture). The most popular programmes included *Select, Kitchen, Sushi* and *TRL*. For example, guest cooks who appeared on *Kitchen* included TV host Maurizio Costanzo, skier Alberto Tomba, singer Jovanotti, Formula One driver Eddie Irvine, actress Veronica Pivetti, actor-director Maurizio Nichetti, and many others.[19] The talk show's format was consolidated, but its immediacy and attention to detail made the show stand out among national television programmes. The day's guests were invited to talk about themselves through their work and their projects, between frying onions and preparing a stir-fry. Andrea Pezzi hosted both *Kitchen* and *Sushi*.

> On MTV, *Sushi* is a brand new program, prepared by Andrea Pezzi... The guy is a driving force for MTV. Television that's...musical, practical, trendy, not at all conservative and woe if it were, malleable and susceptible to the demands of time. MTV is risking and rising. *Sushi* is on Friday nights at 9 pm – bedlam TV. A handful of talk shows, a slice of live music, two pinches of sit-com. A loft studio on two floors. Upstairs they talk, downstairs they play. *Sushi*, you can even try to eat it. It goes beyond the usual stuff (*Il Messaggero*, Veneto, 11 April 1999).

18 As in the case with its sister stations, at MTV Italia nothing was left to chance; the identity of the channel emerged in even the smallest details. Commercial breaks, for example, largely consisted of three types of ads: commercial products, programme promos and idents (one of the first idents for MTV Italia was "No sense makes sense on MTV").
19 The then mayor of Rome, Francesco Rutelli, was invited to the Kitchen and started preparing a mozzarella and tomato salad. The show's producer, Peruzzo, decided to suspend the episode for the sake of ensuring political opponents equal air time. In this case, he wanted to give Berlusconi the chance to decide whether he would go to the TV kitchen to be interviewed by Pezzi.

> With MTV's *TRL*, we've fully achieved the mission that represents the
> foundation of the broadcaster's philosophy: think globally, act locally. . .
> The key to the programme is input from young viewers, which is inter-
> esting because while video clips are being played, text messages sent in
> by young people are continuously scrolling at the bottom of the screen.
> They comment, seriously or ironically, bringing up fragments of their life
> experiences. The studio is a place of passage, overlooking the metropolis.
> A video clip itself is a kaleidoscope of a thousand meanings, a thousand
> threads of thought. *TRL* offers a local spin on a global product (*Corriere
> della Sera*, 4 July 2000).

10.1.2.3 The people

Most of the people at MTV are under 30, working at their first job; their training
generally takes place abroad, mainly in London. MTV employees have a strong
sense of belonging to the company.

> Age is an essential prerequisite for people who join in this adventure. Since
> we know exactly who our audience is, it would be disastrous if the person
> talking to our viewers was a fake youngster or was unable to inspire in
> teenagers that "wannabe" attitude they need to have if they're going to
> listen, watch, and follow (Antonio Campo Dall'Orto, 1999).

> There is a strong sense of belonging, attention to the brand not in terms
> of commercial value, but in being MTV. It's really great. Sometimes it goes
> overboard, and that can lead to a narrow-minded attitude, but there is
> passion, we all love music. It is a very open and democratic environment,
> the work is not hyper-fragmented or standardized, everybody does a lit-
> tle of everything because it's a small company. I myself am involved in
> music programming and scheduling, I work very closely with marketing
> and research, I look at the research findings, and so on. It is a very cohe-
> sive environment, there are no wars here between departments because it
> is a small ship and if there is fire anywhere on board, the whole ship sinks
> (Alberto Rossini, 2001).

> The point of living in London is to train people, and part of that is putting
> them in contact with other MTVs. Here you can compare yourself with
> others, see what they do, what has been done up to now; you can learn
> a certain kind of language that has always existed at MTV, a certain style,
> a certain standard, and how to use certain equipment. We want people
> to have an international approach. For example, you can tell that *Viva* is
> made by Italian set designers who have always worked in Italy (Orsucci,
> 2001).

This applied to people who worked both behind the scenes and in front of the
cameras, the faces of MTV. Many of the members of MTV Italia's VJ team were under
25, almost all were university graduates, and some were working in television for
the first time. Camila Raznovich (Milan, 1974) was one of the first presenters hired
to work at MTV Italia, after three years of hosting MTV Europe; *Loveline* (2002) was
her programme. Enrico Silvestrin (Rome, 1972) was also one of the faces of MTV

Europe; in Italy, he anchored various programmes including *Sonic*. After presenting *Serenate* on Rai 2 (writer Fabio Fazio), Andrea Pezzi (Ravenna, 1973) moved to MTV with the programmes *Hot, Tokusho, Sushi* and *Kitchen*. He immediately became the most popular (and respected) face of MTV. In February 2002, he started playing the lead in the MTV sitcom *Bradipo*; he has also worked as a writer and presenter for Italia 1. Victoria Cabello (London, 1975), had been a presenter on MTV since 1997 and special correspondent for MTV Italia to the annual MTV Europe Music Awards, where she interviewed celebrities on the red carpet.[20] She also covered the 2000 edition of the MTV Video Music Awards from New York and the MTV Movie Awards in Los Angeles. Beyond individual presenters, there were also many artistic duos at the network: Marco Maccarini (Turin, 1976) and Giorgia Surina (Milan, 1975), first for *Select* from London then for *TRL*; Kris Grove (Pittsburgh, 1971) and Kris Reichert (Toronto, 1972); Francesco Mandelli (Erbe, 1979) and Fabrizio Biggio (Florence, 1974); Luca Bizzarri (Genoa, 1971) and Paolo Kessisoglu (Genoa, 1969).[21]

10.1.2.4 The competition

MTV Italia's television competition came from three fronts: Italian general channels Italia 1 and Rai 2, which targeted a similar segment of the audience; different types of theme-based channels (entertainment, documentary),[22] since music was not the sole interest of the target audience (14–34 year-olds); and other music channels, some of which, with respect to MTV, had a different focus, different programming style, different interfaces, etc.[23]

20 On assignment abroad she played the role of interviewer and tormentor of movie stars and artists: she gave a cake to Jennifer Lopez, kissed Richard Gere on the mouth, jumped into the arms of George Clooney, and greeted Ricky Martin Eskimo style.

21 MTV presenters included Daniele Bossari (Milan, 1974), Valeria Bilello (Sciacca, 1982), Massimo Coppola (Salerno, 1972, programme: *Brand: New*), Giampietro Cutrino nicknamed Gip (Padua, 1974, MTV programme: *Mad*), Paola Maugeri (Rome, 1971, programme: *A Night With*), Giorgio Pasotti (Bergamo, 1973), Cristiana "Nanà" Paolucci and Fabio Volo (Bergamo, 1972, programme: *Ca'Volo*).

22 The competition from these channels intensified especially with the advent of Sky Italy (2003) and even more so with the switch to digital terrestrial television (2004).

23 102.5 Hit Channel (unencrypted satellite), COUNT DOWN (unencrypted satellite, whose target and programme themes were very close to MTV's), DEEJAY TV (first television experience of the publishing group L'Espresso, adaption of the radio network, first in Italy in terms of audience among private stations), MAGIC (with particular attention to video clips from the past), MATCH MUSIC (with an accent on "Made in Italy"), ROCK TV (pay-to-view locally transmitted on the D+ digital platform), VIDEO ITALY (unencrypted, television adaption of Radio Italy), VIVARETEA (unencrypted and transmitted on network frequencies). While MTV Italia was relocating to TMC2, Rete A was awarded the concession to host *Viva*. The *Viva* broadcaster, based in Cologne, offered young, trendy music and signed an agreement with Rete A. In the spring of 2001, it started broadcasting in Italy, replacing MTV's schedule. Less than a year after it was launched, MTV's main rival went off the air.

The competition prompted us to rethink the programming focus of the entire network and we are now much stronger. The events in Genoa and 11 September also contributed; we reconsidered our relationship with the public, our way of doing TV, which we've had to adapt to make it a little less lightweight. We are still music television, but we've made room in our programming for analyses, current events, problems that young people are facing, sex. Italian TV? It doesn't offer anything new. We are what's new. We are the only ones who focus on kids and young people. Over the past 10 years, the major networks have moved farther and farther away from the under-35s, losing the only segment of the public that allows us to stay in touch with today's culture (Antonio Campo Dall'Orto, 2002).

10.1.2.5 The events

On 18 September 1998 the first ever MTV Day was held at the Arena Parco Nord in Bologna. Performers included 99 Posse, Blindosbarra, Bluvertigo, Elisa, Marlene Kuntz, Mau Mau, Neffa, Prozac+ and Ustmamò. The turnout exceeded all expectations and Luca De Gennaro (Artistic Director of MTV Italia) lists this as one of the most satisfying moments of his career. Exactly 365 days after this successful debut, the second MTV Day took place, which ran from 3 pm to past midnight and attracted over 60,000 spectators. Since then, every year MTV Italia never fails to celebrate its birthday,[24] enriching the festival to turn it into a platform for disseminating messages to younger generations, most importantly discouraging them from taking Ecstasy.

MTV's audience loves music and listens to everything you have to offer, beyond the hits. . . At certain events, the venue and the equipment aren't good enough so I prefer to lip sync, but in Bologna, everything is highly professional. For example, Director Niki Parsons listened to our CD for a month to get an idea of the best way to shoot our performance (Morgan, lead singer of Bluvertigo, 2000).

10.1.2.6 The web

An essential tool for presenting MTV Italia's identity was the web. In November 1998, taking advantage of the promotional campaign for the MTV Europe Music Awards in Milan, the first MTV Italia website was launched (www.mtv.it). In 1999, the first human resources dedicated to the internet joined the ranks of MTV. They worked in the strategy & research department, coordinating product development with an external agency. The initial mission of the site was to provide a virtual space to foster real contact with the target audience, focusing on areas such as interactive chat rooms. The first initiative was also launched to integrate the TV site with the

---

24 The only exception was 2001. Following the terrorist attacks of 11 September 2001 in the USA, MTV Day was cancelled. This event also spurred MTV Italia to add a new element to its identity, an interest in current affairs.

web chart, the ranking system generated by online voting. From 2000 to 2002, the site was progressively structured along two main lines: interactivity and content. The first was increasingly developed within the MTV Community through interactive programmes such as *Select* and *TRL*, which had strong online integration and were the first shows to offer voting and commenting via text on live TV. In terms of content, departments dedicated to web programmes were established, with initial investments following MTV Italia's programming approach. MTV.it became an important musical reference, investing in up-to-the-minute news, creating an artist archive and offering premiere video content and online music exclusives. At the same time, the website team grew and began to specialize in two areas: product development and content, and business; technical development was still outsourced. Advertising revenues became more structured and new business activities started up, aimed at the mobile telephone and broadband services in particular. The first agreements with telecom operators were made (news service via SMS and MMS, production of logos and ringtones, interactive services on air) and MTV developed the first MTV LIVE broadband product. The growth in business and revenues also generated the need for a more structured organization. Starting in 2001, digital activities were grouped into the Online Division, led by Gian Paolo Tagliavia, previously Head of Agencies at MTV Pubblicità.

Tagliavia identified his staff as one of the site's strengths:

> There is no shortage of ideas, also because the people who work in our department, like those who work at MTV in general, are people who we have the presumption to consider better than average, not because they have bigger brains or better taste, but because their level of commitment to what they do is much higher than any other kind of work (Gian Paolo Tagliavia, 2001).

10.1.3 Success

MTV did not kill the radio stars: it reinforced their global success, energizing the rock and roll culture, and giving singers greater visibility. Yet MTV had an even greater impact on culture, influencing music, fashion, politics, art, advertising, television and the film industry.

In 2001, MTV entered 84.6 million homes in North America, 28.1 in Latin America, 124.1 in Europe and 137.9 million in Asia. The US saw a 5% rise in revenues, while MTVNI achieved around a 19% increase (US$600 million), with the best results in Mexico (27%), and Russia and China (80%). According to an analysis by Merrill Lynch & Co., these figures would double by 2004 (*Bloomberg Business Magazine*, 2002). MTV also started gambling on emerging technologies. In Scandinavia, MTV Live debuted, which allowed viewers to enjoy virtual games such as "Trash Your Hotel Room" (users could become rock stars and virtually destroy a hotel room). In July 2000, MTV Asia launched LiLi, a virtual VJ who interacted with the audience both on-air and online in five different Asian languages. LiLi became so famous that Ericsson started marketing a line of mobile phones inspired by her. In Japan, a wireless MTV internet service allowed users to download entertainment news, vote for their favourite VJ and choose the music they wanted to hear.

There was success and innovation for MTV Italia too. Viewers doubled in two years, and advertising revenues in 2002 jumped by 11% compared with the national market, which according to Nielsen, would lose 3.1%. These were the essential items in the 2002 MTV Italia budget presented by Giorgio Ferrari, General Manager of MTV Pubblicità. As for ratings, MTV Italia decided not to make Auditel data public. Instead the company commissioned Abacus to carry out a viewer survey in the second and third week of November. Results counted average daily contacts of 8,229,000 units, compared with 7,233,000 in May 2001 and weekly contacts totalling 14,297,000 (+9%); 40% of viewers watched MTV every day, 11% watched 4 or 5 times a week. Advertising revenues for 2002 amounted to €48 million (of which €1.5 million were obtained online), in part thanks to innovative marketing, also linked to events and sponsorship. A total of 450 brands invested in MTV Italia.

MTV Italia established itself as the most important channel in the MTV Europe network, second in the world after the United States in terms of number of viewers and financial size. According to company management, the key to success was having built a rich and varied network identity in five years. The result was an "eclectic" television line-up that offered plenty of music as well as a number of original formats spanning sitcoms, comedy and musical entertainment, in addition to talk shows, cartoons and four series that were the most talked-about foreign TV shows of their day.[25] The MTV Italia line-up cost €22 million in 2002, and offered 5 hours of live TV every day. The programming schedule was in constant synergy with the network's www.mtv.it website, which counted 400,000 visitors and 25 million page views per month.

> We would like to enrich our programming and add shows and crazy-surreal fictional entertainment. Monty Python genre, although there's nothing like it. We already know that people will criticize us and say that these are stupid programmes, too provocative, but we want to break away from the rest of the TV panorama. If you hit channel 7 or 8, or wherever MTV is on your remote control, you know straight away that you're watching something different, something you can't see on RAI or Mediaset. We come from a season where the other TV stations, due to budget cuts, have avoided experimenting and have become even more homogeneous (Campo Dall'Orto, 2002).

25 *The Osbournes*, a sort of hard rock version of *Big Brother* where the cameras followed the family life of Black Sabbath's lead singer for 24 hours a day, *The Andy Dick Show*, *Banzai* and *Pets*.

10.2 The new millennium: an evolving market

The new millennium began with a sharp discontinuity in the relationship between MTV and the outside world. In fact, on one hand, MTV affected cultures and habits, on the other, the new generation along with cutting-edge media and technology affected the strategies and actions of the broadcaster.

10.2.1 Consumption that needs to be interpreted

"Today research means inspiration. That's where we start. It gives shape to our strategies. It gives shape to both the business side and to the creative side. It shapes our brand and inspires content and marketing" (Bob Bakish, President and CEO of Viacom International Media Network, 2011).

MTVN and MTVNI based their offerings on ad hoc research into their target audience. In fact, the regionalization strategy of MTVNI and the genesis of MTV Italia in 1997 were both based on the findings from Turned On Europe, a broad sociological survey of young people across European borders. Likewise, the whole history of MTVN and of the various local MTVs was guided by periodic studies. For example, MTV Lab, the research observatory of MTV Italia, constantly monitored young people in relation to both broad social issues and their relationship with the world of MTV. Among recent surveys, the most extensive were:

- Ragazzi Perbene (Italian study, 2004)

- Senza Te (Italian study, 2005)

- Circuit of Cool (international study, 2006)

- Beta Life (international study, 2007)

- 10 Years Young (Italian study, 2007)

- Youthopia (international study, 2009)

- We are Millennials: the International MTV Brand Study (international study, 2011)

10 Years Young was a study comparing Turned On Europe findings with 14- to 24-year-old Italians ten years later. The Turned On Europe methodology consisted of conducting 1,200 face-to-face interviews with 14- to 24-year-olds in six European countries. Ten years later a similar study was conducted to reveal the differences in attitudes and values acquired over a decade, across a spectrum of topics (family, sex, money, politics, religion, transgression, school, work, fears, dreams, the future and MTV). The methodology here involved 600 CATI (computer-assisted telephone interviews) with 14- to 24-year-olds, a representative sample of the Italian population, with 26 ethnographic sessions in Rome and Milan. The participants in this study were teenagers in the first decade of the 21st century: the children of baby boomers facing a world that witnessed 9/11. They were called on to live in a

risk-laden society, and they were gearing up to do so. This was the Me Generation described by Jean M. Twenge (2007): a generation that had never known a world that put "duty" before "self". They believed that the needs of the individual should come first (but this wasn't a question of being selfish; instead their catchphrases were "be yourself", "believe in yourself", "you must love yourself before you can love someone else"). They were individuals first, before being part of a greater whole. To think of themselves collectively, they needed a virtual filter; they need file sharing and a story on a blog where the internet dissolves private spheres. They rejected the passivity of listening; they were good at defending themselves, floating quietly along on the surface; they understood the profound power of the horizontal society that sustained them and they reclaimed the right to make their own decisions: by uploading themselves and their lives (exaggerating only occasionally). They transitioned from using words to convey an ideal to using technology as a tool for building collective consciousness, which for the first time they produced themselves.

We are Millennials: the International MTV Brand Study defined the key features of the segment of the public that MTV was targeting: teenagers. The Millennials are the evolution of the Me Generation: born between the 1980s and 1990s, 100% digital natives, and three times more numerous than the generation that came before them, Generation X. MTV attempted to narrate how dreams, lives and habits have changed through a survey conducted in 15 different countries (6,500 young people contacted through TV, questionnaires, forums and focus groups). The results were surprising: mental and physical boundaries no longer existed; they'd been eliminated by Facebook, Twitter, and YouTube. Millennials are projected towards the future; always connected, attached to their unconventional families, ready to get involved to do good. They dream of happiness and success, believe that love, truth and faith are more important than old-fashioned clichés such as "sex, drugs and rock & roll". They are 80 million strong, hyper-connected and informed like never before. They are determined individualists, but compared with the generation that preceded them they are far more attentive to the common good. They have no desire to rebel, but they are convinced they will change society. For the time being Millennials have debunked the predictions of those who feared that technology would isolate them from the world. In fact, the exact opposite is true. "Only when the Millennials go into politics," prophesied the economist Jeffrey Sachs (2011), "will things change."

10.2.1.1 The network

If all the activities of Millennials were added together, we would find that their day does not last 24 hours but 30. This is the effect of multitasking, which means doing two or more things at the same time. Here are some telling statistics: 41% preferred to stay at home rather than go on vacation and give up the internet; 63% would consider a day without social networking "a nightmare"; one in three would become anxious if they couldn't check their email every 24 hours. A young person between 12 and 24 years of age participates in at least 48 digital conversations per day; 34% send text messages to friends in the next room. Even TV was social: they watch alone, but comment collectively ("When people watch television they always have a mobile device with them," stated Google CEO Eric Schmidt.)

10.2.1.2 The common good

Millennials have little faith in politicians, and 80% said they admired "people who follow their dreams". There are some similarities between the generation of 1968 protesters and Millennials: children of an economic and demographic boom, they've invented a new language; they can communicate faster and faster. They engage outside of political parties, as confirmed by experiments such as Anonymous, Occupy Wall Street and Indignados (2011–2012). Responding to the question about who their idols were, many said, anyone who could find a job today. In contrast to their 1968 counterparts, they aren't dreaming of utopia; they are reformers rather than revolutionaries, with their feet on the ground and their eyes on their smartphones.

10.2.1.3 Their models

For 77% of respondents, their model was their mother, then their father, then friends. On their bedroom walls they hang pictures of their parents, reflecting the fact that families, as non-traditional as they may be, still continue to represent a fortress, a safe space. In fact, building a traditional family was an important goal for 75% of the young people surveyed. Models outside the family are few. Those mentioned include Barack Obama and his communicative power, Mark Zuckerberg and his instinct, Lady Gaga and her role as a global icon, because she celebrates defects and even with her outrageous costumes, manages to remain authentic. Authenticity is an indispensable value for 81% of young people. Millennials are the first global generation; their values, habits and ways of thinking converge on every continent. But they are not a tribe; they take the lead in social change, they realized much earlier than previous generations that nothing stays the same, everything is moving and it is in this movement that they claim their rights and the chance to express themselves. "The 'M' is for Millennials" – the headline of a *TIME*[26] magazine article on MTV (Poniewozik, 2009) – a reality that has certainly helped shape the profile of this generation.

26 On 8 February 2010, for the first time, the new logo of the network appeared on the MTV USA website without the words "music television". Since then, the restyling of the brand has been extended to all international companies of the group, including MTV Italia. The old logo has been replaced by two new icons, one black on a white background and the other white on black. The new design reflects the gradual but decisive shift in the focus of programming from music to other forms of entertainment. TRL has been cancelled, and the broadcaster's new programmes include reality shows such as *Jersey Shore* and *The Hills*.

What MTV has done for twenty-five years now is to unite the suburb with the city, the country with the metropolis, America with the rest of the world. It has spoken to the youth of the globe, to white kids and black kids. After MTV, lying is no longer possible, you can't tell the difference between races. They, the young people of today, know nothing is true. Up to two or three generations ago it was different, the kids, the vast majority of youngsters, lived in their own little world, perhaps in the deep countryside of America or in some country at the end of the earth. They were separated from everything, far away from contact with others. You could tell these kids anything, they would have believed it. . . I strongly believe that the wonderful fact that a black guy, Barack Obama, has become president of the United States of America, and the artistic blending, the cultural exchange that this television has exposed to the young has played a great role (Will Smith, American actor, 2009).

10.2.2 The digital revolution

On 15 June 2000 in Sun Valley, Idaho (USA), the five majors[27] of the record industry refused an offer from Napster, the website that allowed users to download music illegally for free. Napster shut down the following year, but the majors certainly did not get what they had hoped for; putting an end to file sharing was still wishful thinking. The internet, the proliferation of compressed and downloadable music files, the boom in websites for free file sharing (first and foremost Napster and LimeWire), the emergence of MP3 players and the development of a number of peer-to-peer networks (P2P) – all of these factors radically transformed the market. Amazon was already an active player; iTunes was in the pipeline. Consumers were rapidly embracing the opportunities offered by new technologies and CD sales continued to decline.

In 2003 in Italy, a working agreement was signed between the music industry and distribution to help relaunch the sector. The organizations at the table were FIMI (Italian Music Industry Federation) and members of Confindustria,[28] ANCRA/Confcommercio, FISMED/Confesercenti and Vendomusica, respectively trade associations representing production and distribution in the recording industry. Recognizing the crisis plaguing the music industry, the particularly negative economic situation that was stunting growth, and the uncontrollable proliferation of digital piracy, these parties signed a memorandum of understanding to launch joint action at the national and European level. Both MTVN and MTV Italia found themselves facing financially debilitated stakeholders, who were certainly in no position to promote and invest in what these television channels were offering them, much less able to provide support and incentives.

In addition to Napster and similar sites that followed, another virtual reservoir appeared soon afterwards that revolutionized the habits of many internet users:

27 Universal, Sony, EMI, Warner and BMG.
28 Italian Manufacturers' Association

YouTube. This online platform was established in February 2005, enabling users to share videos for free, using Adobe Flash technology to play content. The aim was to host videos made directly by the people who uploaded them, but also to offer access to third-party material uploaded without permission. Thus, the same videos that MTV offered on a rolling basis and framed in ad hoc programmes were now accessible on the internet on demand. In June 2006, the company announced that around 100 million videos were viewed daily, with 65,000 new videos added every 24 hours. The same year, *TIME* magazine elected YouTube "Person of the Year".

> MTV now has a terrible competitor. Not the other themed networks dedicated to young people and music but rather the Network, with a capital N. MTV suffers from the same disease that record companies have suffered from since young people learned to download music from the internet, view their videos, and build a sort of personal program schedule. The greatest effort now that MTV has to make is to free itself from the curse of "background television": turn it on, listen, do something else, as if MTV were a radio. Is it worth keeping a network like this, among the generalists? (Grasso, 2007)

10.3 M: multi-channelling and Millennials (2002–2007)

10.3.1 Investments by Viacom and MTVNI

The first five years of the new century saw Viacom engaged on multiple fronts. Their strategy was to make the new television's three points of strength their own: convergence with the web; programmes on demand; and space for user-generated content. Tom Freston was initially the strategist. One of the founders of MTV, President and CEO of MTVN for 17 years, Freston contributed to the geographical expansion and penetration of the network; he had an animation studio built and developed digital products, services and business. Appointed Co-President and Co-COO of Viacom in 2004, Freston oversaw MTVN, Paramount Pictures, Famous Music Publishing and Simon & Schuster, and was paid $20 million (in salary and bonuses) plus $32 million in stock options in 2004 (the last year in which data on remuneration was made public). Freston was tasked with keeping Viacom "hip, happy and hot"; that is, growing the group in television, internet and telephony, staying creative while managing the transition towards new media and convincing the biggest sceptics on Wall Street. Revenues from digital media, around $150 million in 2005, would reach $500 million in 2008, according to Viacom estimates.

"We will live or die in this next phase. We go from being TV-centric to brand-centric. Our brands have to prosper on every platform that's out there – TV, digital TV, online, wireless, video on demand, and so forth. We've got to prosper or else" (Tom Freston, 2006).

MTVNI first focused on mobile telephony, making 67 offers to operators around the world to provide content via mobile phones, from music videos to sitcoms. Since 2005, integrated activity on air, mobile and WAP, has allowed young people across Europe to download part of the content of MTVNI.[29] "[The mobile] will be a big, big and compelling screen for our audience" (Jason Hirschhorn, Chief Digital Officer of MTVN, 2005).

The Freston era was marked by a positive, shared corporate culture. MTVN had a reputation as a great place to work, where creative minds enjoyed freedom and rewards in the form of generous compensation. Freston's inner circle included Judy McGrath,[30] Chair; Van Toffler, President; Cyma Zargami, Head of Nickelodeon; Bill Roedy at MTVNI; and Doug Herzog, who oversaw TV Land, Spike, and Comedy Central. This team of managers had been with the company since the 1980s. Herzog (who left for a time to work for Rupert Murdoch and Barry Diller) confirmed: "MTVN has created and nurtured the best creative culture in the field, without exception."

> I've never been as jazzed or as excited or as optimistic as I am right now. I look at the Internet and the whole digital interactive world as an amazing opportunity for us. We are the kings of the short attention span (Freston, 2006).

The event that led Freston to lose not only his credibility as a strategist but also his job was his hesitation in acquiring Myspace, the social network in vogue at the time. Rupert Murdoch's News Corporation did so instead for $580 million. The 20% drop in the price of Viacom shares in the first half of 2006 was attributed to this missed opportunity. In September of the same year, Sumner Redstone (Chairman of Viacom) fired Freston, one of the pillars of Viacom and MTVN.[31] In fact it was Myspace that revealed MTV's weakness on the web: despite the music videos, the powerful brand and deep connections with its audience, it was not as attractive as it should have been. MTV may have been the king of the short attention span, but young people on the internet were especially interested in connecting and interacting with each other, creating new material together and circulating professionally produced content (without worrying about copyright). In January 2006 MTV. it

29 MTVNI and Motorola presented MTV Load, an additional phase in the global collaboration that Motorola signed with MTVNI as well as one of the most important and significant marketing operations between the two international companies.
30 McGrath was known for her ability to manage talent and the chaos generated in creative industries. In 2006, *Business Week* reported some commandments from her bible: "Listen to all your people. Make change part of your DNA. It is not companies that innovate, but people. Use research as a tool for creativity" (*Business Week*, 2006).
31 "Absolutely, there were geysers like Friendster and Myspace," said Hirschhorn, Chief Digital Officer at MTVN, a few months after the failed acquisition. "But we can't chase everything that is desirable: if you look at all potential goldmines on the internet over the years, many of them no longer exist." Myspace was sold in 2012 by News Corp for $35 million.

reached around 7.5 million individual users (Nielsen/Net Ratings) compared with almost 30 million for Myspace. This was the new 12- to 24-year-old audience: "Generation P" – called the programmer generation because they want to customize their entertainment.

Top management realized there was no more time to waste. So they appointed Mika Salmi (guru of Silicon Valley, Founder and CEO of Atom Entertainment, the online games site acquired by MTVN) as President of Global Digital Media. The aim was to develop what the company called "a world of exciting games, music, entertainment and a meeting place for young audiences". Thanks to Salmi, the music network became the online leader: MTV and associated trademarks had over 300 websites, including some of the 30 richest broadband sites. With 90 million visitors in 2007, advertisers were enthusiastic. One of the first acquisitions was the video entertainment site iFilm ($49 million), focusing on professional videos and users.

A much more sizeable portion of MTVN resources was absorbed by the new frontiers of video games. In 2005, the company poured $160 million into the Neopets site, a virtual community that everyone could join and create their own virtual pet. Next in line was the GameTrailers website. In addition, MTVN, together with producer Jerry Bruckheimer, founded a studio for creating video games, and bought Harmonix for $175 million. Music video games were the lifeline for a music industry in decline (as much if not more so than digital music sales).[32] In fact, they appeared to be a veritable gold mine. Red Octane, which held the rights to Guitar Hero, was bought by Activision for $100 million, and the Beatles became a video game.[33] Guns N' Roses made their comeback on the music scene with their new original album, *Chinese Democracy*, which fans had been waiting for for 17 years. Prior to its release, the single "Shackler's Revenge" premiered on the Rock Band 2 video game produced by MTV. In less than a year (November 2007 – July 2008), Rock Band sold 3.4 million copies in the United States. The winning move was selling individual songs to players for about $2 each; during the same period, the company sold 21 million, with an average of six songs per player.[34] At the same time, to tap the "P" side of the target generation, MTVN started creating a series of vertical sites. The goal was no longer to capture the attention of the entire audience, but instead to attract only people who were really interested in a specific topic. For

32 An example: in June 2008, Mötley Crüe launched the single *Saints of Los Angeles*; during the first week on iTunes, Apple's online store, 14,000 copies were sold. Instead with Rock Band, offered through the Xbox Live service, the song sold more than three times that number (48,000). This despite the fact that individual tracks sold for twice as much on average for video games compared with MP3 songs ($2 vs. $1). However, the music video games industry, which seemed destined for a bright future, instead plunged into a deep crisis due to saturation in the hardware market. Turnover fell from $1.5 billion in the US alone in 2008 to $875 million in 2009, while 2010 figures showed a further drop of 50%. That same year, Viacom sold Harmonix.

33 The Beatles: Rock Band is a music video game developed by Harmonix Music System for MTV Games.

34 iPod owners, in comparison, bought an average of 20 songs per iPod (for half the price).

example, the dance.mtv.com site was designed along the lines of MTVN's *America's Best Dance Crew* programme; users could upload videos of amateur dancers showing off their moves. Also, on mysupersweetparty.com, inspired by episodes of *My Super Sweet 16*, users could plan their birthday parties and make wish lists for gifts and clothes. In 2008, MTVN operated around 50 such vertical sites. The model was to realize an idea quickly using Web 2.0 technology and, ultimately to promote or eliminate sites depending on how they performed. The barriers to entry were low: less than six weeks and less than $50,000 per site, outsourcing to Russia, Argentina, Israel and India.

Meanwhile, Viacom was engaged in waging war on iTunes and YouTube. In 2006, thanks to a historic agreement between Microsoft and MTV, Urge was created, also known as the iTunes-killer. Born from a partnership between the two giants, in addition to the collaboration of CMT (Country Music Television) and WH1, Urge was one of the most visited music sites in the network with very similar functioning to that of rival iTunes.[35] Next it was YouTube's turn, when Viacom sued Google and its subsidiary YouTube, demanding $1 billion in compensation for the continuous and systematic violation of copyright.[36]

However, the investments outlined above were not enough and music on television (video clips and shows) stopped attracting audiences. A telling example: the 17th annual MTV Movie Awards (California, 1 June 2008) reached about 3 million viewers, 18% less than the previous year and about half the audience of a few years earlier. What's more, a significant number of fans watched the show presented by Mike Myers online but not on MTV.com.

35 The offer consisted of 2 million audio files, 100,000 concerts, 18 music genres and 500 original playlists, more than 130 radio stations, music programmes created ad hoc, 25 music blogs, an archive of interviews, biographies and exclusive material as well as the possibility to send your favourite music directly to your PC and portable player. For $14.95 per month, Urge allowed users to view and download anything. Thanks to Genus technology, if payment stopped, the songs and videos disappeared from the device, but as soon payment restarted, the same content "magically" reappeared.

36 In March 2007, Viacom filed suit with the Federal Court of the Southern District of New York alleging that the search engine and its newly acquired video community had posted at least 160,000 movies (with 1.5 billion views) without permission. The aim was to stop Google and YouTube from continuing to disseminate "material covered by copyright". In June 2010, the Vice President of Mountain View, Kent Walker, announced that YouTube had won the Viacom suit, explaining that in the opinion of the court, YouTube was protected by the Digital Millennium Copyright Act. In 2008, Mediaset sued YouTube for €500 million in the Civil Court of Rome (serving notice in London and Los Angeles as well) for "illegal dissemination and commercial exploitation of audio-video files owned by the companies of the group." The suit covered only the "actual damages" plus "the losses incurred for non-sale of advertising space on the programmes illegally distributed on the web" such as Zelig and Striscia la Notizia.

10.3.2 Investments by MTV Italia

MTV Italia, for its part, reacted to the transformations in the audience and technology. Through various initiatives, the channel strengthened its presence in more innovative media. The first gamble was on telephony. The Italian telephone company TIM allowed its subscribers to watch TV on their mobiles (LA7, MTV, CFN/ CNBC and Coming Soon programmes), a service that was free of charge until 31 December 2003). Meanwhile, logos and ringtones were marketed via MTV.it. The turning point came in July 2008, when MTV Mobile "Powered by TIM" became available, the service designed for young people by MTV-TIM. Antonio Campo Dall'Orto and the Head of Consumers of Telecom Italy, Luca Luciani, presented MTV Mobile aboard a Spanish Vueling aircraft with MTV corporate colours on a flight from Milan to Barcelona. Milan hosted MTV Mobile Bang festivities, a big outdoor concert open to the public.

On the television front, at the same time MTV Italia partnered with Sky and Alice. In 2003, the "music video" area of Primo Sky included MTV, Rock TV, Match Music, Video Italia and Deejay TV. The same year, the Sky platform decided to expand its offering and add two new theme-based channels to the basic package created by MTV (MTV Brand: New) dedicated to people who followed the latest trends and emerging artists, and MTV Hits, which focused on the most listened to songs and top hits. The adventure on paid TV continued, and in the last quarter of 2007, Sky and MTV launched MTV Italia Gold, a channel that hosted the best music videos of the 1970s, 1980s and 1990s. In addition, Pulse was launched for the very young, as well as VH1, a cult channel that brought together the best songs by foreign artists from past and present. During the same time period, in 2006, Telecom Italia and MTV Italia signed an agreement to broadcast four of the best-known international music channels produced by MTV on Alice Home TV,[37] exclusively for Italy: VH1, VH1 Classic, MTV Base and MTV2.[38]

10.3.2.1 The programming

MTV Italia emerged as a dynamic, innovative, cross-media channel, with a variety of programming content: the trash of some American productions, pop from certain presenters, and the more engaging themes of some own programmes and initiatives. In 2003, the network co-produced the reality show *Fashion House* with Channel 4 (UK) and TV 3 (Sweden), a *Big Brother*-type programme centring on 20 designers from Italy, France, the UK and Sweden. This show aired simultaneously

---

37 Alice Home TV is the internet TV service of Telecom Italy (IPTV). With twisted pair cabling and an ADSL connection with up to 20 megabits per second, this service lets users view movies, sports, news and music directly on television and browse the internet with broadband.

38 The four new MTV channels were included in the basic subscription to Alice Home TV, in addition to the MTV Italia channel and other music content such as live concerts and on-demand TV.

on MTV Italia and other European channels. From the UK, MTV Italia imported *Skins*, a series that was all sex, drugs, profanity and mobiles. The stars of the show were a group of 17-year-olds from Bristol.[39] *Comedy Lab*, hosted by Marco Maccarini, was similar to *Zelig* and *Colorado Café*. This was also the time when MTV Italia was full of familiar faces and glamour: Ambra Angiolini introduced *Stasera Niente MTV* (*No MTV Tonight*), from *Isola dei Famosi* came Elena Santarelli, and from Mediaset Elisabetta Canalis. Fabio Volo was one of the most popular presenters. He travelled the world for three years, and did a daily show based on his experiences. The first year was from Barcelona with the Italian-Spanish programme (2006), then the Italian-French from Paris, and finally the Italian-American "Homeless edition, On the Road" from the United States. At the same time, MTV Italia ventured into more serious products, often unrelated to music: producing special reports that gave an inside look at the tough lives some people live, circulating information about AIDS and drug use, providing viewers with a range of knowledge to enable them to make their own choices. Finally, MTV Italia joined the No Excuse campaign and shares the United Nations objectives for 2015.

> If we behave like teachers it's over. The public sees us as a friend who knows more, a person to trust. The kids ask us for help to escape from a situation that they don't understand. With regard to the war in Iraq, 58% of respondents of the study turned to MTV for the latest news, 56% used the national news. . . The turning point could create confusion among our audience, someone will ask us to go back to music and do nothing else. But it is thanks to this that we have accumulated a stock of credibility that we are now trying to invest in other fields (Antonio Campo, 2004)

MTV Italia could rightly call itself a community-builder, a proactive force among young people, establishing a communicative pact that focuses on a shared sense of "us". All this is possible thanks to MTV Italia's ability to bring together different socio-cultural desires, aspirations and attitudes under one banner, and corporate bylaws that transcend more commercial and media-related concerns. "We are usually more divergent, while MTV manages to unite us all" (quote from an interviewee, MTV Day 2007).

39 Another programme that aired at that time was *Pimp My Ride*. On this show, young people would come on with their old run-down cars and they would be revamped and loaded with elaborate accessories, bordering on bad taste (examples include aquariums, Buddhist gongs, jacuzzis, tools for bowling ball maintenance, ping pong tables, etc.). Also part of the line-up was the reality show *Dismissed*. Each episode featured a good-looking girl or guy and two "hopefuls", either of the same sex or the opposite sex. After spending the day together, the person running the date decided which of the two hopefuls to get to know better and who to dismiss. Riding on the success of these two shows, in 2008, *A Shot at Love with Tila Tequila* debuted. In this show Tila, who never made any secret of her bisexuality, spent ten weeks in her mansion with 16 straight guys and 16 lesbians, in search of her ideal partner. The show included tests and competitions, sometimes mixed with softcore sex scenes with explicit displays of affection.

Francesco Mandelli made a variety of special reports for MTV Italia in developing countries where young people had a chance to find freedom through sport. Massimo Coppola wrote and directed *Avere Vent'Anni* (*Being Twenty*), an investigative journey aired late at night, every night, focusing on an inconspicuous generation. The second season in 2005 won accolades: a positive response from critics at the Cannes Film Festival, the "Young People" award from the Bizzarri Foundation and "Best Programme of the Year" at MEI (Meeting of Italian Independent Labels) in Faenza.

> The praise is excessive, the format has been compared to the films of Soldati, Pasolini. . .imagine that! We just tried to describe the daily life of young Italians without sensationalizing. . . We've gone back to exploiting the descriptive power of television. Our format is low-cost, like Rai 3 used to use for its programmes. Today, instead, [this format] finds space on a channel like MTV. . . Reality has far exceeded the imagination. Today it's much more interesting than any fiction. Maybe that's why the show was popular: so normal, so revolutionary (Massimo Coppola, 2006).

During the third season *Avere Vent'Anni* followed four aspiring Italian MPs (Caruso, Carfagna, Scotto and Meloni) on their election campaigns for 15 days with a digital camcorder to see if they really connected with young people. Meanwhile Camila Raznovich presented a talk show in the early evening, three themed episodes on AIDS, racial integration and computer science. In *R'n'R – Rock in Rebbibia*, a reality show shot in a Roman prison, each episode featured an Italian artist giving a lesson in rock to the eight detainees, aged 18 to 43, who made up a band.

Over the years, the programming focus of MTV Italia has streamlined music programmes and expanded its offerings to include entertainment. The broadcaster has proved itself capable of engaging spectators year round. It was the TV channel that young people wanted to watch and talk about and be a part of; they identified with MTV and learned from it.

10.3.2.2 Off-screen

The multifaceted nature of MTV Italia also increasingly emerged off-screen. Nowadays you may run across a flash mob organized by the network, or find yourself the middle of a pillow fight.[40] You can listen to Piero Pelù in the Puccini Room at the

---

40 On 23 June 2007 MTV Italia organized a pillow fight in Milan, between via Borsieri and Piazza Minniti.

Milan Conservatory for the Storytellers cycle,[41] or attend Comicittà, the entertainment festival organized by MTV Italia and the Sky Comedy Central channel.[42]

Events were undoubtedly MTV Italia's forte, as the growing success of MTV Day demonstrated. "Live and Loud" was the MTV Day 2004 slogan, reflecting MTV Italia's desire to nurture 8 million viewers daily not only with video clips and fun, but also with small doses of reflection and commitment scattered here and there in the programming. Since 2003, other events have been added to the calendar, in addition to the annual MTV Day: Coca-Cola Live@MTV,[43] the TRL Awards, Brand: New Day, festivals organized with the cast of the programmes and participating in various all-night events around Italy, Respect the Planet, MTV 1 Night Official Tour and MTV Party in Town.

Other investments were channelled into the internet as well as a project linking multiple platforms. MTV.it went through a growth and structuring phase, developing new technical skills internally, and taking advantage of all the online traffic revolving around the use of video clips on the internet. Entirely run by MTV Italia, the site provided programming support, pages dedicated to specific initiatives and on-demand service, and of course, all the charts. Developed with purely commercial objectives, MTV. it immediately became a very profitable alternative monetization channel.

Referring to the platform that MTV Italia was becoming, Campo Dall'Orto spoke of a "super-mega music club" where the public could enjoy a kaleidoscope of offerings, such as *Flux*, a magazine of events, programmes and videos on air 24/7, accessed via TV, internet and smartphone. The community was made up of 5,000 people who exchanged information and ideas on the website www.yos.it. Audiovisual projects could also be created and rated by users, and the best projects would be aired. There was no real line-up; this was a flow of images, clips and shorts that lasted from 10 seconds to 4–5 minutes. If users liked something they could even download it to their mobile phones. In addition to music, there was room for animation, video art, short films, promos and cartoons selected with the same avantgarde spirit. *Flux* evolved over time into QOOB. Browsing www.qoob.tv, users could look at the images in a transversal and personalized way through the six channels

---

41 Storytellers is an initiative based on music, writing experiences and memories aired live, streaming on MTV.it since 2005. This is a series of concert-encounters between musicians and audiences, in an intimate venue such as a theatre, a university hall or auditorium, where artists play and talk, describing how they came up with a song and then performing it, responding to questions from the audience and revealing their secrets and their techniques. After Jovanotti, Giorgia, Ligabue, Ivano Fossati and Bob Geldof, the grand finale spotlighted the Florentine artist Piero Pelù.

42 Seven days of comedy around Milan. Elio and Le Storie Tese were asked to present the show after the success of the Dopofestival di Sanremo (2008).

43 In 2009, this became Coca-Cola Live @ MTV – The Summer Song, an annual concert taking place in September featuring the summer hits of that year, similar to Festivalbar.

proposed by the editors – animation, fun, reality, shorts, music, art – or they could create new ones.[44]

> We want to break down the linear relationship between television and the viewer, where the production manager decides what goes on the air and when, and replace it with a participatory model in which viewers at home decide the schedule and watch it whenever they want. . . The viewer becomes a co-creator. We decided to finance a mini-drama created by a person we've never met. The contract will be signed via the internet. Next year, we'll fund the debut of a director, which we'll distribute in a new way. . . We'll produce content exclusively for certain media (Antonio Campo Dall'Orto, 2006).

Another product was MTV Overdrive, integrating TV and the web. In other words, Overdrive is an on-demand internet service that allowed viewers to tailor their TV by creating a customized schedule, their own playlist of videos, news, interviews, live performances, and programmes. They could also send it to friends.

> Today, 70% prefer "linear" TV, in three years it will be 50% and in five, 30%. Overdrive is the link between TV and the web. Young people no longer accept a linear model in which we producers manage the flow. Today if you are watching TV, it is by choice, not by accident. We are moving towards a future where everyone will choose what to watch and when. Hence, Overdrive is like a library: take what you want and watch it in the order you prefer. MTV is continuously regenerated. This mobility means enrichment, and new distribution systems allow us to set up other channels to transmit content. The "TV diet" will break down and we want everyone to see us as their music guide (Campo Dall'Orto, 2006).

MTV Italia gradually turned into a media group, starting with television and branching into different platforms. The channel embodied the transition from syndicated television with the offering subdivided into timeslots to television subdivided by platform: from internet to mobile phones, from iPods to the traditional cathode ray tube. In 2006, Campo Dall'Orto was still convinced that the permanent centre of gravity of MTV would be music, and wanted each platform to have its own creative specificity. The idea was not just to recycle programmes, but to create new programmes and content specifically designed for the medium in question.

10.3.2.3 The organization

In 2004, MTV Italia started giving the HR department higher priority, as well as more responsibility and autonomy. More than 400 people[45] were part of MTV

---

44 From 1 January 2009 QOOB went totally digital: the channel on digital terrestrial television was turned off to make room for the myriad possibilities of digital production and more typical Web 2.0 distribution.

45 Aggregate figures of MTV Italia and MTV Pubblicità, considering employees, agency staff and co-workers.

Italia; despite the increasing complexity of platforms and content, their training was still largely based on the radio and television sectors. Organizational roles and processes were not always defined; they aligned with the entrepreneurial vision of Campo Dall'Orto, the respected and feared strategist. ("Antonio said so" was the phrase most often uttered in the offices of Corso Europa.) They were the architects of a successful, exciting and unique story. Their connection with the company was strong: the channel was seen as the temple of music television, MTV was a kind of cult and working there was "cool".

10.4 Rethinking the model (2007–2008)

In 2007, MTV Day abandoned the traditional stage of Bologna for the first time and was split into two eight-hour pop marathons celebrating ten years of TV led by Antonio Campo Dall'Orto. Piazza San Giovanni in Rome and Piazza Duomo in Milan were packed with a total of over 100,000 fans; 123 Italian bands and singers performed on stage with futuristic lighting and big screens. The popular Italian singer Jovanotti performed first in Milan and then rushed to the capital to close the concert there with a duet with Negramaro. He thanked MTV to the tune of his hit *Falla Girare*: "For giving voice to those who do not have one, for the fight for a more righteous world where a child, two hours by plane from here, doesn't have to die from a disease that we treat with a pill" (Jovanotti, 2007).

MTV Italia had a lot to celebrate on its tenth birthday: from music TV to a go-to channel for the public offering a variety of genres – only 50 programmes in ten years, but shows that had left their mark. What's more, the channel celebrated its birthday with strong advertising growth of 10% in the first three months of 2007, a turnover of €100 million, which made it the second largest in the world after MTV USA, and an image among young people who saw it as credible and compelling. At the international level, the crowning achievement of MTV Italia came the following year when Campo Dall'Orto, CEO of MTV Southern Europe since 1999, became Executive Vice President of MTVNI: he would decide the programming and creative strategies of the brand on a global level, reporting directly to Robert Bakish, President of MTV Networks International.

However, it was clear that for MTVN and the national MTVs, the prospects were far from promising, with a new generation to connect with, new media bringing new competitors, and more advanced and rapidly changing technologies. Financial sustainability was no longer taken for granted; on the horizon loomed the risk that the television offering might lose its appeal, with repercussions for the audience and advertising revenues, which were already decimated by the economic crisis. Hence, while in Italy Total Request Live (TRL) was celebrating its tenth anniversary, the USA format changed. The loss of viewers of the trendiest music programme in recent years was serious enough to convince Viacom's top management to kick-start a cost savings plan: two episodes a week of the request programme were paradoxically pre-recorded; the New York studio was used only three days instead of five; 250 jobs at MTVN were cut.[46]

Not very encouraging figures were quick to follow for MTV Italia as well. Advertising revenues had in fact decreased since the early months of 2008. Due to the global crisis, investors cut back sharply on investments and demanded more and more ratings data to justify the money they did spend. In addition, with the switch to digital terrestrial, the number of unencrypted channels exploded from 9 to 100. So MTV Italia faced new competition from themed channels that were attracting businesses and viewers.[47] Because of the decline in revenues, experimentation and big budgets gradually gave way to a large number of reality, talent and game shows made in the USA. The young VJs remained but the main formats were less innovative. The reduction in EBITDA (earnings before interest, taxes, depreciation and amortization) of MTV Italia compared with 2007 (€5 million) was almost entirely attributable to the decline in advertising revenues (down by 12.7%), only partially offset by a reduction in costs and included a €1 million debt incurred from an initial reorganization.

"No sense makes sense on MTV" wavered and MTV Italia needed the resources to redesign the channel's offerings, modulating the content carefully, so as to win back both the young audience and the advertisers with an original, targeted offering.

The urgency of rethinking the model was also felt by the Italian partner.[48] Giovanni Stella, Executive Vice President of Telecom Italia Media, stressed the need for "very hard and conscientious work on the cost side. We know this, and in the forthcoming quarters, resizing will be undertaken in a much more powerful and meaningful way. We know that the drop in advertising is not temporary" (Giovanni Stella, 2008).

. . .end of flashback. September 2008, Tagliavia is on the phone to Campo Dall'Orto
"If we want to stay successful, we have to make a lot of changes," warned Campo Dall'Orto. After hanging up, Tagliavia was a little less happy and a little more

---

46 *TRL* debuted in September 1998 from a studio overlooking Times Square in New York. The American audience peaked in 1999 with almost a million viewers on average, with a large percentage of those in the strategic 12–17 demographic. Today the numbers are 350,000 total viewers; 200,000 teenagers stopped tuning into MTV's top afternoon show.

47 The transition to digital terrestrial television led to a revolution on the Italian television scene. In late 2010, in northern Italy, the transition from analogue to digital was completed, and the number of viewers who ticked the "Other Digital Terrestrial TV" box on the Auditel ranking skyrocketed. These channels scored 3.88% shares in 24 hours and 3.14% in prime time in the month of November 2010, and in December increased to 5.88% over 24 hours and 4.94% in the early evening. Groups such as RAI and Mediaset, despite the proliferation of channels, either maintained or eroded their overall audience numbers in November. Real Time made the ratings of the Discovery Group soar, close to 1% over the entire day; RTL 102.5 TV had a 0.42% share between 9 and 12.

48 Telecom Italia Media, majority shareholder with 51%.

worried: betting on MTV Italia was a wager he had to win. First, he organized trips to New York and London to meet with American colleagues and learn about the macro strategies of MTVNI. After returning to Milan, he also thought about backup for facing the challenge. To take the helm at MTV Pubblicità he called Ivan Ranza, former Managing Director of Blei, the RCS media distribution centre specializing in foreign media (and a colleague of Tagliavia years before at MTV Italia).

At the end of the month during a press conference, Tagliavia stated:

> The reorganization that MTV Italia started implementing this summer was necessary to better govern the explosion of activities and the structure of our universe. A journey that began some years ago and that today has led us to every medium and technology platform, analog and digital, web and mobile. Now that we have reached ubiquity, the goal is to make our media more and more relevant to the audience. Namely, we want to bring value to the communities that revolve around our brand, becoming inspiring and activating a system of relations in constant motion. . . We are living the most fascinating ten years of the history of media. There is tremendous momentum. The fragmentation of the media prevails, the audience is in a constant state of flux. In this scenario, the real challenge is to maintain the trust that young people give us. This must be done without chasing them or trying to please them because today's kids reject easy answers and prefer challenging paths. This is why the motto that guides all MTV activities is "challenge your thinking".

References

Bloomberg Business Magazine (2002, February 17) MTV's World. *Bloomberg Business Magazine.* Retrieved from http://www.bloomberg.com/bw/stories/2002-02-17/mtvs-world

Business Week (2006, February 20). Can MTV stay cool? *Business Week.*

Corriere della Sera (2000, July 4). Mtv: in ferie i videoclip odiati dai negozianti. *Corriere della Sera.*

Grasso, A. (2007, September 16). La Tv dei Giovani e la Sfida Internet. *Corriere della Sera.* Retrieved from http://archiviostorico.corriere.it/2007/settembre/16/dei_Giovani_Sfida_Internet_co_9_070916099.shtml

Il Messaggero (1999, April 11). Sushi, MTV prova una nuova minestra di successo *Il Messaggero.*

Poniewozik, J. (2009, April 28). Corporate Press Release Theater: The 'M' Is for Millennial. *TIME Magazine.* Retrieved from http://entertainment.time.com/2009/04/28/corporate-press-release-theater-the-m-is-for-millennial.

Sachs, J. (2011). *The Price of Civilization: Reawakening American Virtue and Prosperity.* Random House.

Smith, W. (2009). Finalmente orgoglioso di essere americano. *L'Unita.* Retrieved from http://www.unita.it/italia/laquo-finalmente-orgoglioso-di-essere-americano-raquo-1.26466

Twenge, J.M. (2007). *Generation Me: Why Today's Young Americans are More Confident, Assertive, Entitled – and More Miserable than Ever Before.* New York: Free Press.

Annex: Examples of programmes broadcast on MTV Italia from 1997 to 2008

Select (1998–2004, music programme)

Select was a video jukebox where the viewers could request music videos by their favourite singers via email or phone and then speak directly to the show's presenters. In addition, the programme premiered new videos by the most important songwriters, with the hosts giving viewers lots of "fun facts".

A Night With. . . (1998, 2006–2007)

A programme dedicated to the work of national and international artists, hosted by Paola Maugeri for the first few seasons, and later by Carolina Di Domenico. The programme told the story of the biggest music stars, accompanied by exclusive interviews and videos of their top hits and their best live performances.

TRL – Total Request Live (1999–2010)

The programme showed performances by many singers and groups based on the top ten chart, as ranked by online viewer voting (http://en.wikipedia.org/wiki/MTV#Total_Request_Live_.281998.E2.80.932008.29).

Celebrity Deathmatch (1998–2002, cartoon)

The show, produced in claymation (stop motion animation with clay figures), was a hugely popular MTV broadcast. It was a parody of a wrestling match in which famous people in every field were challenged to fight to the death in the ring, one-on-one or on opposing tag teams (hence the title *Celebrity Deathmatch*). At times the clashes between celebrities were based on real world rivalries, but more often, the pairing was simply to decide who was best in a given field (e.g. Sean Connery against Roger Moore for the title of best 007), or between people with similar names (Jim Carrey against Mariah Carey or Al Yankovic against Al Gore); sometimes the match ups made no sense whatsoever (the fight between Bill Gates and the dancer Michael Flatley, due to a transcription error).

Cowboy Bebop (1999–2000, TV series, animation)

The story of a bounty hunter and space cowboy from the future, Spike Spiegel and his companions (Jet Black, Faye Valentine, Edward and Ein the dog, a Pembroke Welsh corgi), as they journey through the solar system.

Inuyasha (2001, 2004–2007, TV series, animation)

The story of Inuyasha, a half-demon dog who, along with co-star Kagome Higurashi and his team, had to find all the fragments of the Jewel of Four Souls (a powerful gem that made its owner extremely strong). They raced to do so before Naraku, the half-demon enemy responsible for numerous abuses against Inuyasha and other characters.

MTV Trip (2000–2002, reality show)

The two presenters travelled around Europe in a Fiat 130 with a Bologna licence plate fitted out as a hearse, chatting and creating parodies, skits and funny shorts in the towns where they stayed.

Loveline (2001–2008, 2010 show)

In a red room, Angela Rafanelli (and Camila Raznovich before her) talked openly about sex and emotions to an audience made up mainly of young people. During the show, the audience in the studio (through anonymous cards) and at home (via phone) could ask questions directly and clear up any doubts they had. The programme included various daily features.

Dismissed (2002–2005, reality game)

Each episode features a good-looking a girl or a guy, and two "hopefuls", who might be either the opposite sex or of the same sex. The two hopefuls had half a day each to decide what to do with the protagonist; they also had the opportunity to be alone with him or her for quarter of an hour, to "trash" the other hopeful. At the end of the day, the protagonist would decide who to get to know better and who would be "dismissed".

Very Victoria (2005–2008, show)

Two interviews per show with celebrities. Each guest was accompanied onto the set by two valets, Loris and Andreas, and every interview ended with an unusual gift for the guests.

Skins (2007–, TV series)

The story revolves around the lives of a group of 16- to 18-year-olds living in Bristol, UK. Each episode deals with a particular character, delving into his or her story, but many situations develop during the course of the series. The title of the series is the slang word for the paper used for rolling cigarettes and joints.

Il Testimone (The Witness) (2007–, information and analysis)

Featuring stories, events and people that never see the front pages of newspapers. Pif the presenter shoots each episode with a small camcorder he carries with him during his investigations. His special shooting technique allows viewers to get a glimpse of stark reality, ideal for conveying the social message in each episode.

Afterword

Elio Borgonovi

Full Professor, Bocconi University, and Member of the ASFOR Annual Case Writing Competition evaluation committee

On reading this book, two questions emerge. How does the case methodology drive change in management education? What contribution can a collection of specifically Italian cases provide?

The first question relates to the criticisms of the methodology itself. In particular, Henry Mintzberg argues that the case represents an over-simplification of reality and so is of little help to managers in how to actually make decisions, operate and behave. He also expresses doubt that strong frameworks can be designed and shared with students using case discussions. For all these reasons, Mintzberg is in favour of a methodology in which participants in MBA and Executive Education programmes build their learning process through sharing experiences, and through discussion between the student and the professor based on concrete management situations. New technology can support this methodology, as everyone has access to much information about companies, public institutions, not for profit organizations and the challenges they each experience. This criticism is relevant to Executive Education and the MBA whose participants have some years of experience. However, cases can still be of high value for Master's and other management programmes aimed at participants with little experience.

Another criticism that is often cited is that the case methodology can turn into an instrument to reinforce the mainstream management culture. In particular, the case methodology is considered an expression of the Harvard Business School approach and the business schools that accept this teaching/learning method. The typology of cases (analytics, problem solving, organization relations, stakeholder approach, etc.), and the format in which they are delivered through the use of teaching notes for instructors, has permeated management education across the globe. As the majority of cases refer to the USA and Anglophone countries, the discussion about cases is not simply confined to the method but how it can be seen as a driver of ways of thinking and socioeconomic contexts.

The publication of Italian cases seeks to address these particular concerns. First of all, teachers/instructors of management education programmes gain insight into a wider range of situations. Italy is a country in which smaller family businesses are a significant part of the economy (see the cases of iGuzzini, Mediolanum, Hotel Stella and Ametista), public–private relations are important (see the cases of Fahrenheit Resort and Telespazio) and, moreover, the change management processes are strongly influenced by the socioeconomic, political and institutional environments (see the cases of MTV Italia, UniManagement, and Magneti Marelli and Mopar). The case of Dynamo Camp is an enlightening example of a social business and of the adaptation of the model initiated by Paul Newman to the Italian socioeconomic and institutional environments. What we see is not simply philanthropy but an example of a manager who became an entrepreneur in the for-profit field and then a social entrepreneur. He was able to create synergies among the volunteers, philanthropists and professionals involved in the camp activities.

It is well known that one of the strengths of the Italian culture is creativity. It follows that the authors of this collection of cases do not necessarily follow a standardized approach. When we read cases or even papers published in top journals, we see a standard format. This collection presents a diversity of formats and this is indeed one of its key features. The authors' aims are to provide the reader with all the essential information and data to stimulate a multi-dimensional approach. Of course, this is not completely new. However, the case approach has been oriented towards quantitative analysis. In the real world, good managers are those who are open to the multi-dimensional solutions to concrete problems.

This collection of cases contributes to the promotion of a multicultural approach. It provides teaching materials for a mix of cases written about organizations in different countries by local authors, each of whom has been trained in their own country's education system. While the case clearing houses do contain cases related to different countries, they are often written by authors who have been trained in the US or Anglophone universities. In many management education programmes there is a contradiction. Lectures or courses on multiculturalism are introduced, but the majority of the cases that are presented refer to one cultural paradigm.

In conclusion, I do hope that the effort of ASFOR, together with Greenleaf Publishing, in promoting the case competition and then in selecting the best cases, will be considered helpful and fruitful for instructors and participants in the management education community.

About the authors

Corey Billington has successfully blended a career as a business leader, university professor, and entrepreneur. He is best known as being a key originator of the field of supply chain management and has published many of the seminal papers that established this field of research and industrial application. Corey Billington is Visiting Professor at the University of Wyoming and at ETH in Zurich. In the past he was the Vice President of Supply Chain Services at HP and spent 25 years pioneering supply chain management techniques. Corey has a PhD in Industrial Engineering & Engineering Management from Stanford University.

Maria Carmela Ostillio has been a Core Faculty Member of SDA Bocconi School of Management since 1988 and is the Scientific Coordinator of Brand Academy at SDA Bocconi School of Management. She directs the Brand Management course of the MSc in Marketing Management at Bocconi University. She has published papers in her research fields, marketing and corporate communications and brand management, and has published on several other topics including: direct and interactive marketing, marketing one to one, customer database and marketing information systems.

Niccolò Cusumano is a non-academic faculty member in the Department of Policy Analysis and Public Management at the SDA Bocconi School of Management. He is currently completing an international PhD in Management, Innovation, Sustainability and Healthcare at the Sant'Anna School of Advanced Studies in Pisa. Cusumano is a Research Fellow at IEFE (Centre for Research in Energy and Environmental Economics) at Bocconi University and a member of the Impact Investing Lab SDA Bocconi School of Management.

Rhoda Davidson specializes in working with senior managers to resolve tough strategic challenges using innovation techniques. She lectures in Strategic Management at Surrey University in the UK and is a Visiting Faculty at ETH in Zurich, Switzerland. In the past she spent ten years at IMD, a leading business school in Switzerland, designing and delivering strategic innovations programmes for large multinational companies and she has also worked for five years for McKinsey & Co. She has PhDs from Oxford University and Geneva University, and an MA from Cambridge University.

Olga E. Annushkina is SDA Professor of Strategic and Entrepreneurial Management, Department of SDA Bocconi School of Management, Milan. Her key research interests include strategic management, strategy implementation, international business, emerging markets and scenario planning.

Giulia Ferrari is an operational and strategic marketing specialist with a degree in Management for Art Culture and Communication and a Master's degree in International Management, both from Bocconi University. She has worked for Confindustria, MTV Italia and is currently PR & Communication Manager in Brazil for an Italian multinational.

Gabriele Gabrielli is Professor of Human Resources Management at LUISS Guido Carli University (Italy). He coordinates the People Management Competence Centre & Lab at LUISS Business School. He is President of Lavoroperlapersona Foundation.

Stefano Grugnetti holds a Master's degree in Strategy and Management from ISTAO. He began to work on quality management systems, occupational safety and privacy in a nonprofit organization in the field of social and health services. He later enriched his professional experience as a partner in a telecommunications company and gained expertise in human resources management and in administration and accounting. Since 2009 he has been a partner with Pharos Consulting, a consultancy, training and research company.

Paolo Gubitta is Full Professor of Business Organization and Entrepreneurship at the Department of Economics and Management, University of Padova, and Scientific Director of Entrepreneurial Lab at CUOA Business School. Since 2006, he has been Adjunct Professor at the College of Business of University of Michigan Dearborn (US). More recently, he held Visiting Professor positions at Tel Aviv University (2014), University of Lugano (2013–2014), Guangzhou University (2012) and Sun Wah College of International Business (2011). Since 2012, he has been a member of the Academic Advisory Board of the GE Capital International Research Project on Mid-Market. His main research topics are entrepreneurship, small business and family firms, and knowledge-intensive business firms.

Laura Innocenti (PhD) is External Professor of Organizational Behaviour and Human Resources Management at LUISS Guido Carli University (Italy) and develops training and research programmes for the People Management Competence Centre & Lab at LUISS Business School. Her research interests involve HRM practices, diversity management and organizational climate.

Giorgio Invernizzi is Full Professor in Strategic Management at Bocconi University and SDA Professor of Strategic and Entrepreneurial Management at SDA Bocconi School of Management. His special interest areas are: strategic management, corporate-level strategy, strategic management accounting, corporate governance and business planning. He has authored many books, including: *Corporate Level Strategy* (with Collis, Montgomery and Molteni; McGraw-Hill, 2012); and *Strategic Management Accounting* (Egea, 2005).

Carmela La Cava is an expert in designing innovative executive development and change programmes to support business leaders in the achievement of their goals. She is a Senior

Adviser at the UniCredit Group and a core team member of UniManagement, the corporate learning centre. Carmela has been a driving force in the development of the UniQuest programme for top talents. In the past Carmela spent ten years at Accenture working in human resources and change management. She has an MBA from ISTUD and a degree in Political Sciences, Labour and Industrial Relations from LUISS Guido Carli University (Italy).

Antonella Moretto is Assistant Professor at the Department of Management, Economics and Industrial Engineering at the Politecnico di Milano. In 2013, she was awarded a PhD with honours at Politecnico di Milano with a thesis about the internationalization of Italian fashion companies in emerging markets; in July 2009, she obtained an MSc with honours in Management Engineering at Politecnico di Milano. During the period 2013–2015, she collaborated as a consultant in the area of operations and supply chain management. Her main research interests are related to purchasing and supply management, supply chain design, sustainable supply chain management and global supply chain management for luxury fashion companies.

Giacomo Morri (PhD, MRICS) is Senior Professor in the Accounting, Control, Corporate Finance and Real Estate Department at SDA Bocconi School of Management, and Real Estate Finance Lecturer at Bocconi University. At SDA Bocconi he is in charge of real estate open program executive education. His research interests span from real estate investment, valuation and financing to more traditional corporate finance topics. He has authored several scientific articles and books, including *Property Finance* (with Antonio Mazza; Wiley, 2015).

Atul Pahwa is a strategy and innovation consultant who works across a spectrum of industries to help companies reshape and retool themselves to take advantage of business disruptions. His strengths lie in working on projects around disruptive innovations, business model innovation and corporate strategy. In the past he spent seven years working at IMD, a leading business school in Switzerland, as a Research Associate analysing key business strategies. Atul has an MBA from Babson College in the US.

Lorenzo Palego holds a degree in Literature and a Master's degree in Business Management from ISTAO. He has worked as project manager for both international and Italian NGOs. Palego then specialized in the field of business training, carrying out international market analysis, business translation (interpreting for English, French and German) and consultancy for company internationalization. He has been working at ISTAO since 2009, where he is now coordinator of the Executive Education area and of the Master's course in International Business Management. Since 2012 he has been a partner at Navigancona.

Sara Paoletti holds a degree in Economics and Commerce from Ancona University and a Master's degree in Business Management from ISTAO. She has wide experience in the field of marketing analysis and in the preparation of business plans, coordinating numerous working groups at an international level. She has worked at ISTAO since 1996 in various positions and currently coordinates placement activities and relations with companies. In 2001 she became partner of CSIL, Centre for Industrial Studies, and in 2014 she founded Tasting Marche.

Margherita Pero is Assistant Professor at the Department of Management, Economics and Industrial Engineering of Politecnico di Milano. She teaches business processes reengineering and operations and supply chain management at the School of Management of Politecnico di Milano. She is director of the FlexEMBA programme at MIP – Politecnico di Milano Business School. In 2009, she was awarded a PhD at Politecnico di Milano with a thesis dealing with new product development and supply chain management processes alignment. In June 2004, she gained an MSc with honours in Management Engineering at Politecnico di Milano. Her main research interests are related to production planning, supply chain design and management, and supply chain management–new product development coordination.

Francesco Perrini is Head of Sustainability Lab at CDR (Claudio Demattè Research), SDA Bocconi School of Management and Senior Professor of Corporate and Real Estate Finance. He is Full Professor of Strategy and SIF Chair of Social Entrepreneurship and Philanthropy at the Department of Management and Technology, Bocconi University, Milan. He has been a researcher at Bocconi University since 1990, focusing on strategic management; corporate finance and real estate; valuations of investments; crisis and corporate restructuring; corporate sustainability; social entrepreneurship and strategic philanthropy.

Silvia Profili (PhD) is Associate Professor of Human Resource Management at the European University of Rome where she is President of the Master of Science in Economics and Management of Innovation. She is Vice Director of the Executive MBA programme at LUISS Business School (Rome). She has been a visiting scholar at the Wharton School, University of Pennsylvania. Her research interests include HRM practices, employees' attitudes and behaviours, and age diversity in the workplace.

Dino Ruta is Professor of Human Resources and Sport Management at the SDA Bocconi School of Management, Milan. He obtained a PhD in Business Administration at the University of Bologna. His research activities are focused on people strategy, leadership and sport management. He directed the Master's in Organization and Human Resource Management at Bocconi University from 2009 to 2014. He teaches the Human Resource Management course as part of the full-time MBA at SDA Bocconi School of Management and is a visiting professor at Columbia University (USA).

Severino Salvemini is Full Professor of Organization Theory at Bocconi University, Milan. He is Director of the Undergraduate Degree in Economics and Management of Arts, Culture and Communication (CLEACC) and President of the CRORA Centre for Research on Business Organization. In 1988 and 1989 Salvemini directed the "International Teachers Programme". He has also taught at the University of Trento (1985–1987) and the University of Bologna (1990–1993). He has taught in Business Schools such as the Stockholm School of Economics, HEC in Paris, Ecole Nationale des Ponts et Chaussées in Paris, Institut d'Administration d'Enterprise in Aix-en-Provence, and INSEAD in Fontainebleau.

Alessia Sammarra (PhD) is Professor of Human Resource Management and Organizational Behaviour at the University of L'Aquila (Italy). She has been a visiting scholar at the University of Illinois at Urbana-Champaign, USA. Her research interests lie in the areas of HRM practices–performance link, innovation, and employees' work attitudes and behaviours. She is Chair of the Human Resource Management Track at the European Management Academy.

Chiara Solerio is a faculty member in the Department of Marketing, Bocconi University. She has worked as a research assistant for the department and completed her PhD at the Catholic University of Milan. Her research interests include branding and consumption experience, both from consumers' and companies' perspectives. Solerio has published several case studies of successful Italian companies.

Alessandra Tognazzo is a Post-doctoral Research Fellow at the Department of Economics and Management "Marco Fanno", University of Padova and is Adjunct Professor of Family Business. She received her PhD in 2012 at the University of Padova and in 2010 was a visiting PhD student at the Master's in Research in Management, IESE Business School, Barcelona. She is the author and co-author of several books and is currently publishing some research articles in international journals about leadership, family business, entrepreneurship and innovation.

Veronica Vecchi (PhD) is Senior Professor of Public Management at SDA Bocconi School of Management where she teaches Business–Government Relations and PPPs (public–private partnerships). She is Director of Executive Education of Bocconi India and coordinates the Bocconi Monitor on Public–Private Partnership and the SDA Bocconi Impact Investing Lab. She is author of several scientific publications on PPPs.
She advises International Institutions, such as OECD, World Bank and Interamerican Development Bank on PPP as well as national authorities.

Clodia Vurro is a Lecturer of Management and Corporate Sustainability at the Department of Management and Technology at Bocconi University. She obtained a PhD in Business Administration and Management from Bocconi University, where she currently teaches management, global sustainability, social entrepreneurship and innovation. She is a senior fellow of the Sustainability Lab at SDA Bocconi and a faculty member of the Master in Green Management, Energy and Corporate Social Responsibility. Her research interests span from CSR and corporate sustainability to social entrepreneurship, impact investing and tools and methodologies for social impact assessment.

About the editors

Elio Borgonovi, Full Professor Bocconi University and Member of the ASFOR Annual Case Writing Competition evaluation committee

Elio is a Full Professor of Economics and Management of Public Administration at Bocconi University and Member of the ASFOR Annual Case Writing Competition evaluation committee. In 1978 he founded CERGAS (Centre for Research on Health and Social Care Management), of which he is currently president. He is a senior professor at SDA Bocconi (Public Management and Policy Department). He was the Dean of SDA Bocconi from 1997 to 2002. He has been a member of the steering committee of ASFOR and a past president.

Vladimir Nanut, President ASFOR

Vladimir is Founder and Dean of MIB School of Management and Full Professor of Business Strategy at the University of Trieste. He has also held the role of Director of the Economics and Business Department at the University of Trieste and has been a Member of the Academic Senate. In addition to his academic activities, Vladimir has had many professional roles: Vice President of the Regional Finance Company of Friulia; President of Friulia Factor; Chairman of L.A. Life (Allianz Group); board member and auditor of several banks and industrial/service companies; and a strategic management consultant. In 2010 he was appointed President of ASFOR, where he has also held roles as Vice-President, Deputy Director on Internationalization and President of the Accreditation Commission.

Luigi Serio, Referent for ASFOR Annual Case Writing Competition

Luigi is Adjunct Professor of Economics and Business Management at the Faculty of Economics and Sociology, Catholic University of Milan. He leads the Master's programme in Human Resources Management at ISTUD Business School and coordinates all the initiatives related to the "case writing" for the members of ASFOR.